Capitalism

Capitalism

A Conversation in Critical Theory

Nancy Fraser and Rahel Jaeggi

Edited by Brian Milstein

polity

First published in 2018 by Polity Press

Polity Press
65 Bridge Street
Cambridge CB2 1UR, UK

Polity Press
101 Station Landing
Suite 300
Medford, MA 02155, USA

ISBN-13: 978-0-7456-7156-7
ISBN-13: 978-0-7456-7157-4 (pb)

A catalogue record for this book is available from the British Library.

Library of Congress Cataloging-in-Publication Data

Names: Fraser, Nancy, author. | Jaeggi, Rachel, author.
Title: Capitalism : a conversation in critical theory / Nancy Fraser, Rachel Jaeggi.
Description: Medford, MA : Polity, 2018. | Includes bibliographical references and index.
Identifiers: LCCN 2018001732 (print) | LCCN 2018002836 (ebook) | ISBN 9781509525263 (Epub) | ISBN 9780745671567 (hardback) | ISBN 9780745671574 (paperback)
Subjects: LCSH: Capitalism--History. | Critical theory. | BISAC: PHILOSOPHY / History & Surveys / General.
Classification: LCC HB501 (ebook) | LCC HB501 .F694 2018 (print) | DDC 330.12/2--dc23
LC record available at https://lccn.loc.gov/2018001732

Typeset in 10.5 on 12 pt Sabon by Servis Filmsetting Ltd, Stockport, Cheshire
Printed and bound in the UK by CPI Group (UK) Ltd, Croydon

For further information on Polity, visit our website: politybooks.com for

Daniel Zaretsky Wiesen
Julian Zaretsky Wiesen
Jakob Jaeggi

Inheritors of the history we have made
Bearers of our hopes for a better future

Contents

Preface

We wrote this book in a turbulent time and in an unconventional way. Established certainties were breaking down all around us. Crises of finance and ecology were deepening before our eyes, becoming subjects of overt contestation throughout the world. At the same time, other societal impasses, of family, community, and culture, were churning a bit further below the surface – not yet major foci of social struggle, but crises-in-the-making nonetheless, preparing to explode in full view. Finally, the accumulated turmoil appeared to coalesce in a full-scale crisis of political hegemony in 2016, as voters across the globe revolted en masse against neoliberalism, threatening to oust the parties and elites that had sponsored it in favor of populist alternatives, Left and Right. These were what the Chinese (and Eric Hobsbawm) call "interesting times."

Interesting – especially for philosophers engaged in developing a critical theory of capitalist society. Each of us had been engrossed in that project separately for several years before joining forces to write this book. We made the decision to do so on the assumption that the deepening turbulence around us could be read precisely as a *crisis of capitalist society*, or, rather, as a crisis of the specific form of capitalist society we inhabit today. The times, it seemed to us, were crying out for this sort of analysis. And what better preparation for the task than our shared background in critical theory and Western Marxism, our history of impassioned political-intellectual engagement with one another, and the capital-critical philosophizing that each of us had been doing individually for quite a while?

We saw our chance when John Thompson proposed that we do a book for Polity's "Conversations" series. But we adapted his proposal to our own purposes. Instead of focusing on the overall trajectory of

Nancy Fraser's thought, as he initially suggested, we decided to center our "conversations" specifically on the question of capitalism and on the work that *both* of us were doing on that theme.

The decision taken, the process of writing this book underwent its own twists and turns. We oscillated back and forth between two conceptions of what we were doing. The idea, at the start, was to record a series of reasonably well-planned conversations on aspects of the topic – to converse orally in person and to edit the transcripts in a way that preserved their semi-spontaneous, conversational feel. That conception survives, more or less, in some chapters of the finished book, especially the Introduction and chapter 4. But it gave way in other chapters to a different conception, involving heavier editing and substantial rewriting. The change reflected the way our work on this book intersected with the work that each of us was also doing concurrently on her own. Chapters 1 and 2 ended up focusing largely on Nancy Fraser's "expanded" view of capitalism as "an institutionalized social order" that harbors multiple crisis tendencies. These chapters were substantially revised, for the most part by her. Chapter 3, by contrast, follows Rahel Jaeggi's mapping of the various genres that comprise a critique of capitalism, their respective internal logics and mutual relations. Mostly revised by her, this chapter also presents Jaeggi's "practice-theoretical" view of capitalism as a "form of life."

Those individual emphases aside, this book was a joint effort through and through. However unconventional, its format is faithful to the actual creative process we engaged in together – in recorded discussions, private conversations, and public presentations in Berlin, Frankfurt, Paris, Cambridge (UK), and New York; in the course of family vacations in Vermont; and in the graduate seminar on Critiques of Capitalism that we co-taught at the New School for Social Research in spring 2016. The book as a whole, we firmly believe, is much greater than the sum of its parts. It emerged from, and reflects, a serendipitous combination of circumstances: that we share many intellectual reference points and political views; that our philosophical approaches nevertheless diverge; and that we enjoy a deep friendship centered on intense if intermittent communication. The result is a book that is richer and deeper than either of us could have produced on her own.

Along the way, we incurred several debts of gratitude, both jointly and individually. Nancy Fraser gratefully acknowledges research support from the Einstein Foundation of the City of Berlin and the JFK Institute for American Studies at the Free University of Berlin; the Rosa Luxemburg Foundation; the Center for Advanced

Studies "Justitia Amplificata" (Frankfurt) and the Forschungskolleg Humanwissenschaften (Bad Homburg); the Centre for Gender Studies and Clare Hall, University of Cambridge; the Research Group on Post-Growth Societies, Friedrich Schiller University (Jena); the Collège d'études mondiales and the École des hautes études en sciences sociales (Paris); and the New School for Social Research (New York). She is grateful, too, to Cinzia Arruzza and Johanna Oksala for inspiring exchanges on Marxism, feminism and capitalism in the course of team-taught seminars at the New School; to Michael Dawson for pushing her to theorize the place of racial oppression in capitalist society; and to Robin Blackburn, Hartmut Rosa, and Eli Zaretsky for great conversation and probing feedback.

Rahel Jaeggi gratefully acknowledges research support from the German Heuss Professorship scheme, the New School for Social Research, the Research Group on Post-Growth Societies at the Friedrich Schiller University in Jena, Germany, and the Humboldt University-Berlin. She also thanks Eva von Redecker and the other members of her research group (Lea Prix, Isette Schuhmacher, Lukas Kübler, Bastian Ronge, and Selana Tzschiesche) for contributing at various stages and in various ways; Hartmut Rosa, Stefan Lessenich, and Klaus Dörre for encouraging discussions and for helping to bring the topic back to the agenda; Axel Honneth and Fred Neuhouser for continuous inspiration; and Martin Saar and Robin Celikates for being those intellectual companions without whom academic life would not be the same.

Both of us thank Blair Taylor and Dan Boscov-Ellen for superb research assistance, which far surpassed the merely technical; Brian Milstein for skillful editing and manuscript preparation in the final stages; John Thompson for the initial suggestion that we write this book and for the patience with which he awaited its completion; Leigh Mueller for copy-editing, and Victoria Harris and Miriam Dajczgewand Świętek for help with proofreading.

Nancy Fraser and
Rahel Jaeggi

Introduction

Jaeggi: The critique of capitalism has been in a kind of "boom period" of late, or, as we say in German, it "hat Konjunktur." For a long time, capitalism had largely been absent from political and intellectual debates. It was even absent from the agenda of "critical theory" – the tradition to which both you and I are affiliated. But now the interest in capitalism is surging – and I don't mean just interest in market economics, globalization, modern society, or distributive justice, but interest in *capitalism*. And of course, there are good reasons for this – not least the 2007/8 financial crisis. As we know, this crisis cascaded rapidly from the financial sphere into the fiscal and economic spheres, and from there into politics and society, rattling governments, the European Union, the institutions of the welfare state, and, in some ways, the very fabric of social integration. Not since the interwar period have people in Western societies felt themselves so exposed to the instability and unpredictability of our economic and social order – a sense of exposure that was only magnified and compounded by the responses of their ostensibly democratic governments, which seemed to range from sheer helplessness to cold indifference.

What is remarkable is how rapidly the critique of capitalism has come back into vogue. It was not long ago at all that the word "capitalism" was still in virtual disrepute, both in the academy and in the public sphere. Granted, some of the critiques we've been seeing are diffuse or rudimentary, simplistic and even inflationary. But you and I both agree that a renewed critique of capitalism is exactly what we need today, and it is important that critical theorists like you and I should focus again on capitalism.

1

Fraser: Yes, indeed, the return of interest in capitalism is very good news for the world in general, but also for you and me. Both of us have been engaged separately in trying to rekindle interest in this topic. For a long time now, each of us has tried to bring key ideas from the critique of political economy back into critical theory: in your case, the concept of "alienation"; in mine, the concepts of "crisis" and "contradiction."[1] And each of us has also sought to rethink the very idea of what capitalism is: in your case, a "form of life"; in mine, an "institutionalized social order."[2] But until recently we were voices in the wilderness. Today, however, that has changed. It's not just you and I, but lots of people, who now want to talk about capitalism. There is widespread agreement that capitalism is (again) a problem and a worthy object of political and intellectual attention. As you said, this is perfectly understandable. It reflects the pervasive sense that we are caught in the throes of a very deep crisis – a severe *systemic* crisis. What we face, in other words, is not just a set of discrete punctual problems, but a deep-structural dysfunction lodged at the very heart of our form of life.

So even if people don't know exactly what they mean by capitalism, the mere fact that they are using the word again is heartening. I read it as signaling a hunger for the sort of critical theory that discloses the deep-structural roots of a major systemic crisis. And that's significant – even if it's true that, in many cases, the use of the word "capitalism" is mainly rhetorical, functioning less as an actual concept than as a gesture toward the need for a concept. In these times, we, as critical theorists, should pose that question explicitly: What exactly does it mean to speak of capitalism today? And how can one best theorize it?

Jaeggi: We should be clear what we mean by the notion that it is *capitalism* that is making a comeback. Certainly, there have always been social movements and advocacy groups concerned with various forms of social or economic justice; and the topic of "distributive justice" has had a heyday in certain parts of the academy. Also, economic questions have frequently arisen in debates about globalization, the future of national autonomy, and inequality and poverty in the developing world. Then, too, the term "capitalism" has continued to float around as a synonym for "modernity" in some circles, where the "critique of capitalism" ends up referring to cultural criticism in the vein of Baudrillard and Deleuze. But none of these approaches grasps capitalism in the sense we are talking about here. None sees it as an overarching form of life, grounded – as Marx would say – in a mode of production, with a very specific set of presuppositions, dynamics, crisis tendencies, and fundamental contradictions and conflicts.

Fraser: Yes, I agree. Fortunately, however, the current interest in capitalism transcends the limited, partial approaches you've just mentioned. What drives it, as I said, is the widespread sense of deep and pervasive crisis – not just a sectoral crisis, but one that encompasses every major aspect of our social order. So the problem isn't simply "economic" – it's not "just" inequality, unemployment, or maldistribution, as serious as those things are. Nor is it even only the 1% versus the 99% – although that rhetoric inspired many people to start asking questions about capitalism. No, the problem runs deeper than that. Above and beyond the matter of how wealth is "distributed," there is the problem of what counts as wealth in the first place and how that wealth is produced. Similarly, behind the matter of who gets how much for what sort of labor lies the deeper question of what counts as labor, how it is organized, and what its organization is now demanding from, and doing to, people.

To my mind, this is what should be at stake when we talk about capitalism. Not only why some have more and others less, but also why so few people now have stable lives and a sense of well-being; why so many have to scramble for precarious work, juggling multiple jobs with fewer rights, protections, and benefits, while going heavily into debt. But that is not all. Equally fundamental questions surround the deepening stresses on family life: why and how the pressures of paid work and debt are altering the conditions of child-rearing, eldercare, household relations, and community bonds – in short, the entire organization of social reproduction. Deep questions arise, too, about the increasingly alarming impacts of our extractive relation to nature, which capitalism treats both as a "tap" for energy and raw materials and as a "sink" to absorb our waste. Nor, finally, should we forget political questions, about, for example, the hollowing out of democracy by market forces at two levels: on the one hand, the corporate capture of political parties and public institutions at the level of the territorial state; on the other hand, the usurpation of political decision-making power at the transnational level by global finance, a force that is unaccountable to any demos.

All of this is central to what it means to talk about capitalism today. One implication is that our crisis is not only economic. It also encompasses care deficits, climate change, and de-democratization. But even that formulation is not good enough. The deeper issue is what underlies all these intractable difficulties: the growing sense that their simultaneous appearance is no mere coincidence, that it signals something more fundamentally rotten in our social order. *That* is what is pointing so many people back to capitalism.

Jaeggi: These multiple crises are forcing us to ask whether there is not some kind of deeper failure in the capitalist social formation. Many people now suspect that it is no longer good enough to look only at these bad effects when it is likely that an entire form of life has become dysfunctional. And this means they are willing to look more deeply at the various social practices that this social formation comprises – not just inequality or ecological degradation or globalization, as you said, but the very practices that make up the system that generates these conflicts, right down to the way we understand things such as property, labor, production, exchange, markets, and so on.

But if we're agreed that the critique of capitalism is once again back on the agenda and that this is a welcome development, we should also ask where it went in the first place. What happened to marginalize capitalism for so long? How might we understand its disappearance from critical theory? It seems that, over the last several decades, we have seen a turn toward a "black box" view of the economy. This is certainly true of philosophical liberalism and other schools of thought that focus narrowly on questions of "distribution." Take left-wing Rawlsians or socialists like G. A. Cohen: they take an otherwise radical and egalitarian approach to matters of distributive justice, but they tend to avoid talking about the economy itself.[3] They talk about what comes out of the economic "black box" and how to distribute these outcomes, but they don't talk about what's going on inside it, how it works, and whether these goings-on are really necessary or desirable.

But the trend isn't confined to liberalism and theories of justice. Capitalism used to be a core problem for critical theory. For virtually all the great thinkers in this tradition – from Marx to Lukács to Horkheimer and Adorno to the early Habermas – capitalism was central. But sometime in the mid- to late 1980s, it pretty much dropped out of the picture. What happened? Did we all just become so ideologically "one-dimensional" that even critical theorists lost sight of the sources of our unfreedom? That sounds rather crude as an explanation. I suspect there are reasons intrinsic to the theoretical development of our intellectual tradition that have led to the abandonment of the topic.

In a sense, Habermas's *Theory of Communicative Action*, with its controversial thesis about the "colonization of the lifeworld," was the last attempt to ground critical theory in a large-scale social theory.[4] It is certainly inspired by Marx, Lukács, and the intuitions of earlier critical theory in a way that can't be said of some of his later disciples. Nevertheless, Habermas relies on systems-theoretic ideas about functional differentiation to such an extent that he in effect removes the economic sphere from the realm of criticism. The economy is understood as something that functions autonomously, a "norm-free" domain driven by its own logic.[5] This amounts to another kind of "black box" approach, as all we can do is protect against the invasion of the economic into other areas of life. The capitalist economy is a "tiger" to be "tamed" by political or otherwise external means, but we no longer have critical access to the economy itself.

Now this is not to rehash the old debate between *transforming* capitalism through reform and *overcoming* it through more radical means. How "tamed" capitalism can be and still be "capitalism" is largely a semantic issue, which we needn't get into now. At the same time, the excesses and threats posed by contemporary capitalism might give us pause over whether the idea of "taming" capitalism is still adequate. "The historical connection between democracy and capitalism"[6] is very much in question today, and perhaps this is why it is only now that new takes on economic issues are beginning to develop.

Fraser: I fully agree with you that Habermas's *Theory of Communicative Action* marked a turning point in critical theory. Like you said, it was the last great systematic attempt, but it failed to generate successor works of comparable ambition and breadth. Instead, its legacy proved to be a tremendous increase in disciplinary specialization among Habermas's followers. In the subsequent decades, most of those who think of themselves as critical theorists went on to do freestanding moral, political, or legal theory, with hardly anyone taking up large-scale social theory (the Research Group on Post-Growth Societies in Jena being a recent and welcome exception). The effect was to abandon the original idea of critical theory as an interdisciplinary project aimed at grasping society as a totality. No longer linking normative questions to the analysis of societal tendencies and to a diagnosis of the times, people simply stopped trying to understand capitalism as such. There were no more efforts to identify its deep structures and driving mechanisms, its defining tensions and contradictions, or its characteristic forms of conflict and emancipatory possibilities. The result was not only to abandon the central terrain of critical theory; it was also to muddy the once sharp boundary that separated it from egalitarian liberalism. Today, those two camps have drifted so close as to be barely distinguishable, making it hard to say where liberalism stops and critical theory begins. Perhaps the best one can say is that (so-called) critical theory has become the left-wing of liberalism. And that is something that I have long felt unhappy about.

Jaeggi: Actually, Axel Honneth has criticized this tendency to buy into freestanding normativism for a long time as well. He is one person who, in a Hegelian manner, has stayed in touch with social theory and, reconstructing the institutional spheres of modern societies, has started to re-think the "system of needs," the sphere of the market and economy in general, anew.[7]

Fraser: Good point. But he's the exception that proves the rule. The overwhelming majority of critical theorists have shown little interest in social theory. And if we want to understand the relative absence of the critique of capitalism in recent years, we also need to factor in the spectacular rise of poststructuralist thought in the late twentieth century. In the US academy, at least, poststructuralism became the "official opposition" to liberal moral and political philosophy. And yet, despite their differences, these ostensible opponents shared something fundamental: both liberalism and poststructuralism were ways of evacuating the problematic of political economy, indeed of the social itself. It was a very powerful convergence – a one–two punch, if you like.

Jaeggi: Could one say that, from both sides, liberal-Kantian normativism and the poststructuralist critique of normativity, we now find a situation in which the unity of the analysis and critique has fallen apart? Beyond the explicit concern with capitalism, the central idea of critical theory from the very beginning was its continuation of the Hegelian–Marxist framework for analyzing and criticizing society. It was motivated by this very special idea that, without being moralistic, social analysis should already have some transformative and emancipatory aim contained within it. But now it seems, with the dominance of political liberalism and the enormous influence of Rawls, that this unity has broken up, so we now have empirical social theory on one side and normative political theory on the other.

Fraser: You are absolutely right about Rawlsian liberalism – and, I would add, its poststructuralist opposition. The intellectual dominance achieved by the combination of these two camps effectively killed the left-Hegelian project, at least for a time. The link between social analysis and normative critique was severed. The normative was abstracted from the social realm and treated as something freestanding, regardless of whether one's aim was to affirm it (as in the case of the liberals) or to reject it (as in the case of the poststructuralists).

Jaeggi: But perhaps there were good reasons to turn away from capitalism and the economy. Maybe this was something that needed to be done, even by left-thinkers and critical theorists. Older Marxist-inspired theories tended to encourage an overly "economistic" way of seeing society, and we needed to gain some distance from that. So while capitalism dropped out of the picture, this also made room to explore a wide array of cultural issues, such as gender, race, sexuality, and identity. And critical study of these things in a way that did not subordinate them to economics was something we sorely needed. But I would say that it's time to restore the balance. It's not enough to avoid economism. We must also take care not to lose sight of the importance of the economic side of social life.

Fraser: I agree with your suggestion that the turn away from political economy was not a simple mistake – for two different reasons. The first is that there have been real gains in addressing questions of misrecognition, status hierarchy, ecology, and sexuality. These were all matters that an orthodox, sclerotic, and reductively economistic paradigm pushed off the table. Recovering them and giving them a central place in critical theory represents an important achievement. This is why I've always insisted on a "both/and" approach – both class *and* status, redistribution *and* recognition. It is also why I've insisted that we cannot simply return to an older received critique of political economy, but must rather complicate, deepen, and enrich that critique by incorporating the insights of feminist thought, cultural theory and poststructuralism, postcolonial thought, and ecology.

But there's also a second reason why the turn away from political economy wasn't a simple mistake. Rather, it was a response, however unwitting, to a major historical shift in the character of capitalism. We know that capitalist society was undergoing an immense restructuring and reconfiguration during the period in question. One aspect of this shift was the new salience of "the symbolic" (the digital and the image, derivatives trading and Facebook), which thinkers as diverse as Fredric Jameson and Carlo Vercellone have sought to theorize.[8] That is linked, of course, to the decentering of manufacturing in the Global North, the rise of the "knowledge economy" or "cognitive capitalism," the centrality of finance, IT, and symbolic labor more generally. It may sound ironic, but there's a political-economic story that helps explain why people abandoned political economy and began to focus one-sidedly on issues of culture, identity, and discourse. Although those issues *appear* to be something other than political economy, they cannot actually be understood in abstraction from it. So this is not just a mistake; it's also a clue about something going on in society.

Jaeggi: There's an old quote by Horkheimer, in which he says, "Economism . . . does not consist in giving too much importance to the economy, but in giving it too narrow a scope."[9] In other words, we shouldn't turn away from the economy, but rather we need to try to re-think economy and its role in society in a "wider" sense. My sense is we haven't yet arrived at a conception that would be wide enough, and part of the tendency to abandon the topic of capitalism comes from this "fear of economism" that we've been internalizing since the early days of the Frankfurt School. This drives much of my interest in social ontology, forms of life, and trying to understand the economy as a "social practice."[10] In a practice-oriented approach, the economy and its institutions comprise a subset of social practices that are interrelated with other practices in a variety of ways, which, taken together, form part of the socio-cultural fabric of society. This way of thinking has the benefit of avoiding the opposition between "the cultural" and "the economic," a dichotomy I don't find particularly helpful.

How would you place your own work in respect to this dichotomy and these trends? You've long framed your project as being about "redistribution" as well as "recognition." Would you characterize your recent work on capitalism as a move away from this "black box," redistribution-focused way of thinking? Or would you say your past work on the redistribution versus recognition debate already harbored a concern with capitalism?

Fraser: I have always tried to resist what you've called the "black box" approach. And the question of capitalism has never been absent from my conscious thoughts, even when it was not the explicit focus of a given project. Coming as I did out of the democratic-socialist wing of the New Left, I always took it as axiomatic that capitalism was the master frame within which every question of social philosophy and political theory had to be situated. That went without saying

8

for my generation. So when I wrote in the 1980s about the "struggle over needs," the androcentrism of the "family wage," or the idea of so-called "welfare dependency," I was trying to clarify aspects of what was then called "late capitalism" – and what I would now call "state-managed capitalism."[11]

An analogous point holds for my work in the 1990s and 2000s. In that period, I was grappling with a major shift in the political culture of capitalist society: which I called the shift "from redistribution to recognition."[12] Far from being an exercise in freestanding moral philosophy, this work was an early attempt to grasp an epochal historical mutation of capitalist society, from the "state-managed" variant of the postwar era to the "financialized" capitalism of the present. For me, in other words, "redistribution" was never meant as a euphemism or substitute for "capitalism." It was, rather, my term for a grammar of political claims-making that gestured toward a structural aspect of capitalist society but pictured it ideologically as an economic "black box," if you like, and which became a major focus of social struggle and crisis management in the state-managed regime. I was interested in disclosing how and why capitalist society generated this sort of *economic* black box of distribution, separated from the equally problematic *cultural* box of recognition. Far from endorsing the black box view of distribution, then, I was trying to clarify where it came from and why it was juxtaposed to recognition. I traced the provenance of both those categories (as well as their mutual opposition) precisely to capitalism, which I viewed as the broader totality within which redistribution and recognition, class and status, had to be understood.

Still, I take your point that my current work spotlights the problem of capitalism in a different and more emphatic way. Today, capitalist society is the explicit foreground of my theorizing, the direct object of my critique. That's partly because the character of financialized capitalism as a deeply crisis-ridden regime is much clearer to me now. But it's also because, for the first time since the 1960s, I can see the palpable fragility of capitalism, which now manifests itself openly with visible cracks. This fragility spurs me to look at it in a head-on way – and to focus especially on its "crisis tendencies" and "contradictions."

Jaeggi: Getting back to this kind of theorizing may not be so easy, however, especially if we're talking about returning to the kind of "grand theory" that most critical and social theorists have long abandoned – the kind that deals in large historical processes, systemic conflicts, and deep-seated contradictions and crisis tendencies. Marx was looking for the unfolding of one kind of crisis, but today we are confronted with a variety of crises and conflicts. Do we need large-scale social theory to think about capitalism in crisis?

Fraser: We do need "grand theorizing," in my view – and we always have. But you are right: it's by no means easy to develop a large-scale social theory of capitalism for our time. One problem, as you said, is the multi-dimensionality of the present crisis, which is not only economic and financial, but also ecological, political, and social. This situation cannot be adequately grasped by economistic theorizing. But neither can we be satisfied with vague gestures to "multiplicity," which have become so fashionable. Rather, we need to disclose the structural grounds of multiple crisis tendencies in one and the same social totality: capitalist society. There are many traps here. Neither doubling down on received Marxian models nor simply jettisoning them altogether will suffice. We need somehow to create a new understanding of capitalism that integrates the insights of Marxism with those of newer paradigms, including feminism, ecology, and postcolonialism – while avoiding the respective blindspots of each.

In any case, the sort of large-scale social theory I am developing now is centered on the problem of crisis. This may be putting my head in the lion's mouth, because no genre of critical theory has been so heavily criticized as "crisis theory." That genre has been widely rejected, even dismissed, as inherently mechanistic, deterministic, teleological, functionalistic – you name it. And yet, we are living in a time that literally cries out for crisis critique. I would go further and say that we are living in the throes of an epochal crisis of capitalism, so we have an urgent need to reconstruct crisis theorizing today. This is the genre of large-scale social theory that I am pursuing now and that I want to discuss with you here.

Jaeggi: We certainly have a lot of common ground here. In my *Forms of Life* book I also argued for a crisis critique of forms of life, which I take to mean a form of immanent critique that finds its starting point not "positively," in already shared values, but in the immanent crises and contradictions inherent in the dynamics of forms of life – in the fact that forms of life can "fail," even if the failure itself is normatively infused.[13]

And yet to focus on crises and contradictions builds on a wealth of suppositions. Quite a few critical theorists have long defined their task in reference to the old line by Marx to Arnold Ruge, as being

10

about the "self-clarification of the struggles and wishes of the age."[14] They took this to imply a focus on the social movements and the people engaged in these kinds of struggles, with the role of the critical theorist being that of someone who clarifies the issues surrounding them. Now, this might be a somewhat "lightweight" interpretation of the historical dynamics Marx had in mind when talking about the "struggles and wishes" of the present. After all, what he had in mind was primarily one struggle – class struggle – with a strong historical and materialistic dynamic as its moving force in the background.

You yourself have cited this passage, and your work has always been great in reflecting the social struggles and movements taking place. But your orientation now seems to have undergone a change. It's not as if you are now turning away from the struggle dimension – you're certainly not – but you have begun to push beyond the "subjective" elements of struggle and languages of claims-making to the more "objective" dimensions of contradictions and crises, which turn more on the dynamics of systemic elements operating independently of whether or not people actually thematize them via struggle. So there are implications we should be aware of, as well as a host of new questions that come along with this kind of shift from one dimension to the other.

I would be interested in how one would balance these two dimensions. One option might be to use the lens of present-day social struggles diagnostically to trace underlying contradictions. Another might involve looking, in a more foundational way, at the conditions of social integration and division as a basis for thinking about systemic contradictions – though theorizing at this kind of level is often a tricky proposition.

Fraser: Yes, that's true. There has indeed been a shift in emphasis in my recent work. As someone deeply schooled in Marx, I've always believed that capitalism harbored "real" objective crisis tendencies, but in the past I didn't take it upon myself to try to analyze them. Perhaps this was because my formative political experiences were the social movements and struggles of the 1960s – I became preoccupied with questions of struggle and conflict at a moment when capitalism's crisis tendencies did not take the form Marx described in *Das Kapital*. More recently, I have been influenced by ecological thought, especially the ecological critique of capitalism, which posits some real, seemingly objective limits to capitalist development, and which seeks to identify the contradictions and self-destabilizing tendencies of a social system that is consuming its own natural conditions of possibility. This kind of thinking did not play a major role in my earlier work, but it has come into focus for me in recent decades. The ecological paradigm understands capitalist crisis in a way that is as systemic and as deeply structural as the Marxian paradigm, almost as if the two crisis complexes were parallel. I'm not satisfied with the idea that they are parallel, however, and believe we need to understand their imbrication with one another – as well as with other, equally "objective" tendencies to political and social crisis. This is something we'll talk about later, I'm sure.

But you asked about the relation between the "objective" and "subjective" strands of a critical theory. (At some point, we should problematize that terminology; there may well be better ways to name the distinction you have in mind.) I'm convinced we have to look both at the "real contradictions" or systemic crisis tendencies, on the one hand, and at the forms of conflict and struggle that develop in response to them, on the other hand. In some cases, the struggles are explicit and conscious "subjective" responses to the "objective" dimension. In other cases, they are symptomatic of it. And in still others, they may be something else entirely. In other words, the relation between the two levels, the "objective" and the "subjective," is a problem. We cannot assume the perfect synchronization that Marx thought he had discerned between capitalism's system crisis, on the one hand, and the sharpening class struggle between labor and capital, on the other, according to which the latter perfectly reflected or responded to the former. In the absence of any such auto-harmonization, we must treat the relationship between these two poles as an open question and a problem to be theorized. This is an especially pressing question today, when we are facing an evident structural crisis, but (as yet anyway) no corresponding political conflict that adequately expresses the crisis in a way that could lead to an emancipatory resolution. So the relation between system crisis and social struggle must be a major focus of our conversation in the chapters that follow.

"the relation between system crisis and social struggle"

1

Conceptualizing Capitalism

What is capitalism? The problem of the many and the one

Jaeggi: What is capitalism? This question begs for an essential defini-tion of some sort, a set of core features that distinguish capitalist societies from non-capitalist societies. I think we both agree that capi-talism has social, economic, political dimensions that should be seen as standing in some kind of interconnected relation to each other. Yet a skeptic might claim it's not so easy to specify the core elements of capitalism. After all, haven't we learned from the "varieties of capitalism" debate that capitalism doesn't look the same everywhere in the world?[1] Might we not conclude that capitalist societies look so different from one another that there is no true common denomina-tor? If this were the case, we face a real problem. If we cannot specify the core elements that make a social formation capitalist, how can we talk about a crisis of capitalism? Without those core elements, there would be no way to establish that the present crisis is really a crisis of capitalism and not a crisis of something else. The same holds for our resources to *criticize* capitalism: how can we claim that the instances of social suffering we want to address are actually related to *capital-ism*, if we don't even have a sufficiently clear and coherent concept of capitalism that allows us to identify its core elements?

Fraser: Good point. I myself start with the assumption that the present crisis *can* be understood as a crisis of capitalism. But that assumption needs to be demonstrated. And the first step is to answer the capitalism skeptic, so to speak, by showing that we can indeed speak of "capital-ism" as such, despite its many varieties. This requires explaining what we mean by capitalism, defining it in terms of some core features that obtain across the broad range of societies we call "capitalist." After all, it makes no sense to talk about *varieties* of capitalism if they don't share some common underlying features in virtue of which they are all varieties *of capitalism*. So the challenge for us is to say what makes a society capitalist without homogenizing the great variety of ways in which capitalist societies can and do differ from one another. We will then need to clarify the relation between the core features we identify and the variety of forms in which they are instantiated across space and time.

Jaeggi: This issue has at least two dimensions: one vertical and the other horizontal. There is not only the question of varieties of capitalism with respect to the thesis that we confront contemporaneous *capitalisms* in the plural, coexisting in different societies at the same time. In addition, we are confronted with the historical development of different *stages* of capitalism. There are tremendous differences between earlier configurations of capitalism and present-day capitalism, and we could ask whether it's still a good theoretical move to call all of them "capitalism." How can we equate or relate the early stages of industrial capitalism with modern neoliberal and global capitalism? Is it even appropriate to use the same conceptual framework to analyze both the competitive capitalism of the nineteenth century and the "monopoly capitalism" of the twentieth, which the early Frankfurt School called "State Capitalism?" I think our first task should be to get at what core elements have to be in place for a social formation to count as some instantiation of capitalism.

Fraser: The historical point is important. I'm inclined to the view that, whatever else it is, capitalism is intrinsically historical. Far from being given all at once, its properties emerge over time. If that's right, then we have to proceed cautiously, taking every proposed definition with a grain of salt and as subject to modification within capitalism's unfolding trajectory. Features that appear central at the outset may decline in salience later, while characteristics that seem marginal or even absent at first could assume major importance later.

As you just suggested, inter-capitalist competition was a driving mechanism of capitalist development in the nineteenth century, but it was increasingly superseded in the twentieth, at least in leading sectors of what was widely understood as "monopoly capitalism." Conversely, whereas finance capital seemed to play an auxiliary role in the Fordist era, it has become a major driving force in neoliberalism.

14

Finally, the governance regimes that embed and organize capitalism at every stage have been transformed again and again in the course of the last 300 years, from mercantilism to laissez-faire liberalism to state-led *dirigisme* to neoliberal globalization.

These examples point to capitalism's inherent historicity. What is at issue here are not simply different "varieties of capitalism," which might exist side-by-side, but rather *historical moments*, which are linked to one another in a path-dependent sequence. Within this sequence, any given transformation is politically driven and, to be sure, traceable to struggles among proponents of different projects. But this sequence can also be reconstructed as a directional or dialectical process in which an earlier form runs up against difficulties or limits, which its successor overcomes or circumvents, until it too encounters an impasse and is superseded in turn.

Considerations like these complicate the search for a core definition. I don't think they make such a definition impossible, but they do suggest we should proceed with care. Most importantly, we have to avoid conflating relatively fleeting historical forms with the more enduring logic that underlies them.

Core features of capitalism: an orthodox start

Jaeggi: Here's a proposal to get us started. Let's begin by positing three defining features of capitalism: (1) private ownership of the means of production and the class division between owners and producers; (2) the institution of a free labor market; and (3) the dynamic of capital accumulation premised on an orientation toward the expansion of capital as opposed to consumption, coupled with an orientation toward making profit instead of satisfying needs.

Fraser: This is very close to Marx. By starting in this way, we'll arrive at a conception of capitalism that will, at least at first sight, appear quite orthodox. But we can de-orthodoxize it later, by showing how these core features relate to other things and how they manifest themselves in real historical circumstances.

Let's start with your first point: the social division between those who own the means of production as their private property and those who own nothing but their "labor power." I don't mean to suggest that capitalist society harbors no other constitutive social divisions; I want to discuss some others very soon. But this one is certainly central: a definitive feature of capitalism and a historical

15

"achievement" of it, if that's the right word. This class division supposes the break-up of prior social formations in which most people, however differently situated, had some access to means of subsistence and means of production – access to food, shelter, and clothing, and to tools, land, and work – without having to go through labor markets. Capitalism destroyed that condition, separating the vast majority from the means of subsistence and production and excluding them from what had been common social resources. It enclosed the commons, abrogating customary use rights and transforming shared resources into the private property of a small minority. As a result of this class division between owners and producers, the majority must now go through a very peculiar song and dance (the labor market) in order to be able to work and get what they need to continue living and raise their children. The important thing is just how bizarre, how "unnatural," how historically anomalous and specific this is.

Jaeggi: Yes, and this leads us to the second point: capitalism depends on the existence of free labor markets. Capitalist societies, as we know them, have tended to abolish unfree labor of the sort found in feudal societies. They institutionalize free labor on the assumption that the workers are free and equal. This is the official version, at least, but it is contradicted in reality by capitalism's coexistence for over two centuries with New World slavery. But this aside, the labor power of "free workers" is treated as a good that one party to a legal contract (the worker) owns and sells to the other party (the employer-capitalist).

Historically speaking, this is a tremendous change with tremendous implications, one that alters daily life as well as the economic structure of the societies involved. Even without seeing societies divided, in a reductionist way, into economic base and ideological superstructure, we can say that their form as a whole changes once this is established. Moreover, since the free labor market is constitutive for capitalism, the normative ideals of freedom and equality find their place in an actual institution. They are not just a masking decoration; to some extent, they really are objectified and present. The capitalist labor market wouldn't work without legally free and independent contractors. This is true even if at the same time those ideals are corrupted exactly in and through the labor market. Which brings us to the fact Marx pointed out so vividly: labor in capitalism is free *in a double sense*.[2] The workers are free to work but also "free to starve" if they do not enter the labor contract.

16

Fraser: Exactly. Those conceived as "workers" are free, first, in the sense of legal status. They are not enslaved, enserfed, entailed, or otherwise bound to a given place or particular master. They are mobile and able to enter into a labor contract. But the "workers" are also free in a second sense: they are free, as we just said, from access to means of subsistence and means of production, including from customary use rights in land and tools. In other words, they are unencumbered by the sort of resources and entitlements that could permit them to abstain from the labor market. Their freedom in the first sense goes along with their vulnerability to compulsion inherent in the second sense.

That said, I want to underline your point that the view of the worker as a free individual is not the whole story. As you said, capitalism has always coexisted with – I would say, relied on – a great deal of unfree and dependent labor. And as I'll explain soon, not everyone who works or produces has been considered a worker or accorded the status of a free individual – which is why I put the word "worker" in scare quotes before. The point, then, is that, in discussing the worker's double freedom, we are talking only about one chunk of capitalist social reality – albeit a very important, even defining, chunk.

Jaeggi: Right. We'll have to come back to that point later. For now, however, I want to stress that the notion of freedom in a "double sense" doesn't mean that freedom and equality in capitalism are fictitious or some kind of lip service. These notions are ideological in the deep sense that Adorno invoked, when he said that ideologies are true and false at the same time.[3] The point is that freedom and equality are actually realized in capitalism and in fact *must* be realized in order for the system to work. And yet at the same time they are not realized: the reality of capitalist work relations seems to undermine and contradict these norms – and not accidentally so.

Fraser: I would say that capitalism realizes thin, liberal interpretations of freedom and equality, while systematically denying the social prerequisites for realizing deeper, more adequate interpretations – interpretations that it simultaneously invites and callously frustrates.

Jaeggi: Let's talk about our third feature: the dynamic of capital accumulation. This seems to be one of the defining characteristics of capitalism.

17

Fraser: Yes, it certainly is. Here we find the equally strange song and dance of self-expanding value. Capitalism is peculiar in having an objective systemic thrust or directionality: the accumulation of capital. Everything the owners do is and must be aimed at expanding their capital. Not to expand is to die, to fall prey to competitors. So this is not a form of society in which the owners are simply enjoying themselves and having a grand old time. Like the producers, they too stand under a peculiar compulsion. And everyone's efforts to satisfy their needs are indirect, harnessed to something else that assumes priority – an overriding imperative inscribed in an impersonal system, capital's own drive to unending self-expansion. Marx is brilliant on this point. In a capitalist society, he says, Capital itself becomes the Subject. Human beings are its pawns, reduced to figuring out how they can get what they need in the interstices by feeding the beast.

Jaeggi: Max Weber and Werner Sombart have also spelled out how bizarre this form of life really is. From Weber, we have the famous remarks according to which the capitalist "Erwerbsstreben" ["pursuit of wealth"] has become an end in itself, one that is precisely *not* directed toward the fulfillment of needs, wishes, not to mention happiness.[4] And, despite its nostalgic and pre-modern tenor, Sombart's book on modern capitalism is especially interesting on that matter because it's filled with vignettes about how difficult it is to keep the capitalist dynamic going, to keep it alive. For example, in France quite a few successful capitalist entrepreneurs at a certain point sold their factories to buy huge villas and enjoy their lives – to get off the treadmill and out of the rat race. Sombart calls this phenomenon the "degenerative fattening of capitalism" ("die Verfettung des Kapitalismus"), whereby capitalists lose their initiative to accumulate.[5] We can also look to the many novels, such as Gaskell's *North and South*, which deal with the transition from a precapitalist to capitalist mode of life.[6]

The lesson we can learn from them is that these attitudes and the "spirit of capitalism" are far from self-evident. So, when we speak with Marx of capital becoming the real subject, this still leaves open crucial philosophical questions as to whether we really face a purely systemic self-perpetuation, or whether this manner of speaking obfuscates some more fine-grained prerequisites, including the social attitudes that sustain the perpetuation of profit-seeking. Economic practices are always already embedded in forms of life, and taking this into account complicates the effort to define capitalism as a system that could be specified independently of them – especially

18

if we want to avoid the stark division, which you yourself have criticized, between an innocent "lifeworld" and a free-wheeling "system" of economic dynamics.[7] That division treats capitalism as a self-perpetuating "machine" that feeds on people but is in no way driven by them. But perhaps we should keep the question of what "feeds" capitalism on hold for the time being.

Markets: a defining feature of capitalism?

Jaeggi: Now, perhaps we should add a fourth feature to our list of a still rather orthodox definition of capitalism: the centrality of markets in capitalist society. Aside from the labor market, markets more generally seem to be the principal institutions for organizing material provision in a capitalist society. In capitalism, it is typically via market mechanisms that goods are provided.

But the relation between capitalism and markets is complicated: although the two are intertwined, they are far from identical. Capitalism is more than a "market society." Markets have existed in non- or precapitalist societies, and, conversely, we might think of a socialist society that includes market mechanisms. So it is important to investigate the relation between them.

Fraser: I agree. The relation between capitalism and markets is quite complicated, I think, and needs to be carefully unpacked. I would start, once again, by recalling Marx. For Marx, the market is closely related to the commodity form. And the commodity form is only the starting point for theorizing capitalism, not the end point. It is presented in the opening chapters of *Das Kapital* as the realm of appearances, the guise in which things appear initially, when we adopt the commonsense standpoint of bourgeois society, the perspective of market exchange. From that initial perspective, Marx quickly leads us to another, deeper one, which is the standpoint of production and exploitation. The implication is that there is something more fundamental to capitalism than the market: namely, the organization of *production* through the exploitation of labor as the engine that generates surplus value. That at least is how I read Marx, as wanting to replace bourgeois political economy's focus on market exchange with a deeper, more critical focus on production. It's there at the deeper level that we discover a dirty secret: that accumulation proceeds via exploitation. Capital expands, in other words, not via the exchange of equivalents but precisely through its opposite: via

19

the *non*-compensation of a portion of the workers' labor time. This already tells us that market exchange per se is not the heart of the matter.

Jaeggi: But don't you think that a marketizing tendency is already built into the first three core features of capitalism that we just identified? After all, when you imagine those three coming together to form a dynamic system, what you get is a picture of a world in which more and more things are bought, sold, and traded on markets.

Fraser: Perhaps. But for me the crucial question is: what kind of markets? As you said, markets exist in many non-capitalist societies, and they take an amazing variety of forms – a point that is central for Karl Polanyi.[8] So our question should be: what's specific to markets in capitalist societies?

Jaeggi: Yes, I agree, especially since this matter easily lends itself to ideological mystification. Do you realize that, in Germany, the term "capitalism" has more pejorative connotations than it does in the English-speaking world, and, as a result, German economists prefer not to talk about capitalism at all? In their view, if you're using the word "capitalism," you're already being too critical. Textbooks typically use the euphemistic expression "market society." A similar move (in your country) has been made by the Board of Education in Texas by ordering that all history textbooks no longer refer to "capitalism" but instead call it "the free-enterprise system."[9]
   This locution is ideological – not least because it obscures an important question: what actually *is* the relation between markets and capitalism? Could we have markets without capitalism? For example, societies with markets but without private ownership of the means of production, as market socialists have advocated? And what about the converse: is it still a capitalist society if its economy features such a huge degree of monopolization that a certain amount of goods are not exchanged via the market? In short, can we have capitalism without markets and markets without capitalism?

Fraser: That's a good way to formulate the problem. To answer it, I would like to distinguish some different kinds of markets and some different roles markets can play. Let's think, first, about markets in consumer goods, which distribute the means of subsistence to individuals in the form, first, of wages or income, and then of commodities. Is this sort of market definitive of capitalism? I don't think

20

so! Granted, it seems to follow logically from the point about "free" labor. As we already noted, it is a characteristic of capitalism's economic logic that propertyless workers have no direct access to the means of subsistence. They can only get the necessities of life by selling their labor power for wages, which they then use to purchase food, shelter, and other essentials. The flip side of this is a tendency, over time, to transform the means of subsistence into commodities, available only through purchase with money.

Nevertheless, that point is not decisive. The key phrase here is "over time," as the process is rather uneven. On the one hand, it can proceed quite far, as we know from the "consumer capitalism" of the twentieth century, which built an entire accumulation strategy around the sale of consumer goods to the working classes of the capitalist core. On the other hand, many people in the periphery were not (and are still not) fully included in this sort of consumerism, for reasons that are not accidental but in fact structural. And even for those who did become consumers, the process can be at least partially reversed, as we know from the present-day experience of neoliberal crisis, when, even in the capitalist heartland, many people find it necessary to engage in in-kind transactions of various types, including barter, non-formalized reciprocity, and mutual aid – just think of Athens or Detroit today.[10]

Jaeggi: But how should we interpret this? Is it a regression to a precapitalist condition or a remnant of precapitalist society? Or do these phenomena indicate something systemic about capitalism itself – along the lines of the thesis that total commodification wouldn't even be possible?

Fraser: There's nothing precapitalist about this, in my view. Immanuel Wallerstein has often stressed that capitalism has generally operated on the basis of "semi-proletarianized" households.[11] Under these arrangements, which allow owners to pay workers less, many households derive a significant portion of their sustenance from sources other than cash wages, including self-provisioning (the garden plot, sewing, etc.), informal reciprocity (mutual aid, in-kind transactions), and state transfers (welfare benefits, social services, public goods). Such arrangements leave a significant portion of activities and goods outside the purview of the market. They are not mere residual holdovers from precapitalist times; nor are they on their way out. They were intrinsic to Fordism, which was able to promote working-class consumerism in the countries of the core only by way of semi-proletarianized households that combined male employment with female homemaking – as well as by inhibiting the development of commodity consumption in the periphery. And, as I just said, semi-proletarianization is even more pronounced in neoliberalism, which has built an entire accumulation strategy by expelling billions of people from the official economy into informal gray zones, from which capital siphons off value. This sort of "primitive accumulation" is an ongoing process from which capital profits and on which it relies.

Jaeggi: But again, is this a historical contingency or something systemic: a functional necessity for capitalism to rely on non-marketized or non-commodified resources?

Fraser: I think it's systemic. Marketization is not ubiquitous in capitalist societies – and the reasons for that are non-accidental. In reality, marketized aspects or zones of life coexist with non-marketized ones. This is no fluke or empirical contingency, in my view, but a feature built into capitalism's DNA. In fact, "coexistence" is too weak a term to capture the relation between marketized and non-marketized aspects of a capitalist society. A better term would be "functional imbrication" or, still better, and more simply, "dependence." Karl Polanyi helps us understand why: society, he tells us, cannot be "commodities all the way down" – that's my paraphrase.[12] Polanyi's idea is that markets depend for their very existence on non-marketized social relations, which supply their background conditions of possibility. I think that is right.

Jaeggi: That's a striking and important claim, which is definitely worth unpacking. To start pressing for further clarification: what does it mean that societies "can't" be commodified all the way down? What poses as the "or else . . . !" here? One can say this is a question of "functional" necessity, that society will no longer "work" properly should commodification become totalized. This suggests there is some objective limit commodification cannot be permitted to cross. But one could also frame the problem more subjectively or normatively, saying excessive commodification is "wrong" or "bad," that the members of these societies simply *don't want* things to be commodities all the way down because it disrupts or erodes a certain "ethos" society might hold and value. It's important to be clear on these terms and to clarify how these functionalist and normative aspects of social critique hang together and require each other. I believe we need a normative–functionalist vocabulary to capture the crises, failures, or mis-developments we face. But still, a functional argument alone doesn't do the work. It's not that it isn't "possible" to commodify all the way down; rather, it isn't possible without creating severe immanent contradictions, which may remain latent for a time but which can also generate real social conflicts.[13]

Fraser: I'm not sure we disagree here. When I say that "society can't be commodities all the way down," I mean that efforts to totalize marketization are self-destabilizing: they jeopardize the market's own background conditions of possibility, which are not themselves marketized. This is one interpretation (the best one, I think) of what Polanyi meant by "fictitious commodification."[14] And it's close to Hegel's claim in *The Philosophy of Right* that society cannot be contract all the way down: if a sphere of contractual relations is possible only on the basis of a background of non-contractual social relations, then efforts to universalize contract necessarily undermine it, by destroying the non-contractual basis on which it depends.[15] This is indeed an "objective" structural argument, but it's not functionalist in a way that's objectionable. It doesn't pretend to say anything about the other crucial, "subjective" half of the equation: how do those living in society experience the fallout? For that, I agree with you: we need a different kind of analysis, focused on the "commonsense," the normatively laden interpretive frames, through which social actors live societal dislocation.

Jaeggi: I would hold that the entanglement between the normative and the functional dimensions must go even deeper in order to make this point. It's not that the "norms" are on the subjective side whereas "function" is on the objective side. There's definitely more to be said about this topic, but let's pursue it later, in chapter 3, when we consider how best to criticize capitalism. For now, I want to resume our discussion of the role that markets actually play in capitalist society. What we've said so far is that capitalism contains a tendency to proliferate markets in consumer goods, but the realization of that tendency is quite variable in space and in time. We noted, too, that non-capitalist societies also have markets in consumer goods, which suggests that such markets are not strictly definitive of or proper to capitalism. But what about markets in other things, such as inputs into production, which are not themselves consumed by or distributed to individuals? Could markets in those sorts of things be distinctive of capitalism?

Fraser: Yes, that's exactly what I mean to suggest. I would distinguish between the use of markets for *distribution* and their use for *allocation*. Whereas markets that function distributively mete out tangible divisible goods for personal consumption, those that function allocatively direct the use of general societal resources in projects that are intrinsically trans-individual or collective, such as production, surplus accumulation, research and development, and/or investment in infrastructure. On the basis of that distinction, we can distinguish market socialism from capitalist society. Market socialism would use markets distributively, to mete out consumer goods, while using non-market mechanisms (such as democratic planning) for allocative purposes, such as allotting credit, capital goods, "raw materials," and social surplus. Capitalism too uses markets distributively, as we have said. But where it is really distinctive is in using markets allocatively – to direct society's use of its accumulated wealth and collective energies. Here, I think, lies the distinctive function of markets in capitalist society: their use to allocate the major inputs to commodity production and to direct investment of social surplus.

Jaeggi: In what you've said, I can see two different "allocative" market functions that are specific to capitalism: allocation of productive inputs and allocation of surplus.

Fraser: Right. The first idea is neatly captured in a striking phrase of Piero Sraffa: capitalism is a system for "the production of commodities by means of commodities."[16] This system marketizes all the major direct inputs to commodity production, including credit, real estate, raw materials, energy, and capital goods, such as machinery, plants, equipment, technology, and so on. This point is also central for Marx. He gave markets in capital goods a prominent place in his account of capitalism's system logic, where they were said to comprise one of the two major "Departments" of capitalist production (the other being goods for individual consumption).[17] And Polanyi made markets in "land" and "money" as central as markets in labor power in distinguishing capitalism from other social formations in which markets also exist.[18] For both thinkers, capitalism is distinctive in this way. Whereas non-capitalist societies have marketized luxury goods and some ordinary goods, only capitalism has sought to marketize *all the major direct inputs of production*, including, but not only, human labor power.

Jaeggi: The second point, too, seems to be quite central for Marx: capitalism uses market mechanisms to determine how the society's surplus will be invested. There is no other kind of society, as far as I know, in which it is left to "market forces" to decide such fundamental questions about how people want to live. Which also means: a shift in the relation between the political and the economic – and a transformation of both sides at the same time.

Fraser: This is for me the most consequential and perverse feature of capitalism, this handing over to market forces of the most important human matters – for example, where people want to invest their collective energies, how they want to balance "productive work" vis-à-vis family life, leisure, and other activities; how much and what they want to leave to future generations. Instead of being treated as matters for collective discussion and decision-making, they are handed over to an apparatus for reckoning monetized value. This is closely related to our third point, about capital's inherent self-expansionary thrust, the process through which it constitutes itself as the subject of history, displacing the human beings who have made it and turning them into its servants. The removal of fundamental questions from the purview of human determination, the ceding of them to an impersonal mechanism geared to the maximal self-expansion of capital – this really is perverse. And it's really distinctive of capitalism. Whatever else socialism might mean, it must entail collective democratic determination of the allocation of social surplus!

Jaeggi: I agree completely. This is exactly where I would locate alienation, which I take to be a certain kind of powerlessness and unfreedom that results from this "displacement" and subjection of the very human beings who created it and set it in motion.

But we should also discuss the "structuring force" exerted by markets in capitalist societies. This may be another distinctive feature of capitalism that distinguishes it from non-capitalist societies. I'm thinking especially of the claim that, under capitalism, the structure of commodity exchange is deeply infused into social life. There are different versions of this claim, but the basic idea is that to treat something as a commodity produced for sale is to alter our relation to it and to ourselves. This involves de-personalization or indifference and orients relations to the world in terms of instrumental, as opposed to intrinsic, values. In this way, the market exercises a qualitative structuring force: it shapes the "worldview," the "grammar" of our lives. We might want to refrain from a totalizing picture of a society entirely controlled and determined by this logic, but it still points to an important insight.

Fraser: That's a good Frankfurt School formulation! And it makes sense, certainly, to say that the labor market (and the whole institution of "free" labor surrounding it) is a major structuring force in capitalist society, which impresses its stamp quite deeply on social life. Over time – and here again, the phrase signals capitalism's inherent historicity – markets in labor power assume not just an allocative function, but also a deeper, more formative function. They change the internal character of what is traded on them and the surrounding form of life in which they are located. This point is important for both Marx and Polanyi. Markets have long existed, but in many societies they are peripheral, contained, confined to the edges of social life. They don't structure the form of life internally. But with capitalism they start to do that.

Jaeggi: Is this Polanyi or Marx? Because if you ask Polanyi, "What is capitalism?", he would say it's market totalization. He definitely does refer to markets as having this structural function. In which respect is this also true for Marx?

Fraser: Just recall Marx's account of the "real" versus the "formal" subsumption of labor. At first, a market in labor just means that people perform essentially the same work they did before, except now they do it in a factory instead of in their cottage. They receive an hourly wage instead of piece rates, but they still make the entire shirt, as they always did. That's what Marx called the "formal subsumption of labor," in which the labor market's force does not yet go "all the way down." Soon, however, the combination of a market in "free" labor and capital's inherent self-expansionary thrust creates pressure to restructure the labor process internally. The work is divided into small segments, which are parceled out to different workers, each of whom is now required to perform the same small, partial operation over and over again – to stitch hundreds and hundreds of collars, for example, which is not at all the same thing as making a shirt. This is one (rather dramatic) example, from Marx, in which the market has not just an allocative or distributive function, but a constitutive, structuring force.[19] There are other examples as well. I think that Marx and Polanyi are close on this point.

Jaeggi: I agree, though I would still say that only Polanyi sees a scandal in the fragmentation per se, because it dissolves some organic unity of the person. I read Marx as far less of a romantic. For him, the absurdity is that we can come up with such an efficient process

26

and still leave it so fundamentally irrational in its effects. The division of labor into very small parts might be a good thing if we had come to it via a process of collective self-determination and also controlled the allocation of the surplus gained. Instead, the division of labor is instituted in a non-transparent, self-disguising way.

But let's continue with markets. Beside the functions of them we discussed – distributive, allocative, formative – we might also focus on their particular form under capitalism. For example, we could also distinguish capitalist markets by their "disembedded" character, to use Polanyi's word. He distinguished "embedded" markets, which are enmeshed in non-economic institutions and subject to non-economic norms (such as "just price" and "fair wage"), from "disembedded" markets, which are freed from extra-economic controls and governed internally by supply and demand. According to Polanyi, embedded markets were the historical norm; throughout most of history, markets have been subject to external controls (political, ethical, religious), which limit what can be bought and sold, by whom, and on what terms. In contrast, the disembedded market is historically anomalous and specific to capitalism. In theory, at least, disembedded markets are "self-regulating": they establish the prices of the objects traded on them through supply and demand, a mechanism internal to the market, which trumps or brackets external norms.[20]

Fraser: Yes, that's the theory, but the reality is rather different. Markets have never really been truly "self-regulating." Nor could they ever be, in Polanyi's view. Marx, too, can be read this way, as rejecting the reality, in history, of "self-regulating markets." In his famous chapter on the struggle over the working day, for example, he demonstrates that wage levels depend on political power and on the outcome of class struggle, not on supply and demand.[21] So historical reality contradicts economic theory on this point.

Jaeggi: I agree. From my perspective, neither markets nor any other form of economic social practice can ever be fully "disembedded" from the forms of life in which they are situated. In fact, I would go further and say that even to refer to markets as "embedded" in societies already goes too far in positing some kind of normative or functional "separation" between economic practices and other social practices. It makes it sound like the economy is something that exists or functions independently of the rest of society, and then it is "embedded" in it or "disembedded" from it. This is not to say an economy can't be institutionalized in a way that resembles or "presents itself" as one or the other; however, I think the relation between economic and other social practices is much more dynamic in a way that can be obscured by the language of "embedding" or "disembedding."[22]

Fraser: I would stress the *paradoxical* character of capitalism's institutionalized differentiation of its economy from "society." This differentiation is at once real and impossible – which may explain why capitalist society is so perverse and self-destabilizing, so subject to periodic crises.

Jaeggi: Let's recap what we've said here about markets. It's not markets in general, but only certain types or uses of markets that are specific to capitalism. The issue is not the use of markets to distribute consumer goods, but their use in allocating the major inputs to production (including, but not only, labor power) and the disposition of social surplus.

We now have four core features that distinguish capitalist societies: (1) a class division between owners and producers; (2) the institutionalized marketization and commodification of wage labor; (3) the dynamic of capital accumulation; and (4) market allocation of productive inputs and social surplus.

Behind the scenes: from the front-story to the back-story

Jaeggi: But still, this really does sound very orthodox, and presumably we don't want to leave matters at that. Firstly, I sense that both of us take "capitalism" to be about more than just the economy or those social practices and institutions that are *directly* economic. And if we're serious about overcoming the bad habits of economism and determinism that plagued so many previous critiques of capitalism, then we would not want to reduce capitalism to its economic system. But more than that, I think we both agree that these core features we've been discussing did not simply happen of their own accord; rather, they had to be somehow established or institutionalized through various means. We've already said that this form of life was no natural development and that it radically disrupted the forms of life that preceded it, and we also raised some doubts about the notion that the economy is an autonomous, self-regulating and non-normative sphere that functions independently of the rest of society.

In other words, what we need is a conception of capitalism that

28

does not limit itself to only one dynamic and historical force – the economy – which determines everything else in society in a one-sided, one-dimensional way. Rather, we need to somehow account for a more nuanced and complex web of dynamics that encompasses multiple realms of society – of which the economy is an important and central one, but not the *only* one – so that we can look at the various ways they function in relation to one another.

Fraser: Agreed. For me, the whole point of starting with a relatively orthodox definition of capitalism was precisely to set up the next step, of "de-orthodox-ification." So I want to show now exactly why the orthodox definition is inadequate – by demonstrating that the four core features we identified rest on some other things, which constitute their background conditions of possibility. In the absence of those other things, this capitalist economic logic that we've been describing is inconceivable. It only makes sense when we start to fill in its background conditions of possibility. In sum, the "economic foreground" of capitalist society requires a "non-economic background."

Jaeggi: What must exist behind or beyond the immediate purview of capital in order for the system's core features to be possible? What must be present behind markets in labor power and other major direct inputs to commodity production, behind private property in the means of production and private appropriation of social surplus, and behind the dynamic of self-expanding value?

Fraser: I'm going to answer your question by turning yet again to Marx. This may seem strange, given my "de-orthodoxifying" aim. But Marx himself may be less orthodox than we've been assuming. After all, he raises a question very like this one near the end of volume I of *Das Kapital* in the chapter on so-called "primitive" or "original" accumulation. Here, he asks: where did capital come from? How were means of production transformed into private property? And how did the producers become separated from them? In the preceding chapters, he had already laid bare capitalism's economic logic in abstraction from its background conditions of possibility. These latter were taken for granted, assumed as simply given. But it turns out that there is a whole back-story about where capital itself comes from – a rather violent story of theft, dispossession, and expropriation.[23]

What interests me here is the epistemic shift that occurs when we move from the front-story of exploitation to the back-story of expropriation. Actually, there are *two* such shifts in volume I. There

29

"from the front-story of exploitation to the back-story of expropriation" is, first, the shift from the standpoint of exchange to the standpoint of production. In that case, we were led from a world where equivalents are exchanged for equivalents to a world of exploitation, in which the capitalist pays the workers only for the "necessary" portion of their labor time and appropriates the "surplus" for himself to augment his capital.[24] And now, we have come to a second shift: from production to primitive accumulation. In this case, Marx leads us from *accumulation through exploitation*, which is a legally sanctioned form of rip-off that works through – and is mystified by – the labor contract, to *accumulation by expropriation*, which is an overtly brutal process, with no pretense of equal exchange.[25] The latter process, which David Harvey calls "dispossession," lies behind contractualized exploitation and renders it possible.[26]

I don't mean to turn the discussion now to "primitive accumulation" – we'll get to that soon enough, I'm sure. No, what interests me here is Marx's method. In each of the twists I've just outlined, he orchestrates a major shift in perspective, leading us from a standpoint associated with what I'm calling "the foreground" (in the first case, exchange, in the second, exploitation) to one that discloses the relevant background (first exploitation, then expropriation). The effect in each case is to make visible something that was previously in the shadows. Suddenly, that "something" appears as a necessary presupposition for what we (mis)took for the main event, and its revelation casts everything that went before it in a new light. Thus, market exchange loses its innocence once we see that it rests on the dirty secret of exploitation. In the same way, the sublimated coercion of wage labor appears still more unsavory when we see that it rests on the even dirtier secret of overt violence and outright theft. The second shift is especially relevant for our problem. It shows that the long elaboration of capitalism's "value logic," which constitutes most of volume I, is not the last word: that it rests on another level of social reality, in effect – an abode behind the abode.

Jaeggi: In speaking about exploitation's "conditions of possibility," you are using metaphors of foreground and background, front-story and back-story.

Fraser: Right. My strategy is to take this "Marxian method" of looking beneath a given socio-historical complex for its underlying conditions of possibility and to apply it further, including to some matters that Marx himself did not fully explore. I want to show that there are some other, equally momentous epistemic shifts that are implied in his analysis of capitalism but that he did not develop. These still need to be conceptualized, written up in new volumes of *Kapital*, if you like, if we are to develop an adequate understanding of 21st-century capitalism. In fact, I can think of three further epistemic shifts, over and above the shift to expropriation, which are required to fill out our conception of capitalism.

From production to reproduction

Fraser: The first is the shift, theorized by Marxist- and socialist-feminists, *from commodity production to social reproduction.* What are at issue here are the forms of provisioning, caregiving, and interacting that produce and maintain social bonds. Variously called "care," "affective labor," or "subjectivation," this activity forms capitalism's human subjects, sustaining them as embodied, natural beings, while also constituting them as social beings, forming their *habitus* and the socio-ethical substance (*Sittlichkeit*) in which they move. Central here is the work of socializing the young, building communities, and producing and reproducing the shared meanings, affective dispositions, and horizons of value that underpin social cooperation, including the forms of cooperation-cum-domination that characterize commodity production. In capitalist societies, much (though not all) of this activity goes on outside the market – in households, neighborhoods, civil society associations, and a host of public institutions, including schools, childcare and eldercare centers; and much of it does not take the form of wage labor. Yet social reproductive activity is absolutely necessary to the existence of waged work, to the accumulation of surplus value, and to the functioning of capitalism as such. Wage labor could neither exist nor be exploited, after all, in the absence of housework, child-raising, schooling, affective care, and a host of other activities that produce new generations of workers, replenish existing generations, and maintain social bonds and shared understandings. Much like "original accumulation," therefore, social reproduction is an indispensable background condition for the possibility of capitalist production.

Jaeggi: This is a familiar theme in Marxist-feminist theory – that the reproduction of wage labor in the factory depends on and is subsidized by unwaged labor in the household. How would you position yourself in relation to the work of Maria Mies or other approaches in Marxist-feminism that have developed since the 1970s?

31

Fraser: Yes, it is familiar, although you'd be amazed at how many major Marxist thinkers have managed to avoid incorporating it systematically into their work, even today! They ignore a great tradition of Marxist-feminist thought, which goes all the way back to Engels.[27] Continued by Alexandra Kollontai and Sylvia Pankhurst in the Bolshevik era, this tradition was richly expanded by "second wave" thinkers like Mariarosa Dalla Costa and Selma James, Juliet Mitchell, and Angela Davis.[28] There's also my personal favorite among Marxist-feminist theorists, Lise Vogel, whose brilliant 1983 book has recently been rediscovered by a new generation of "social reproduction feminists."[29] This isn't the place to rehearse my agreements and disagreements with the various thinkers in this tradition. But since you specifically mentioned Maria Mies, let me say that she was the first to develop a "world systems" perspective on social reproduction. Her account of the link between European "housewifization" and Third World colonization remains a major contribution and unsurpassed insight.[30] On the other hand, I'm not sympathetic to the "subsistence perspective" she developed with Veronika Bennholdt-Thomsen; nor to the version of ecofeminism she developed with Vandana Shiva – both romanticize a supposed "outside" of capitalism, as I will explain later on.[31]

But let me make one general point about my relation to this tradition. Many of the thinkers I've mentioned construe social reproduction quite narrowly, as concerned only with the reproduction of labor power, whereas I take a broader view of it. For me, social reproduction encompasses the creation, socialization, and subjectivation of human beings more generally, in all their aspects. It also includes the making and remaking of culture, of the various swaths of intersubjectivity that human beings inhabit – the solidarities, social meanings, and value horizons in and through which they live and breathe. In addition, I want to take a broad view of the sites where social reproduction is located in capitalist society. Unlike those Marxist-feminists who associate this activity exclusively with the domestic sphere of the household, I find it occurring in multiple sites, including, as I just mentioned, neighborhoods, civil society associations, and state agencies, but also increasingly in marketized realms.

Jaeggi: You mentioned subjectivation as an element of social reproduction. Does that mean that you want to fold the Foucauldian problematic into the feminist perspective? For that matter, you also mentioned the terms *habitus* and *Sittlichkeit*, which suggests that you also want to include Bourdieusian concerns and the "ethical" and cultural concerns of neo-Hegelian thinkers.

Fraser: Yes, that's right. I am deliberately casting a broad net here. My aim is to develop an *expanded conception of capitalism* that can incorporate the insights of all of those paradigms. I would argue, in fact, that the insights of Foucault, Bourdieu, and the neo-Hegelians who focus on "ethical life" only receive their full meaning and importance when they are situated in relation to capitalism as a historically elaborated social totality. I think a full account of social reproduction must integrate the concerns of Marxist- and socialist-feminists with those of theorists of subjectivation, *habitus*, culture, lifeworld, and "ethical life."

Jaeggi: The Marxist-feminist claim that unpaid reproductive labor is necessary for productive labor has raised quite a heated debate. A lot of that has focused on whether this amounts to a sufficient theory of patriarchy – let alone heteronormativity. But even if we focus on the claim about capitalism needing such a background, this is a strong thesis. I find it interesting that your view is that, by extending the background, you can make the argument hold better. This in fact goes half-way to seeing capitalism as an entire form of life. But for you, though you understand reproduction much more broadly than in most accounts, you also situate it in relation to commodity production, taking it to be one of the latter's necessary background conditions and enabling presuppositions.

Fraser: Yes, I do understand social reproduction very broadly. But the point I want to stress here concerns the very specific way in which social reproduction is *institutionalized* in capitalist society. Unlike earlier societies, capitalism institutes a division between social reproduction and commodity production. Their separation is utterly fundamental to capitalism – and indeed is an artifact of it. And as many feminists have stressed, this division is thoroughly gendered, with reproduction associated with women and production with men. Historically, the split between "productive" waged labor and "reproductive" unwaged labor has underpinned modern capitalist forms of women's subordination. Like that between owners and workers, this division, too, rests on the break-up of a previous unity. In this case, what was shattered was a world in which women's work, although distinguished from men's, was nevertheless visible and publicly acknowledged, an integral part of the social universe. With capitalism, by contrast, reproductive labor is split off, relegated to a separate, "private" sphere, where its social importance is obscured. And, of course, in a world where money is a primary medium of power, the

33

fact of its being unpaid seals the matter: those who do this work are structurally subordinate to those who earn cash wages, even as their work also supplies some necessary preconditions for wage labor.

Jaeggi: I'm not so happy with your account of this development as the "break-up of a previous unity." Some nostalgia seems to be in play here, a nostalgic tone that suggests that the undifferentiated state of pre-modern or feudal societies is somehow more desirable. But wouldn't this then obscure the emancipatory effects, or at least ambivalences, that flow from their break-up? And doesn't it also lend itself to the misleading suggestion that the supposed former unity was "more natural?" I would hold that these "unities" were themselves the result of a historical development. In fact, neither the former "unity" nor its subsequent split-up is a natural state of affairs. Both are historical and social all the way down. So there is a certain danger in your account. It might sound conservative or backward-looking, as if there were an innocent past that we should try to recover. Surely you don't mean to suggest that!

Fraser: No, absolutely not! That's the last thing I want to suggest! So let me clarify. What capitalism disrupted was not an "original unity" to which we should try to return. It was in every case a thoroughly historical, and often hierarchical, form of society, albeit one that did not hive off production from reproduction. That division was quite unknown in feudalism, for example – capitalism alone can claim credit for it. But it doesn't follow that precapitalist societies were gender-egalitarian or otherwise desirable. On the contrary, the rise of capitalism brought many positive, emancipatory developments, as Marx often stressed. He was much better in this respect than Polanyi, who was so relentless in stressing the negative that he overlooked capitalism's upside. Having criticized Polanyi for succumbing to nostalgic communitarianism, I could hardly do the same thing myself.[32] No, I certainly don't want to idealize precapitalist society!

My point is rather that the division between production and reproduction is a historical artifact of capitalism, not a "natural" state of affairs. And it is not given once and for all. On the contrary, the division develops historically and takes different forms in different phases of capitalist development. In the twentieth century, for example, some aspects of social reproduction that had previously been privatized were transformed into public services and public goods; they were de-privatized but not commodified. Today, by contrast, neoliberalism is (re)privatizing and (re)commodifying some of these services, as well

34

as commodifying other aspects of social reproduction for the first time. By demanding retrenchment of public provision at the same time that it is massively recruiting women into low-waged service work, it is remapping the institutional boundaries that had previously separated commodity production from social reproduction. As a result, neoliberalism is reconfiguring the gender order of capitalist society. Equally important, it is turning social reproduction into a major flashpoint of capitalist crisis in the present period.

I maintain, in fact, that all capitalist societies entrench a *tendency to social-reproductive crisis* – over and above the tendency to economic crisis theorized by Marx. As I'll explain in chapter 2, this strand of crisis is grounded in a structural contradiction – in the fact that the capitalist economy simultaneously relies on and tends to destabilize its own social-reproductive conditions of possibility.

Jaeggi: We'll get to that later. Here I want to stick with your idea that the move, in feminist theory, from commodity production to social reproduction inaugurates another epistemic shift, as profound as Marx's shift to "primitive" or original accumulation. In the reproduction case, too, we move from the front-story of exploitation to a back-story of what makes exploitation possible. And in both cases, the new perspective needs to be fully elaborated and integrated into our understanding of capitalism. But you said you wanted to introduce three such epistemic shifts. So what are the other two?

From human to non-human nature

Fraser: The second one is the shift inaugurated in eco-Marxian and eco-socialist thought, which foregrounds another condition of possibility for a capitalist economy. Just as Marx, Harvey, and (one should add) Rosa Luxemburg have revealed the back-story of capital's reliance on "original" and ongoing dispossession, and just as feminists have disclosed the back-story of capital's dependence on women's unwaged labor of social reproduction, so these thinkers are now writing another back-story – this time about capital's free-riding on nature. This eco-Marxian story concerns capital's annexation (*Landnahme*) of nature, both as a "tap" to provide "inputs" to production and also as a "sink" to absorb the latter's waste. Nature here is made into a resource for capital, one whose value is both presupposed and disavowed. Capitalists expropriate it without compensation or replenishment and treat it as costless in their accounts.

35

So they implicitly assume it to be infinite. In fact, nature's capacity to support life and renew itself constitutes yet another necessary background condition for commodity production and capital accumulation. Needless to say, it is also indispensable in sustaining all our *dramatis personae*: owners, producers, reproducers, and expropriated or colonized subjects, none of whom could exist without it.

Like the perspective of social reproduction, this one, too, has been theorized by an impressive group of thinkers – James O'Connor, John Bellamy Foster, Jason W. Moore, Joan Martinez-Alier, and many others.[33] And, like the social-reproduction perspective, this one, too, foregrounds a historical division that is fundamental to capitalism. Structurally, capitalism assumes (indeed inaugurates) a sharp division between a natural realm, conceived as a free, unproduced supply of "raw materials," available for appropriation, and an economic realm, conceived as a sphere of value, produced by and for human beings. Along with this goes a hardening of the pre-existing distinction between "humanity," which is figured as spiritual, socio-cultural, and historical, and (non-human) "nature," which is cast as material, objectively given, and ahistorical. The sharpening of this distinction, too, rests on the break-up of a previous world, in which the rhythms of social life were adapted in many respects to those of non-human nature. Capitalism brutally separated human beings from those latter rhythms, conscripting them into industrial manufacturing powered by fossil fuels and into profit-driven agriculture bulked up by chemical fertilizers. Introducing a "metabolic rift,"[34] it inaugurated what scientists now call "the Anthropocene," an entirely new geological era in which human activity decisively impacts the Earth's ecosystems and atmosphere. Actually, that term is misleading, since the principal culprit is not "humanity," but capital.[35] But the effects are real enough. After three centuries of capital's predations, capped by neoliberalism's current assault on what remains of the ecological commons, the natural conditions of accumulation have now become a central node of capitalist crisis.

Jaeggi: Once again, this can sound a bit romantic and backward-looking. I'm quite glad that my life does not conform to nature's rhythm – I wouldn't want to have to go to bed as soon as it gets dark. And as bad as ecological crises in capitalism are, precapitalist crises, where people were dying as a result of plagues and starving as a result of bad harvests, were also not much fun. Couldn't we view the split between the human and the natural – and the resulting mastery over nature – as a good thing as well?

Fraser: Perhaps. But as with the production/reproduction separation, my point is not to idealize a supposedly original unity, but rather to view the division between the human and non-human histori-cally, as well as to reckon the gains and the losses. That is because this division, too, undergoes a series of structural mutations in the different phases of capitalist development. The current neoliberal phase is full of complexities. On the one hand, we are facing a new round of enclosures – think, for example, of the commodification of water – which are bringing "more of nature" (if one can speak that way) into the foreground of the official accumulation process. At the same time, neoliberalism is also proliferating new technologies that promise to blur the nature/human boundary – just think of new reproductive technologies, the bio-engineering of sterile seeds, and the various "cyborgs" that Donna Haraway has written about.[36] Far from offering a "reconciliation" with nature, however, these develop-ments intensify capitalism's commodification-cum-annexation of it. Certainly, they are far more invasive than the land enclosures Marx and Polanyi wrote about. Whereas those earlier processes "merely" marketized already-existing natural phenomena, their 21st-century counterparts are producing new ones. Penetrating deep "inside" nature, neoliberalism is altering its internal grammar. We could see this as another case of "real subsumption," analogous to the real subsumption of labor we discussed earlier. Finally, we are also seeing halting efforts to assert public political responsibility for sustaining the Earth's biosphere, which would require a profound structural transformation of our way of life – a shift from fossil fuels to renew-able energy. And all this occurs, of course, against the background of looming ecological crisis, which I understand as yet another, struc-turally grounded "moment" of capitalist crisis. As I'll explain in chapter 2, capitalist societies institutionalize an *ecological contradic-tion*: capital simultaneously relies on and tends to destabilize its own "natural" conditions of possibility.

From economy to polity

Jaeggi: What about the third shift? Doesn't capitalism depend on political conditions? One could call state power another background condition for the front-story of capitalism. Political power has cer-tainly shaped capitalist societies and economies more than people are sometimes ready to admit when they conceive of the capitalist economy as a bounded sphere with a logic of its own.

37

Fraser: Yes, that's exactly what I had in mind. Capitalism relies on public powers to establish and enforce its constitutive norms. A market economy is inconceivable, after all, in the absence of a legal framework that underpins private enterprise and market exchange. Its front-story depends crucially on public powers to guarantee property rights, enforce contracts, adjudicate disputes, quell anti-capitalist rebellions, and maintain, in the language of the US Constitution, "the full faith and credit" of the money supply that constitutes capital's lifeblood. Historically, the public powers in question have mostly been lodged in territorial states, including those that operated as colonial powers. It was the legal systems of such states that established the contours of seemingly depoliticized arenas within which private actors could pursue their "economic" interests, free from overt "political" interference, on the one hand, and from patronage obligations derived from kinship, on the other. Likewise, it was territorial states that mobilized "legitimate force" to put down resistance to the expropriations through which capitalist property relations were originated and sustained. Finally, it was such states that nationalized and underwrote money. Historically, we might say, the state *constituted* the capitalist "economy."

Here we encounter another major structural division that is constitutive of capitalist society: the *division between economy and polity*. With this division comes the institutional differentiation of public from private power, of political from economic coercion, of the noisy, strident compulsion of armed force from (what Marx called) the "silent compulsion" of capital. Like the other core divisions we have discussed (those between owners and producers, producers and reproducers, human and non-human nature), this one, too, arises as a result of the break-up of a previous unity. In this case, what was dismantled was a social world in which economic and political power were effectively fused – as, for example, in feudal society, which vested control over labor, land, and military force in the same institution of lordship and vassalage. In capitalist society, by contrast, as Ellen Meiksins Wood has elegantly shown, economic power and political power are split apart; each is assigned its own sphere, its own medium and *modus operandi*.[37]

Jaeggi: The picture you've just sketched sounds very "Westphalian." What about globalization? How does the picture change once the national state is no longer in charge to the extent that you just described? How then are these political background conditions established under conditions of a globalized economy?

Fraser: Good point. We must not imagine capitalism's political conditions of possibility exclusively on the level of the territorial state. We must also consider the geopolitical level. What is at issue here is the organization of the broader space in which territorial states are embedded. This is a space to which capital naturally gravitates, given its expansionist thrust. But its ability to operate across borders depends on international law, brokered arrangements among the Great Powers, and supranational governance regimes, which partially pacify (in a capital-friendly way) a realm that is often imagined as a state of nature. Throughout its history, capitalism's front-story has depended on the military and organizational capacities of a succession of global hegemons, which, as Giovanni Arrighi argued, have sought to foster accumulation on a progressively expanding scale within the framework of a multi-state system.[38]

Here we find some other structural divisions that are constitutive of capitalist society: the "Westphalian" division between the "domestic" and the "international," on the one hand, and the imperialist division between core and periphery, on the other – both premised on the more fundamental division between an increasingly global capitalist economy organized as a "world system" and a political world organized as an international system of territorial states. These divisions are currently mutating as well, as neoliberalism is increasingly hollowing out the political capacities on which capital has historically relied at both the state and geopolitical levels. As a result of this hollowing out, capitalism's political conditions of possibility are also now a major site and flashpoint of capitalist crisis.

We can speak here of a *political crisis of capitalist society* over and above the other strands of crisis I mentioned before. As I'll explain in chapter 2, this strand of crisis is grounded in a specifically *political contradiction* of capitalist society – in the fact that its economy simultaneously relies on and tends to destabilize public powers. Fortunately, there's a raft of excellent work on this point as well, ranging from Polanyi and Hannah Arendt on liberal capitalism, to Jürgen Habermas on state-managed capitalism, and Wendy Brown, Colin Crouch, Stephen Gill, Wolfgang Streeck, and Nancy MacLean on the financialized capitalism of the present day.[39]

Race, imperialism, and expropriation

Jaeggi: You just mentioned the distinction between core and periphery, and we've noted earlier capitalism's entwinement with slavery and racism. Where exactly do these matters fit into your account, and how would you relate them to the various spheres, divisions, and boundaries that you have identified? For example, you said that you modeled your account of the front-story/back-story relation on Marx's discussion of "primitive accumulation," but you haven't discussed that issue in its own right. And it's with regard to relations of colonial and imperial oppression that this topic is often brought up. Marx himself, in fact, stresses this connection.

Fraser: I take imperialism and racial oppression to be integral to capitalist society, as integral as gender domination. Just as we found a structural basis for gender hierarchy in capitalism's constitutive institutional separation of production from reproduction, so we should also look for built-in, constitutive institutional bases for racial and imperial oppression.

Jaeggi: So where would you locate the institutional division that anchors racial oppression? What is the racializing analogue to the gendered division between production and reproduction?

Fraser: As before, my idea turns on the distinction between capitalism's foreground economy and the latter's background conditions of possibility. But in this case, we don't need to reinvent the wheel. We can follow the path laid out by Marx in his chapter on "primitive accumulation," to which you just referred. In that chapter, he tunneled beneath the hidden abode of exploitation to excavate an even more obfuscated realm, which I've called "expropriation." Building directly on Marx's argument, while taking it further than he did, I see expropriation as another abode behind the abode, which makes exploitation possible. And when it is properly understood, the back-story of expropriation clarifies the structural place of imperial and racial oppression in capitalist society. Let me explain.

Expropriation is accumulation by other means. Whereas exploitation transfers value to capital under the guise of a free contractual exchange, expropriation dispenses with all such niceties in favor of brute confiscation – of labor, to be sure, but also of land, animals, tools, mineral and energy deposits, and even of human beings, their sexual and reproductive capacities, their children and bodily organs. Both of these "exes" are equally indispensable to capital accumulation, and the first one depends on the second; you could not have exploitation without expropriation. That is the first step of my argument. The second is that the distinction between the two "exes" corresponds to

40

CONCEPTUALIZING CAPITALISM

a status hierarchy. Whereas exploited workers are accorded the status
of rights-bearing individuals and citizens who enjoy state protection
and can freely dispose of their own labor power, those subject to
expropriation are constituted as unfree, dependent beings who are
stripped of political protection and rendered defenseless – as, for
example, in the cases of chattel slaves, colonized subjects, "natives,"
debt peons, "illegals," and convicted felons. (Recall that I hinted at
this point earlier, when we discussed the worker's double freedom.)
The third and final step is that this status differential coincides with
"race." It is overwhelmingly racialized populations who lack political
protection in capitalist society and who are constituted as *inherently
expropriable*.

Yes

Jaeggi: I understand that you are claiming that expropriation is a
built-in feature of capitalism, a structural and ongoing feature, and
that it correlates strongly with racial oppression. But I still don't see
how it relates to capitalism's institutional divisions. Exactly where
and how is the distinction between exploitation and expropriation
anchored in your picture of capitalism as an institutionalized social
order? You seemed to imply that the distinction was not just economic
but also political, that it correlated with freedom and subjection, with
access to and deprivation from political protection. So are you saying
that the line between the two "exes" is drawn politically? That it is
grounded in the economy/polity division, which is constitutive of
capitalism as you understand it?

Fraser: Yes, that's exactly what I'm saying. The distinction between
expropriation and exploitation is simultaneously economic and political. At one level – call it "economic" – these terms name mechanisms
of capital accumulation, analytically distinct yet intertwined ways
of expanding value. In the case of exploitation, capital pays for the
workers' socially necessary costs of reproduction in the form of wages,
while appropriating the surplus their labor creates. In expropriation,
by contrast, it simply seizes labor, persons, and land without paying
for their costs of reproduction. That's the nub of the distinction when
viewed economically. Viewed politically, however, it's about hierarchical power relations and status differentials, which distinguish
rights-bearing individuals and citizens from subject peoples, unfree
chattel slaves, and dependent members of subordinated groups. In
capitalist society, as Marx insisted, and as we ourselves noted before,
exploited workers have the legal status of free individuals, authorized
to sell their labor power in return for wages; once separated from the

41

means of production and proletarianized, they are protected, at least *in theory*, from (further) expropriation. In this respect, their status differs sharply from those whose labor, property, and/or persons are still subject to confiscation to capital's benefit; far from enjoying protection, the latter populations are defenseless, fair game for expropriation – again and again.

This status differential is forged politically. The paradigmatic agencies that afford or deny protection are states. And it is largely states, too, that perform the work of political subjectivation. They codify the status hierarchies that distinguish citizens from subjects, nationals from aliens, entitled workers from dependent scroungers – all categories that invite racialization. These distinctions are essential for a system that pursues accumulation simultaneously along two tracks. They construct and mark off groups subject to brute expropriation from those destined for "mere" exploitation. In codifying and enforcing those distinctions, states supply yet another indispensable precondition for capital accumulation.

Jaeggi: I can see how states are engaged in codifying the subjective statuses that underwrite expropriation and exploitation, respectively. And I see how those statuses are connected with race. But you have insisted throughout our discussion that capitalism's political order is inherently geopolitical. Aren't transnational arrangements also implicated in political subjectivation and in the racial hierarchies associated with it?

Fraser: Yes, that's right. We can't understand the dynamics of racialization if we limit our thinking to the national frame. We already said that capitalism's economy has always relied on trans-state political powers to facilitate flows of value across borders. But these powers are also implicated in fabricating the political statuses essential to capital accumulation. Obviously, the "Westphalian" system of sovereign territorial states underwrites the border controls that distinguish lawful residents from "illegal aliens," as well as the limits of political community that demarcate citizens from non-members; and those status hierarchies are racially coded – just think of current conflicts over migration and asylum. But that is not all. Capitalism's other, unofficial geography, its imperialist division of "core" and "periphery," is at work here as well. Historically, the capitalist core appeared as the emblematic heartland of exploitation, while the periphery seemed to be the iconic site of expropriation. And that geography was explicitly racialized from the get-go, as were the status hierarchies associated with it: metropolitan citizens versus colonial subjects, free individuals versus slaves, "Europeans" versus "natives," "Whites" versus "Blacks." So yes, you are right. To understand the status divisions that underlie capitalism's racial formations, we need to attend simultaneously to all these levels: national/domestic, international/"Westphalian," and colonial/imperialist.

Jaeggi: Okay. That point is clear. But tell me: what is the relation between your view that expropriation is central to capitalism and Marx's account of primitive accumulation? According to Marx, capital was initially stockpiled through the outright theft of resources, land, animals, labor, the commons, without any pretense of contract. Such confiscations simultaneously generated the private property of the capitalist class while separating workers from the means of production.[40] And subsequent thinkers have developed this idea. I am thinking of Rosa Luxemburg's concept of "Landnahme" and David Harvey's idea of "dispossession."[41] How would you situate your view of expropriation in relation to these thinkers?

Fraser: I already said that my view – that exploitation rests on the even more hidden abode of expropriation – is inspired by Marx's account of "primitive" or "original accumulation," with which it has clear affinities. But what I am arguing here differs in two respects. First, primitive accumulation denotes the "blood-soaked" process by which capital was initially stockpiled at the system's beginnings.[42] Expropriation, in contrast, designates an ongoing confiscatory process essential for sustaining accumulation in a crisis-prone system. I am closer in this respect to Luxemburg and Harvey, who also stress the continuing character of so-called primitive accumulation.

But there is also a second respect in which I differ from Marx. He introduced primitive accumulation to explain the historical genesis of the class division between propertyless workers and capitalist owners of the means of production. Expropriation explains that as well, but it also brings into view another social division, equally deep-seated and consequential, but not systematically theorized by Marx – nor, for that matter, by Luxemburg or Harvey. I mean the social division between the "free workers" whom capital exploits in wage labor and the unfree or dependent subjects whom it cannibalizes by other means. Historically, that second division correlates roughly but unmistakably with the color line. In my view, the expropriation of racialized "others" constitutes a necessary background condition for the exploitation of "workers." In fact, I would say that "race" just *is*

43

"the expropriation of racialized 'others' constitutes a necessary background condition for the exploitation of 'workers'" the mark that distinguishes free subjects of exploitation from dependent subjects of expropriation.

Jaeggi: I agree that there is truth, in a historical sense, to Luxemburg's idea – which Harvey and now you have taken up – that original accumulation and dispossession or expropriation are ongoing features of the capitalist story. But isn't there a further, even more dramatic implication of this modification of Marx's original idea? The original Marxist picture was that these moments of primitive accumulation or expropriation are framed as features of capitalism's distant past, so that, whenever these things occur today, it is only at the margins of capitalism and no longer integral to its continuation. But if expropriation is not just a precondition but an ongoing condition, then capitalism has an ongoing imperative to explore more and more terrain to expropriate. It has to look out for ever-new grounds not just of capital accumulation but of possible dispossession. This is actually a dramatic change with respect to classical Marxism.

Fraser: Yes, it is dramatic, though perhaps no more so than the other back-stories I've been proposing, which together make visible entire "hidden abodes" beneath Marx's front-story. And just as we can build on rich bodies of feminist, ecological, and political thought to develop those other back-stories, so we can build here on the very distinguished tradition of "Black Marxist" thought, which runs from C. L. R. James, W. E. B. Du Bois, Eric Williams, and Oliver Cromwell Cox in the 1930s and 1940s to Stuart Hall, Walter Rodney, Cedric Robinson, and Angela Davis (among many others) in the late twentieth and twenty-first centuries.[43] These thinkers rejected the conventional economistic, class-essentialist, and color-blind assumptions of orthodox Marxism, but without throwing out the baby with the bathwater. That is the stance I take as well.

Building on that illustrious tradition, I maintain that expropriation has always been entwined with exploitation in capitalist society; that even "mature" capitalism relies on regular infusions of commandeered capacities and resources, especially from racialized subjects, in both its periphery and its core; that its resort to them is not just sporadic, but a regular aspect of business-as-usual. In short, the connection is not just historical. On the contrary, there are structural reasons for capital's ongoing recourse to expropriation – hence, for its persistent entwinement with imperialism and racial oppression.

Jaeggi: You've said several times that the connection is structural. But you haven't actually spelled that out. What exactly are the structural mechanisms that drive capital to cultivate a hidden abode of expropriation beneath the Marxian story of exploitation?

Fraser: Well, to begin with, a system devoted to the limitless expansion and private appropriation of surplus value gives the owners of capital a deep-seated interest in confiscating labor and means of production from subject populations. In that way, they obtain productive inputs for whose reproduction they do not (fully) pay. We know that, in exploitation, they are supposed to pay the reproduction costs of the free workers whose labor power they purchase in exchange for wages. But their production costs would soar if they also had to pay the full reproduction costs of other inputs, such as energy and raw materials. So they have a strong incentive to seize land and mineral wealth; to conscript the unfree labor of subjugated or enslaved populations; and to extract stores of fossilized energy that formed beneath the crust of the earth over hundreds of millions of years. Profit rates rise to the extent that capital is able to free-ride on such processes, avoiding responsibility for their replenishment.

But that is not all. Expropriation also lowers the reproduction costs of "free labor." Jason W. Moore explains this point with a memorable line: "Behind Manchester stands Mississippi."[44] He means that goods (cotton, sugar, coffee, tobacco) produced under racialized slavery cheapened the cost of living for industrial workers, allowing capital to pay them lower wages and to reap higher profits. Polanyi tells a similar story about the repeal of the protectionist British Corn Laws in the nineteenth century.[45] By opening up free trade in corn and grain, industrial and commercial interests were able to cheapen the cost of food and thereby to drive down wages of English workers. In other words, by confiscating resources and capacities from unfree or dependent subjects, capitalists could more profitably exploit "free workers." And so what I have taken to calling the two "exes" (exploitation and expropriation) are intertwined.

This shows that expropriation is advantageous for capital in "normal" times. But it becomes even more so in periods of crisis, which occur periodically and for non-accidental reasons in the course of capitalist development. In those times, intensified confiscation of resources serves as a critical if temporary fix for restoring profitability and navigating economic crisis. Expropriation can also help defuse capitalism's political crises, which can sometimes be tempered or averted by transferring value seized from populations that appear not to threaten capital to those that do – another distinction that often correlates with "race." Such divide-and-rule tactics mobilize those racially coded status hierarchies that distinguish citizens from subjects, nationals from aliens, free individuals from slaves, "Europeans" from "natives," "Whites" from "Blacks," entitled workers from dependent scroungers.

What all of this shows is that expropriation and exploitation are not simply separate parallel processes. Rather, the two "exes" are systemically imbricated – they are deeply intertwined aspects of a single capitalist world system. The conclusion I draw is that the racialized subjection of those whom capital expropriates is a hidden condition of possibility for the freedom of those whom it exploits. And that tells us that racial oppression stands in a systemic, non-accidental relation to capitalist society – that the connection between them is structural, not contingent.

Jaeggi: I agree that the phenomena associated with expropriation are more in the foreground now, but we still need to retain the Marxist insight that capitalism is not robbery. This was one of the most important contributions of Marx's theory of exploitation. We do need to push back against the orthodox Marxist idea that everything beyond exploitation is merely a side story, but we should also be wary of telling a similarly under-complex story about capitalism being built on greed and robbery. I'd say what makes your reading interesting is the way these two sides of the coin – exploitation under the guise of the wage contract and outright expropriation and coercion – are mutually dependent on each other. This is what distinguishes capitalist expropriation from the kind we find in feudalism or ancient slave societies, which does not have that other "above ground" or "more legal" side into which it feeds and with which it is mutually dependent.

Fraser: Absolutely, I agree. The last thing we want is to assimilate capitalism to simple robbery. That's why I define expropriation as confiscation plus conscription into accumulation. What is essential, in other words, is that the commandeered capacities get incorporated into the value-expanding process that defines capital. Simple theft is not enough. Unlike the sort of pillaging that long predated the rise of capitalism, expropriation in the sense I intend here channels wealth into capital's circuits of accumulation, where it becomes imbricated with exploitation. This imbrication constitutes the specificity of capitalist expropriation. As I said, it is only by confiscating resources and capacities from unfree or dependent subjects that capital can profitably exploit "free workers." The official "ex" of exploitation rests on the hidden "ex" of expropriation, which is to say on a racialized "caste" of subjects stripped of political protection and rendered defenseless. That caste is the disavowed enabling condition for the official working class, those free "White" or "European" proletarians, who are constructed as rights-bearing individuals and (eventually) as political citizens.

But we should also note that many contemporary forms of expropriation are tricked out with a façade of legality. Think of for-profit prisons and foreclosures on predatory debt, including the subprime mortgages marketed specifically to people of color in the United States. Think also of the new forms of precarious, low-paid service work, the so-called McJobs, largely assigned to racialized minorities and immigrants, which pay less than the socially necessary costs of the workers' reproduction. These too involve an expropriative element, despite the contractual façade. They permit accumulation through processes distinct from, although imbricated with, exploitation.

Economic system, totalizing grammar,
or institutionalized social order?

Jaeggi: Let's return to the big question with which we began: what is capitalism? I'd like to know how you would answer that question now, in light of our discussion. When you use the metaphors of front-story and back-story, what do they really imply? In order really to de-orthodoxize the picture, one would need to come up with a model that differs from the orthodox base/superstructure model in that it gets rid of a certain kind of determinism. As long as the economic foreground is seen as one-sidedly determining the background, as long as the background is conceived in some way as related *qua* "functional necessities" to the economic foreground, you are still within a rather orthodox framework. My take is that we have to re-conceptualize this one-dimensional way of conceiving of the relation. It's definitely not a one-way street, but a two-way street, at the very least – which is to say, a rather complicated story with multiple dependencies in several directions. The slippery slope here might even be that, with enough back-and-forth, we realize, as it were, that we are somewhere in a circle and the whole distinction between back and front starts to reel. I don't want to press this, but rather ask whether you would see the two levels – background and foreground – at least as mutually imbricated and interacting.

Fraser: Well, so far I haven't said anything about how the foreground interacts with the background. I've focused instead on identifying some key topographical divisions that structure capitalist society: production/reproduction, economy/polity, and human/non-human nature. My aim was not to chart the causal flows across those divisions, but to provide an institutional map that can situate and clarify the place of "the economy" within capitalist society.

But I don't want to duck your question. The implications of this view cut against economic determinism. By situating "the economy" in this way, we delimit it. And by revealing its dependence on the non-economic backgrounds of social reproduction, ecology, and public power, we stress the latter's weight and societal importance, as well as their capacity to impact and indeed to destabilize historically entrenched regimes of accumulation. But, of course, the converse is also true; foreground processes of capital accumulation impact and often destabilize the very background structures on which they depend. So, no, there's no economic determinism here.

Jaeggi: Fair enough. But then what exactly *is* capitalism, on this view? Is capitalism only an economic system, the economic sphere within a larger society? Or does your concept of capitalism also include the spheres you identified as the economy's background conditions of possibility?

Fraser: Capitalism is definitely not just an economic system. Granted, it may have looked at first sight as if the core features we identified were "economic." But that appearance was misleading. It became clear, in the course of our discussion, that these are not features of a capitalist economy, but features of a capitalist *society*. The peculiarity of capitalist society is that it treats its central defining and structuring social relations as if they were "economic" and pertained to a separate subsystem of society, an "economy." But that's just an appearance. We very quickly found it necessary to talk about the "non-economic" background conditions that enabled such a system to exist. And we concluded that those background conditions must not be airbrushed out of the picture, but must be conceptualized and theorized as part of our conception of capitalism. So capitalism is something larger than an economy.

Jaeggi: Does this "enlarged" picture lead us back to the view associated with Georg Lukács, which conceives capitalism as a single totalizing system, which impresses the commodity form everywhere,

48

in all spheres of social life? Lukács famously identified capitalism with a grammar of life, based on the commodity form. Supposedly ubiquitous, the commodity form supplied a template for objects in general and for all subject–object relations. Nothing in capitalist society escapes its imprint, including legal, scientific, and philosophical thought.[46] Is that where your view is leading?

Fraser: No, no, no! That's not where I want to go at all. That view is far too totalizing. It renders invisible major swaths of social interaction that are essential components of a capitalist society but are not governed by market norms. It obscures the character of social institutions that supply indispensable preconditions for commodity production and exchange, but which are themselves organized on different bases.

The whole point of the foreground/background perspective is to relativize the commodity form. It's to insist that the commodity form, while causally consequential, is not at all ubiquitous in capitalist society. Granted, it is immediately visible from the standpoint of exchange. And it plays a significant role at Marx's next level, the standpoint of production, where the buying and selling of labor power (that very peculiar commodity which generates surplus value) is what enables the "self-expansion" of capital via exploitation. But the commodity form is decentered when we shift to the still deeper background levels we have disclosed here. Remember, the commodity was not (and is not) the paradigmatic object form in "primitive accumulation." The same holds for social reproduction, ecology, and polity. Those arenas, too, are instituted differently, on different terms, and they operate in accord with different norms.

Jaeggi: So capitalism's commodified zones depend for their very existence on zones of non-commodification. But, furthermore, these non-commodified zones – social, ecological, and political – do not simply mirror the commodity logic, but operate according to a different logic. We are confronted with a variety of different dynamics that have their own logics even if they are, at the same time, entangled. We can trace how they inform each other, enable each other, or even presuppose each other – or, in the weakest sense, how they are related via elective affinities. This would certainly lead to a complex picture, an interesting and "thick" understanding of the web of social and economic relations.

Fraser: Yes, and this is worth spelling out. I am indeed claiming that the social, ecological, and political backgrounds I've identified are

49

not integrated primarily via the norms of the foreground economy. I would even state this more strongly. Each of these background arenas harbors some distinctive normative and ontological grammars. For example, social practices oriented to reproduction (as opposed to production) tend to engender ideals of care, mutual responsibility, and solidarity, however hierarchical and parochial these may typically be. Likewise, practices associated with capitalism's background conditions in non-human nature tend to foster such values as sustainability, stewardship, non-domination of nature, and justice between generations, however romantic and sectarian these may often be. Finally, practices oriented to polity as opposed to economy often refer to principles of democracy, equal citizenship, and the public interest, however restricted or exclusionary these may often be.

Jaeggi: Again, this makes me curious about the exact relation between foreground and background. Is there a double-play of functional dependency and normative contrast? What role does the distinctive normative "grammar" of the background play for you? Does it just help descriptively to tell the two apart, or is it a resource for critique in a stronger way? We can think of conflicting normativities as arising out of contradictions immanent to a given form of life, but one might also style them as the fragments of a more harmonious past reasserting themselves against the corrupting forces of rationality and modernity. Do the normativities you associate with these background domains form "innocent" reservoirs on which we can draw to spell out our critique of the brutal world of the economy?

Fraser: No, that's not at all where I'm heading. Far from wanting to idealize these "non-economic" normativities, my aim here is simply to register their divergence from the values associated with capitalism's foreground, such as growth, efficiency, equal exchange, individual choice, negative liberty, and meritocratic advancement. The divergence makes all the difference for how we conceptualize capitalism. Far from generating a single, all-pervasive logic of reification, capitalist society is normatively differentiated, encompassing a determinate plurality of distinct yet interrelated social ontologies. What happens when these collide remains to be seen (in chapter 2). But the structure that underpins them is already clear: capitalism's distinctive normative topography arises from the foreground/background relations we have identified. If we aim to develop a critical theory of it, we must replace the Lukácsian view of capitalism as a uniformly reified mode of ethical life with a more differentiated, structural view.

Jaeggi: But still, in stressing the distinct "normativities" and "social ontologies" of foreground and background, you seem to be recycling some version of Habermas's system/lifeworld distinction, a distinction that you yourself criticized in the past. I myself have become more and more skeptical about this framework – this "two spheres" picture that has such a strong hold on us in social theory. I believe this is the wrong picture to start with, because it solidifies a view whereby the central issue is the *invasion* or "colonization" of the economic into other, more "innocent" areas of social life. The problem with this strategy is that, while it is intended to criticize the capitalist economy, the economic sphere as such is effectively removed from the realm of criticism. It is treated as something autonomous, self-propelling, and non-normative, which must be accepted as more or less given. As a result, critical theory is reduced to the project of somehow "taming" it and protecting social life from it, instead of engaging it directly. This kind of framework makes it impossible to rethink the economy itself, while urging us to find strategies whereby it becomes unnecessary to do so.

This is why I've been advocating a monistic social theory, which accounts for economic and other areas of life as practices. This, of course, no longer allows us to pit the economy against the rest, or to argue that certain spheres (cultural, social, personal) need to be protected from contamination by the supposedly separate economic sphere. Economic practices are not merely "embedded" in a surrounding or enabling ethical form of life; they are rather *part of the form of life* itself, part of the social order and its respective dynamic. This is an argument on the level of social ontology, and it aims at a different understanding of the economy as such. In order to understand economy in a "wider" sense – following Horkheimer's intuition – we should conceive of economic practices as being interrelated with other practices in ways that make them part of the socio-cultural fabric of society. Taking up a perspective like this is better suited for a more immanent form of critique – one that can hold economic practices up to the normative conditions of fulfillment immanent to their location within a given form of life. The issue would then no longer be the invasion of the economy into society – as in Habermas's colonization thesis – but defects in the shape and content of economic practices themselves.[47]

You yourself have been very critical about the system/lifeworld distinction, so I am wondering how you reconcile your previous criticisms of that paradigm with this foreground/background distinction, which in some ways sounds quite similar.

Fraser: I share your skepticism about the system/lifeworld framework and haven't at all changed my mind about that! But the view I have outlined here is quite different. It isn't premised on the idea that there are two distinct "action logics" that pertain to two distinct types of institutions. Nor does it imply that one such action logic (the "system") is colonizing the other (the "lifeworld"). It certainly doesn't assume that the economic "system" of capitalist society is a "norm-free" zone, devoid of communication, cooperation, and struggle. Nor the converse: it doesn't assume that the household, for example, is a power- and money-free zone, devoid of strategic calculation and structural domination. No, I still find the system/lifeworld framework far too dualistic and dichotomizing – and therefore far too susceptible to the sorts of ideological mystification I criticized in my early paper, "What's Critical about Critical Theory?"[48]

The alternative I am sketching here assumes that capitalist societies institutionalize multiple (more than two!) normative and ontological orientations. Although each of these is often associated with a given institutional sphere, none is strictly bound to any one sphere. Rather, the norms in question are regularly deployed "wrongly," so to speak – which is to say, in the "wrong sphere" – and they can be mobilized against the grain. So there are no sharply defined, sphere-specific "action logics." Rather, there are sedimented patterns of action and interpretation, which are themselves subject to contestation, disruption, and transformation.

Of course, all of this needs to be spelled out in much greater detail. But I can sum up my view in this way: capitalism is best conceived neither as an economic system nor as a reified form of ethical life, but rather as an *institutionalized social order*, on a par with feudalism, to take an example. This formulation underscores its structural divisions and institutional separations. In my view, four such divisions are constitutive. First, the institutional separation of "economic production" from "social reproduction," a gendered separation that grounds specifically capitalist forms of male domination, even as it also enables the capitalist exploitation of labor that provides the basis of its officially sanctioned mode of accumulation; second, the institutional separation of "economy" from "polity," a separation that expels matters defined as "economic" from the political agendas of territorial states, while freeing capital to roam in a transnational no-man's land, where it reaps the benefits of hegemonic ordering while escaping political control; third, the ontological division between its (non-human) "natural" background and its (apparently non-natural) "human" foreground, which pre-exists capitalism but is massively

52

intensified under it; and finally, the institutionalized distinction between exploitation and expropriation, which grounds specifically capitalist forms of imperial predation and racial oppression.

If I were to contrast this approach to the practice-theoretic view that you just outlined, I would say that mine is more structural and institutional. Whereas your view suggests a view of capitalism as an indefinite congeries of more or less linked social practices, mine implies a determinate societal topography. For me, capitalism's institutionalized separations and divisions give the society a specific shape. That's what I mean when I say that capitalism should be understood as an institutionalized social order.

Jaeggi: The expression "institutionalized social order" is very helpful to summarize your view. It allows us to bridge the social theoretical gap between system and lifeworld. This is precisely what I'm doing by analyzing forms of life, though, as you say, I'm not beginning with the institutional level. Rather, I'm approaching the issue first as a question of social ontology and of understanding how the social practices constitutive of forms of life "congeal" into institutions, which can then take on a certain dynamic whereby they appear to take on a life of their own. One of the reasons it is important to me to begin at this level is that it methodologically prohibits us from losing sight of the thoroughly *normative* basis of practices like the economy, even though the capitalist organization of the economy presents itself to us as something "disembedded" and "norm-free." Once we see that there can be no social practice that is non-normative, the very manner in which practices like those associated with the economy seem to depend on their appearing "norm-free" tells us something is amiss. Again, the system/lifeworld division doesn't offer us a path to this avenue of critique.

Your analysis of capitalism as an institutionalized social order also departs from the orthodox account in that it does not see the things in the background as superstructure determined by production. Quite the opposite: it turns out that production depends on them. Nevertheless, one might think that your view remains very orthodox in this functional dependency. Unlike a forms-of-life account, which posits an overall social ontology of practices, you divide society into different spheres. Insofar as you invest too much in "functional" relations between these spheres, you risk reintroducing the "norm-free" lingo by other means. At least, there's a worry of prematurely closing off certain aspects of social life to normative inquiry when we attribute too much to relations of functional dependency. So I'd like to see you allay some of these concerns.

Perhaps we could get at the question of which social ontology you presuppose by clarifying the status of the institutional divisions you just mentioned. Are they porous or sharply bounded? Are they fixed or subject to change? In general, how do you reconcile the view that these institutional divisions are definitive of capitalism with the view you expressed at the outset: that capitalism is intrinsically historical and it unfolds over time?

Fraser: I don't actually think my view of these matters is functionalist. To explain why, I must add an important point. Although I consider these divisions constitutive for capitalism, I don't think they are simply given once and for all. On the contrary, I would say that precisely *where* capitalist societies draw the line between production and reproduction, economy and polity, human and non-human nature, and exploitation and expropriation varies historically under different regimes of accumulation. In fact, this variation can provide the basis for constructing a typology of such regimes. In the view I'm elaborating here, what distinguishes accumulation regimes are the ways in which they differentiate capitalism's foreground and background conditions and relate them to each other. Thus, we can conceptualize mercantile capitalism, competitive liberal capitalism, state-managed monopoly capitalism, and globalizing financialized capitalism as historically specific ways of demarcating economy from polity, production from reproduction, human from non-human nature, and exploitation from expropriation.

I would also say that the precise configuration of the capitalist order at any place and time depends on politics, on the balance of social power, and on the outcome of social struggles. Far from being simply given, capitalism's institutional divisions often become both sites and stakes of conflict, as actors mobilize to challenge or defend the established boundaries separating economy from polity, production from reproduction, human society from non-human nature, exploitation from expropriation. Insofar as they aim to relocate contested processes on capitalism's institutional map, capitalism's subjects draw on the normative perspectives associated with the various zones that I have identified. Their efforts to redraw institutional boundaries inevitably incite counter-efforts. And these *boundary struggles*, as I would like to call them, decisively shape the structure of capitalist societies. They constitute a fundamental type of capitalist conflict – as fundamental as the class struggles over control of commodity production and distribution of surplus value that Marxists have privileged. I want to talk more about them at a later point (see chapter 4). But for now, my point is this: the institutional divisions established at any given time and place are best understood as provisional stabilizations of the outcome of previous struggles – as are the resulting regimes of accumulation.

Jaeggi: This helps to forestall the worry I had that your view was functionalist. After all, you began by stressing that reproduction, ecology, political power, and expropriation were necessary background conditions for capitalism's economic front-story, and you underlined their functionality for commodity production, labor exploitation, and capital accumulation. But it now appears that this functionalist aspect does not capture the full complexity of capitalism's foreground/background relations. It seems to coexist, rather, with another, more political "moment," which characterizes the relations among economy, society, polity, and nature in capitalist society in terms of social struggle.

Fraser: Yes, you're right. The view I've been sketching is not functionalist. But it does incorporate a two-level theory of society: on the one hand, it contains a structural perspective, which stresses the foreground economy's dependence on society's "non-economic" background; on the other hand, it incorporates an action-theoretical perspective, which highlights the self-understandings and projects of social actors. Without buying into Habermas's full theory, we could borrow his terminology and say that this second perspective pertains to the level of "social," as opposed to "system," integration. It is a perspective that affords access to the conflict potentials inherent in a capitalist society. Because it discloses inherent possibilities for social struggle, it clarifies how a critique of capitalism is possible from within it.

Jaeggi: I'm still skeptical of the need to take on this terminology of social *versus* system integration or action *versus* system levels, at least insofar as it gives us an ontology of two realms of social life that are in some sense fundamentally opposed or alien to one another. I'll grant that a systemic view of the economy seems to have the advantage of being able to grasp "mechanisms of societal integration" which "do not necessarily coordinate actions via the intentions of participants, but objectively, 'behind . . . [their] backs.'"[49] The "invisible hand" of the market then is the paradigm case of this type of regulation.

Nevertheless, I believe that, with a practice-theoretic approach, the alternative between an action- and a system-theoretic approach to the economy can be overcome in a meaningful way. To conceive of the economy *as* and *in* a context of social practices doesn't mean that it arises from actions and intentions, or the results of such. Practices are only partially intentional, only partially explicit, and only partially due to the will and actions of people. They are not planned for in advance, but emerge, which means that they can congeal into institutions in ways that make them appear to have achieved their own dynamic. This process is difficult to see for the parties involved; it appears "systemic" and "second nature." But it might then be fruitful to recast these apparently "systemic" phenomena in a practice- and institutional-theoretical framework, because this will avoid the unwanted side-effects of buying into these appearances and understanding economics as a non-normative sphere.

This is what I referred to as the attempt to understand the economy as "part of the social order" and not as its "other," to borrow from Jens Beckert.[50] It is not a distinct system, let alone a norm-free one, but an agglomeration of social practices that are related to other economic and non-economic practices and institutions (which we can think of as states of aggregate practices). They are ensembles within ensembles. A further implication of this is that the very distinction between economics and its "preconditions," and even the way of distinguishing what is inside from what is outside of the economy – these turn out to be less informative and helpful than we have thought.

Fraser: I see your point, but I'm not convinced of your underlying premise, that it's desirable to overcome the distinction between structural–systemic and social–action perspectives. I would say that the problem with that distinction arises only when it gets ontologized – treated as marking out two substantively distinct societal realms ("system" versus "lifeworld") that correlate with two ontologically distinct types of interaction ("purposive–rational" or "strategic" action versus "normatively regulated" or "communicative" action). This is precisely what Habermas did in *Theory of Communicative Action*, and it's what gave the distinction in question a bad name. But I believe that it's perfectly possible – and desirable! – to retain a de-ontologized version of the distinction between structural–systemic and social–action perspectives. In that case, one treats the distinction not as ontological, but as *methodological*. It's a distinction between two different lenses that critical theorists can put on to understand *any* domain of social reality or type of societal interaction. So, it's entirely appropriate, in my view, to use "social" analysis to under-

stand economic interaction, and "structural" analysis to clarify interaction within families. In fact, such counterintuitive orientations are
immensely revealing; they disclose processes that remain inaccessible
to mainstream observers. So, unlike you, I am not seeking to overcome the methodological distinction. I want, rather, to embrace it. In
fact, I would say that it's precisely by combining or articulating the
structural–systemic and social–action perspectives that a theory of
capitalist society can become *critical*. In other words, I still subscribe
to the view I once called "perspectival dualism."[51] I suppose we'll
discuss this issue in more depth later (in chapter 3).

Jaeggi: Yes, we will. But let me try another angle. Your account
relies on a tension between foreground and background, between
something that is the capitalist "inside" and a background, which is
deemed necessary but situated "outside" it. Nevertheless, my sense is
that you also want to resist the "inside/outside" picture of capitalist
society. Is that right?

Fraser: You're right. I *do* want to resist the inside/outside picture
of capitalist society, and here is why. Everything I've said so far
implies that it would be wrong to construe society, polity, and nature
romantically, as "outside" capitalism and as inherently opposed to it.
That romantic view is widely held today by a fair number of left-wing
thinkers and activists, including cultural feminists, deep ecologists,
and neo-anarchists, as well as by some proponents of "plural," "post-
growth," "solidary," and "popular" economies. Too often, these
currents treat "care," "nature," "direct action," or "commoning"
as intrinsically anti-capitalist. As a result, they overlook the fact that
their favorite practices are not only sources of critique but also integral parts of the capitalist order.

   Recall that I have said that reproduction, polity, and nature
arose concurrently with economy, as the latter's "others." It is only
by contrast to economy that they acquire their specific character.
Reproduction and production make a pair. Each term is co-defined
by way of the other; neither makes any sense without the other.
The same is true of polity/economy and nature/society. All three of
these divisions and distinctions are part and parcel of the capitalist
order. None of the "non-economic" realms affords a wholly external
standpoint that could underwrite an absolutely pure and fully radical
form of critique. On the contrary, political projects that appeal to
what they imagine to be capitalism's outside usually end up recycling capitalist stereotypes, as they counterpose female nurturance

to male aggression, spontaneous social cooperation to economic calculation, nature's organicist wholism to anthropocentric individualism. Clearly, these binary oppositions are historically inaccurate, conceptually problematic, and indeed ideological. To premise one's struggles on them is not to challenge, but unwittingly to reflect, the institutionalized social order of capitalist society.

Jaeggi: I think on the level of social theory the connection between foreground and background is nicely fleshed out now. I'm still somewhat puzzled how this translates to the normative level. You reject the idea that there exists an "outside" to capitalism that ensures the possibility of radical criticism and practice. But, at the same time, you claim that capitalism's background normativities afford some critical potential, even though they are "inside" the capitalist order. Perhaps one could say they are "intra-capitalist" but "extra-economic." This is quite a complex view, which indeed scrambles any easy inside/outside opposition!

Fraser: It *is* complex, and necessarily so, because a proper account of capitalism's foreground/background relations must hold together three distinct ideas. First, capitalism's "non-economic" realms serve as enabling background conditions for its economy; the latter depends for its very existence on values and inputs from the former. Second, however, capitalism's "non-economic" realms have a weight and character of their own, which can under certain circumstances provide resources for anti-capitalist struggle. Nevertheless – and this is the third point – these realms are part and parcel of capitalist society, historically co-constituted in tandem with its economy, and marked by their symbiosis with it. All three ideas are necessary for an adequate conception of the foreground/background relations that constitute capitalist society. None alone is sufficient. All must be thought together in an "enlarged" view of capitalism as an institutionalized social order.

Unity of analysis and critique

Jaeggi: I have one last question, inspired by what we said in the Introduction about the difference between a critical theory of society and a freestanding normative theory. We agreed that what distinguishes critical theory is unity of analysis and critique. This means that, in analysis, the attempt to comprehend what is going on in social life – the attempt, for example, to understand the structure of capitalist social integration and its historical transformations – is a crucial part of what it means to criticize it. Analysis forms a part of the critique and critique forms part of the analysis: the critique unfolds in a process which the analysis sets in motion. Of course, this all hinges on whether the analysis brings out the contradictions, conflicts, and emancipatory possibilities inherent in a social formation. Still, if we are taking aim at deep structural dysfunctions inherent in our form of life, then this might indicate a methodological shift in contemporary critical theory – away from those more "Kantian–Rawlsian" concerns with deliberation and justice-claims, and back toward left-Hegelian reflections on the "objective tendencies" of an age. If not replacing the orientation on social actors and movements, this focus on crises at least supplements the focus on social struggles.

Fraser: Well, my aim is certainly to develop a critical theory. And I don't think anyone could mistake what I've laid out here for free-standing normative theory. In proposing an expanded conception of capitalism, I have at the same time constructed a framework for analyzing the society we inhabit now. The framework directs our attention to the institutional divisions that structure this society – to the shifts they are now undergoing and to the projects of various actors who are seeking to challenge or defend those divisions. It invites us to ask: how is the current form of capitalism (financialized, globalized, neoliberal) redrawing the boundaries between commodity production and social reproduction, between private and public power, between human beings and the rest of nature, and between exploitation and expropriation? And what are the implications for our society's characteristic forms of domination, injustice, and suffering – forms that in this conception are centrally concerned not only with class domination and labor exploitation, but also with gender and sexual domination, ecological depredation, imperial predation and racial oppression, and exclusions and marginalizations based in the organization of public power and the division of political space?

The framework also invites us to ask: how are capitalism's inherent "crisis tendencies" expressed today? When viewed in this enlarged way, does capitalism harbor propensities for self-destabilization beyond those identified by Marx, which were conceived as "contradictions" internal to its economy? Does it also harbor systemically entrenched tensions between the economic foreground and the non-economic background – between economy and society, economy and

59

polity, economy and nature? And how are these "contradictions of capitalism" playing out now?

Finally, this perspective encourages us to ask: what forms of social struggle characterize present-day capitalism? Does the notion of "boundary struggles" serve to clarify the political projects of present-day social actors? And does it afford a basis for assessing their emancipatory potential? Above all, what light does this understanding of capitalism shed on the prospects for emancipatory social transformation?

We shall surely address these questions in the discussions that follow. Whatever the answers turn out to be, they will comprise a "diagnosis of the times," in which analysis and critique are brought together. And to the degree it succeeds, this diagnosis will have practical relevance. It won't provide a blueprint for action, to be sure. But it could afford the sort of context-clarifying orientation that guides action, a map on which to locate – and to understand better – "the struggles and wishes of the age."

2

Historicizing Capitalism

Capitalism in time

Jaeggi: In the previous chapter, we conceptualized capitalism as an institutionalized social order and talked about its background and foreground conditions. What I am going to ask in this chapter is how to conceive of capitalism not only as an institutionalized social order but also as a *historical* social order that changes over time, and that has different significant characteristics as things evolve through history. So the first question would be: What does it actually mean to historicize capitalism, and why do we have to do it? How is it that the idea of historicity in capitalism comes out of the idea of it as an institutionalized social order?

Fraser: Your question suggests another reason to reject the view of capitalism as an economic system *simpliciter*. That view is ahistorical, focused on a "system logic" that appears to exist outside of time. It doesn't tell us how "capital's logic" is implanted in actual societies, nor does it tell us how to connect "system" and history. And that contrasts sharply with the approach I'm proposing, which is designed to foreground those connections. By redefining capitalism as an institutionalized social order, I postulated that its economic logic is "embedded," to use Polanyi's term, in a larger framework, which includes the non-economic background conditions of public power, social reproduction, and nature. And that leads directly to history. The way the official economy is situated vis-à-vis public power, social reproduction, and nature changes historically, as does the way those things are organized.

Nevertheless, it's also true that there was something "out of time"

61

about our discussion in the previous chapter. We focused there on the general features of a capitalist social order, but we only hinted about the ways that order develops in and through history. So we should now put our perspective *into* time by conceptualizing capitalist society as developing temporally, in a sequence of historically specific regimes of accumulation. In these regimes, state–economy relations assume various historically specific forms, as do relations between production and social reproduction, on the one hand, and between society and nature, on the other.

Jaeggi: Let's just stay for a second with the relation between history and theory, or the relation between the logic and the history of capitalism. What is it that actually changes here? Is it the background, the "bed" in which the economy is embedded? Or do you think that there are dynamics in each field, as well as within the economy itself? Or is it the relation that changes? What is it that actually produces the historical dynamic that you have in mind?

Fraser: In the model I'm proposing, each component of the institutionalized social order that is capitalism is co-constituted in relation to the others. We can't even make sense of the idea of "an economy" except in contrast to a "polity," nor of "production" except in contrast to "reproduction," nor of (non-human) "nature" except in contrast to (human) "society." Of course, the boundaries between these "spheres" shift historically. But these shifts do more than simply alter the place where economy, production, and society stop, and where polity, reproduction, and nature begin. They also introduce qualitative changes in the nature of each term within those relations. So yes, the bed changes, but so does what is lying in the bed. On this view, it would not make sense for any one of these terms to change without the others changing as well, because they are mutually co-constitutive.

Jaeggi: So then does the distinction between the logic of capitalism and the history of capitalism still make sense? Or would you say that we should historicize capitalism so deeply that the logic itself is historicized?

Fraser: At the most general level, it *does* make sense to talk about the orientation to endless accumulation of surplus value – the so-called "law of value" – as an impelling, dynamic force that operates in one form or another in every society that merits the name "capitalist." But how that force is expressed, the practices through which it works, the constraints and limits it comes up against, and the strategies capital evolves for getting around those limits and for profiting from them – all of that is historically specific. So, yes, there is a constant here, but it is very abstract – so abstract that you won't get very far if you stick to that level of analysis.

Jaeggi: So how do you know that a specific institutional social order is still capitalism, or was already capitalism? For example, merchant capitalism doesn't resemble today's capitalism all that much, and you could come up with a set of conceptual distinctions along which they are farther apart from each other than from non-capitalist social orders, and so forth. If you are critical of certain understandings of an unchangeable logic of capitalism, within the multiplicity of capitalisms, both historically and worldwide, what sort of conceptual standard would you still use to identify an institutional social order as capitalist?

Fraser: There are two different questions here. So far, I have been talking about capitalism as a path-dependent sequence of accumulation regimes that unfolds diachronically in history. Now, you have introduced the question of synchronic varieties of capitalism, which exist alongside one another within the same epoch. And that's a rather different matter. I want to propose that, for now, we put the synchronic question aside and focus on the diachronic. Then we can answer the question of how we know it still is capitalism by returning to what we said in chapter 1. I stand by the analysis there, which posited an expanded view of capitalism, encompassing both the official economy and its background conditions. That constellation of foreground and background serves as a general conception that distinguishes capitalist from non-capitalist societies. Unlike the former, the latter do not institutionalize separations of economy from polity or production from reproduction; and their nature/society divisions are far less sharp. In my view, these separations constitute capitalism's specificity, not least because they represent the indispensable preconditions for an "economy" subject to direction by "the law of value." Without them, such an "economy" could not exist. That's the view I've been developing. Now, however, I want to historicize it, by considering how it is concretely instantiated in different regimes of accumulation.

Capitalism's regimes of accumulation

Jaeggi: So, in the first chapter, we have identified four basic characteristics of capitalism, and now we are going to historicize them by saying that the historical instantiations of each of those moments are changing, and although they are different from each other, they are still instantiations of these characteristics.

Now, when we talk about the history of capitalism, we tend to come up with certain more or less well-defined stages, though scholars might disagree on the details.

Fraser: The stages that I'm going to propose here are quite familiar. They are the same ones invoked by many historians of capitalism: first, mercantile or commercial capitalism, followed by so-called "liberal" (competitive) capitalism, then state-managed (or social-democratic) capitalism, and finally, financialized capitalism. At this level, I have nothing original to add to mainstream discussions. What's new, by contrast, is how I propose to distinguish these regimes. Most scholars focus on the specific ways in which states and markets are related in each, while neglecting the relation between production and reproduction, on the one hand, and between (non-human) nature and (human) society, on the other hand. But those latter relations are equally consequential and equally defining of capitalist societies. So they too belong at the center of our analysis of it. We can go a long way toward understanding capitalism's history by focusing on how social reproduction and nature are organized in each of its phases, as well as on the organization of political power. For any given era, to what extent and in what form are "carework" and "nature" commodified? To what extent and in what way are they internalized as objects of political and/or corporate management? To what extent and in what way is responsibility for them devolved to households and/or neighborhoods, base communities and/or civil society? I hope to contribute something new to discussions of capitalism's historicity by re-describing each of its familiar phases as a historically specific constellation of all these foreground/background relations.

Jaeggi: Ok, so we have four stages, and we are going to talk more about these stages later on. But first, I want to ask you: What do you actually mean by a stage or a phase?

Fraser: By a phase, I mean a *regime of accumulation*. And by that I mean a relatively stabilized institutional matrix, in which the accumulation dynamic is shaped and channeled by a specific organization of its background conditions. The shaping is effected, first, by a specific organization of public power at both the state and geopolitical levels, including political membership, citizenship rights, hierarchies of political subjectivation, and core/periphery relations; second, by a specific organization of social reproduction, including family forms and gender orders; and finally, by a specific ecological organization, including characteristic ways of generating energy, extracting resources, and disposing of waste. Together, these things channel the accumulation dynamic. By implanting it in an institutionalized social order, they give a definite shape and some relative stability to that which is otherwise wild and anarchic.

Of course, stability is never perfect. And capitalism is changing all the time. But there is nevertheless a difference between periods of "normal" historical development, in which change unfolds within a given order whose basic parameters remain relatively fixed, and "abnormal" moments, in which a regime is unraveling. In the second case, unlike in the first, the basic parameters are up for grabs. (I should clarify that I am using the terms "normal" and "abnormal" here in a sense inspired by Thomas Kuhn and Richard Rorty.[1])

System-level dynamics

Jaeggi: So on this abstract level – we are going to concretize things in a moment – what leads from one stage to the other when one of these more or less stabilized situations in institutionalized social orders somehow ceases to be stable? Marx had a very specific idea about this dynamic, and I would be interested in hearing a bit more about the modes of social transformation and change that are in place here.

Fraser: Here I want to distinguish between a "system"-level explanation and a "social"-level explanation. An example of the first is the Marxian idea that entrenched "relations of production" come to act as "fetters" on developing "forces of production." Over time, so the story goes, the "forces" erode the "relations," unraveling the regime and paving the way for its replacement by a new one. This is *not* the explanation I want to propose – it is too technological, deterministic, and mono-causal. But I do want to develop an account that operates on the same level, one which clarifies the role of systemic contradictions in historical transitions.

Here's the alternative I have in mind: I assume, first, that each regime of accumulation represents a provisional way of dealing with some tensions that are inherent in any capitalist society, tensions between economic production and social reproduction, between economy and polity, and between society and nature. I also assume, second, that these tensions constitute "crisis tendencies" above and beyond the ones theorized by Marx. Whereas his crisis tendencies were located *within* capitalism's economy, these arise at the *boundaries* that divide the economy from its non-economic conditions of possibility. We could call them (quasi-)"Polanyian," as opposed to "Marxian," crisis tendencies, since they break out along the established institutional frontiers that structure a given regime of accumulation. So I would say that capitalist societies are always sitting on a plurality of potentially disruptive crisis tendencies: political, ecological, social-reproductive. But this does not rule out the existence of Marxian contradictions as well. I assume that capitalist societies also harbor crisis tendencies that are internal to the economy and are expressed in specifically economic ways, such as falling profit rates, boom–bust cycles, mass unemployment, the siphoning of capital from production to finance, and the like. In some periods, in fact, these two types of crisis tendencies converge. At such times, capitalism's Marxian and Polanyian tensions sharpen and combine to create "system crises" that far exceed the difficulties of "normal times." Periodically, they reach a point of severity at which people react, and here is where we transition to the *social* level of explanation.

Jaeggi: May I interrupt you for a moment, before we start talking about the other level, and return to Marx? For Marx, or at least in some versions of orthodox Marxism, there is only one dynamic – that which stems from the development of the forces of production. As he famously said in *The German Ideology*, ideology has no history.[2] He thus might think of all these other social dynamics you have in mind as things that do not have a history, but which merely *reflect* dynamics that stem from the economic realm. Of course, this would be a very orthodox Marxism, but in this orthodox version, everything else would somehow revolve around the development of the forces of production. This is why we have the powerful idea of the relations of production being the "fetters" on the forces of production. This is where the music plays: everything else is secondary to and dependent on this so-to-speak "master dynamic."

Granted, even in Marx things are not quite this simple. Still, I think we should try instead for a multidimensional picture, in which each of the spheres, each of the parts of an institutionalized social order (or form of life), are seen to have dynamics of their own that then somehow interact. I still like the idea of fettering, or the idea that change and crisis comes about because there is a mismatch between the dynamics of these spheres, and there might even sometimes be a technological change that destabilizes other dimensions of social life. So I am not at all opposed to the idea that a dynamic can be fettered, or that these different spheres of the social can be in a relation of either matching or being mismatched, but I would go for a more complicated picture. And I imagine that you would go for a more complicated picture with respect to crises and the dynamics of transformation as well.

Fraser: Absolutely. I would sign on, to the letter, to the formulation you just gave. The picture we developed in the previous chapter included the idea that different elements of the capitalist order have their own normativities and social ontologies. And that implies the possibility of "relatively autonomous" developments that are not mere "reflections" of economic or technological developments, even though they may be affected by the latter – but also vice versa! Take, for example, the striking decrease in household size that developed in many European societies in the early modern period. This shift, from extended kin residence arrangements to conjugal-centered households, long predated the emergence of industrial capitalism and appears to have facilitated the latter's development – which is why the most sophisticated materialist and Marxian histories of the family assume the relative autonomy of the kinship sphere vis-à-vis that of official production – for example, Göran Therborn's book, *Between Sex and Power*.[3] So, yes, the view of capitalism as an institutionalized social order must reject the base/superstructure model. I also like your idea of mismatches in which different aspects of life unfold at different paces. That idea introduces the possibility of mutual disturbances or interferences – or again, as I would prefer to call them, "boundary tensions." These arise from the contradictory background/foreground relations we discussed in the previous chapter – from the fact that capitalism's economy simultaneously needs and destabilizes its own "non-economic" conditions of possibility. When these "Polanyian" contradictions intensify, people face difficulties in navigating the societal terrain. So, yes, we are on the same page on this.

Jaeggi: To go back to the metaphor of embeddedness, then, it is not that the "bed" is stable and the economy is dynamic. We have a multiplicity of dynamics.

67

Fraser: Agreed. That's a good way of saying what's wrong with Polanyi. He really *does* assume that there is a stable bed ("society") and then this bad economic dynamic comes along and messes it up. What I am saying, by contrast, is closer to Weber and Habermas. They hold that capitalist society encompasses a plurality of "value spheres," each of which has its own "inner logic" of development.[4] My view is akin to that idea, but it differs in a crucial respect: for me the "spheres" in question are not natural kinds but artifacts of capitalism. Each of them gets its distinctive quality (its normativity, its social ontology) from the position it occupies in the larger institutional structure – from the way it is set apart from, and made to contrast with, the other constitutive elements of that structure, including the capitalist economy. So my view is far more historicist and anti-essentialist than that of Habermas.

Social-level dynamics

Jaeggi: Okay, so we have talked a bit about the system side of it. Since you still prefer to talk about the system- and the action-theoretical sides, perhaps now you might give us an idea of how you understand the non-systemic side of it. We are talking about the sphere of action and of social struggle now, right?

Fraser: Exactly. One quick preliminary comment: It's not so much that I prefer the language of "system theory" and "action theory" – I fully appreciate, as you do, why it is problematic. I am using these terms in scare quotes, in order to stress that a proper explanation of capitalist "regime change" must encompass (at least) two different levels. But I would be happy to use other terms to designate them – for example, the structural-institutional level and the level of social-action or inter-subjective agency.

In any case, we're now moving to the social level, the level of experience and social action. Nothing fully counts as a crisis, as Brian Milstein has argued, until it is experienced as such.[5] What looks like a crisis to an outside observer does not become historically generative until participants in the society see it as a crisis. Only then, when a critical mass of people conclude that they can no longer go on in the same way, that something must *give*, do you get social action that transgresses the bounds of the established social order and opens the possibility of major institutional change.

Let's go back again to Marx to illustrate what is meant by a social-level explanation of historical change. Marx thought that as modes of production ran into "objective" system difficulties, class struggles would progressively sharpen and widen, eventually assuming a revolutionary form and transforming the established order. He also thought that at such times the established ruling class would lose its confidence, that the initiative would pass to the rising class, which would eventually remake the social order through revolutionary struggle. Of course, this sounds deterministic and overly unitary. It glosses over important distinctions among different actors, different forms of struggle, and the various processes by which they may (or may not!) converge into a new hegemonic bloc. And, of course, we are speaking here neither about the shift from feudalism to capitalism nor about that from capitalism to socialism, but rather about major shifts *within* the history of capitalism. So we must think about the social-action dynamics of transition somewhat differently. But we do need this level of explanation.

I propose to begin by affirming that class struggles – struggles between labor and capital over the rate of exploitation and the distribution of surplus value – are indeed characteristic of capitalist societies. They appear in one form or another in virtually every phase of its development. But this Marxian type of conflict is not the only type that is definitive of capitalist society. Equally endemic are what I have called "boundary struggles," which erupt at the sites of capitalism's constitutive institutional divisions: where economy meets polity, where society meets nature, and where production meets reproduction. At those boundaries, social actors periodically mobilize to contest or defend the institutional map of capitalist society – and sometimes they succeed in redrawing it. So, in my view, capitalist societies are inherently prone to generate both types of struggle: class struggles, in the Marxian sense, and boundary struggles, in a sense reminiscent of Polanyi. The key question is how these two types of struggle relate to each other – above all, in those historical moments of transformation, when one regime of accumulation gives way to another. To understand such transformations, we need the idea of a "general crisis" in which not just one or two, but *all* (or most) of capitalism's inherent contradictions – economic, social, political, and ecological – intertwine and exacerbate one another. And I don't mean only "objectively," but also inter-subjectively, as when class struggles and boundary struggles converge and combine to produce a new counter-hegemony. That is my understanding of the "social-action" side of "regime change."

Logics of change

Jaeggi: With these two levels in view, let's return to the question of how one stage leads to another. We are already circling around the idea of crisis on objective and subjective levels. Marx pointed out that social transformations and revolutions rely on both passive and active moments. We might define the active moments as the moments of class struggle and boundary struggles and the passive moments as those more "objective" moments of crisis and contradiction. On the latter side – what you've described as the system level – certain practices and institutions have become dysfunctional, whereas on the class and boundary struggle side, it's more about outrage. But even on the side of class struggle – the subjective or, in your terms, social level – it is not *just* about outrage, and it certainly does not only depend on a voluntaristic revolutionary will. Marx put these two sides together. His insight was that crises create a certain kind of potential for those movements to emerge, and that there are objective social conditions required in order for emancipatory movements to evolve.

Bringing this back to your discussion of crises: What is the model you have in mind? Is it that each of these regimes runs into some kind of problem at the system level, which then needs to be resolved by a transformation initiated at the social level? In that case, in talking about these four regimes, we should also spell out how, at a certain point, something just did not work anymore – how, at a certain point, practices and institutions erode, become uninhabitable, unstable, delegitimized, and a new solution and a new set of institutions needed to be produced. But then this only leads to the next issue, which is how to conceive of these kinds of transformation. Is it just, as some Foucauldians might say, a matter of contingency and discontinuity? In my own work, for example, I argue for a more powerful (slightly Hegelian, slightly dialectical) conception of dynamics that is somehow cumulative, that is marked by the fact that new regimes react to crises of the old regime, and these crises demand responses to the problems they pose at the same level that they pose them.[6] Even if one stage then does not necessarily lead to another, and even if there is more than one "logic of history," there is nevertheless some kind of rationality at work.

Fraser: There is definitely something more at work than mere contingency. I agree that Foucault can serve as a negative object lesson, an example of how *not* to think about social transformation. While rightly rejecting historical determinism and teleology, he overshot the mark, ending at the equally problematic view that things simply change all of a sudden and for no reason. In his radically discontinuous view of history, an entrenched episteme or power/knowledge regime simply ends, we know not why, and a new one abruptly appears, but in a way and in a form that's entirely unmotivated – it's as if anything might happen at any time! That's quite different from the view I want to propose. For me, in contrast, each new set of possibilities has its grounds in a concrete problem situation, one in which existing arrangements have run into trouble objectively and are subjectively experienced as problematic. In this sort of situation, social actors face the burning question of how, concretely, to change the organization of society. They seek arrangements that can satisfactorily address the historically specific problems gestated in, but not solvable by, the old regime. So transformation here resembles the Hegelian idea of determinate negation, except I would insist that every concrete crisis situation harbors a plurality of possible paths, and not simply one, as Hegel appeared to assume. But, on the other hand, the number of real possibilities is relatively small, and some things are simply not possible. You don't suddenly go from global financialized capitalism to medieval Spain – that's not an intelligible sequence, and not a genuinely possible historical path.

On this view, moreover, one can retrospectively reconstruct the history of capitalist society as a path-dependent sequence of different regimes. Each regime emerges out of the specific crisis situation of the previous one and seeks to overcome the latter's impasses. But each regime also introduces new problems of its own, which it is unable to resolve, and each is replaced in turn. At least that's always been the case up to the present, and it is likely, I think, to be the case in the future as well. Seen this way, the sequence makes sense retrospectively and appears to possess a directionality.

Regimes of polity-cum-economy

Jaeggi: Let's begin to look at these regimes of accumulation in more detail. I think an interesting way to tell the story of these four stages is by referring to the changing relationships between economy and polity. Capitalism is very often thought of as the institutional order in which economy and politics, economy and state, have become separated. It is nearly a truism that the capitalist economy is somehow independent of the rest of society. But at the same time, it is also not true, and this idea of an economy autonomous from the state is

71

very much a product of ideology. So, what interests me here is the dependency as well as the independence, the connection as well as the separation. How is this spelled out in these different stages and regimes? How, in this historicized picture, have these relationships evolved? Because the matter seems not as simple as: first, there was unity; then, there was separation.

Fraser: The general idea you've just sketched accords very well with my view, by which I mean the idea that capitalism's economy stands in a complex relation to its background conditions. It is, on the one hand, institutionally separated from them, as I initially stressed. But, at the same time, it depends on them for various "inputs," including people, and for various forms of political and social organization without which it couldn't profitably produce and sell commodities, access and exploit labor, and accumulate and appropriate surplus value on a sustained and ongoing basis. So, yes, there is both separation and dependence.

But that is not all. Capitalism's economy also stands in a relation of *denial* vis-à-vis its background conditions. It disavows its dependence on them by treating nature, social reproduction, and public power as "free gifts," which are inexhaustible, possess no (monetized) value, and can be appropriated *ad infinitum* without any concern for replenishment. As a result, the relation is potentially contradictory and crisis-prone, because the ceaseless drive toward ever-expanding accumulation destabilizes the background conditions on which the foreground dynamic depends. All in all, it is a relation of *division–dependence–disavowal*. And that is a built-in source of potential instability, a recipe for periodic crisis (see chapter 3).

But please notice that I have been describing capitalism's foreground/background relations in a way that holds not only for economy/polity but also for production/reproduction and society/nature. And I would like eventually to use this conception to historicize capitalism along all three of those axes in an integrated way. It may be necessary now to discuss them separately, but I want at least to register that this is less than ideal. And I want to repeat what I said before. Most accounts, including those of the Regulation School, focus single-mindedly on state/economy relations.[7] That is one important part of the story, to be sure, but only one. And it needs to be interwoven with other, equally important strands, which concern production/reproduction relations and society/nature relations. Those relations are fundamental to capitalism as an institutionalized social order. Periodizations that overlook them can only mislead. An expanded conception of capitalism must make ecology and social reproduction as central as political orders to its schemas of historicization. An important aim of my project is to bring those neglected aspects into the picture, to put them front and center in capitalism's history.

Jaeggi: Okay, this makes for a really ambitious project, because you need to find a holistic vocabulary of how the spheres interact differently at different times – which is complicated by the fact that a thorough historicization would also affect the definition of those very spheres. Nevertheless, you agreed that there are also autonomous dynamics at play in each of those, at least when we focus on the transitions that interest us most, those that have to do with capitalism. So, bearing in mind that the picture must be pieced together, let's start in small steps and focus on the economy/polity separation once again, and then on the other institutional separations. What shape did the relation between economics and politics take under each of these regimes of accumulation, and how did it change as we move through these four regimes?

Fraser: Let me start with capitalism's initial, mercantile phase, which held sway for a couple of hundred years, roughly from the sixteenth to the eighteenth centuries. In this phase, capitalism's economy was only partially separated from the state. Neither land nor labor was a true commodity; and moral-economic norms still governed most everyday interactions, even in the towns and cities of the European heartland. Absolutist rulers used their powers to regulate commerce internally, within their territories, even as they profited from external plunder and long-distance trade, which were organized capitalistically, through an expanding world market in luxury commodities. So there was an internal/external division: commercial regulation inside the state territory, "the law of value" outside it. This division held for a while but was eventually breached, as the value logic that operated internationally began to penetrate the domestic space of European states, altering the social relations among landowners and their dependents and fostering new professional and business milieus in urban centers, which became seedbeds of liberal, even revolutionary, thinking. Equally corrosive – and consequential – was the rising indebtedness of rulers. Needing revenue, some of them were forced to convene proto-parliamentary bodies, which they could not in the end control. And that led in several cases to revolution.

Jaeggi: And to a new regime?

73

Fraser: Right. Thanks to this combination of economic corrosion and political turmoil, mercantile capitalism was supplanted in the nineteenth century by a new regime, often called "liberal capitalism." In this phase, leading European capitalist states no longer used public power directly to regulate internal commerce. Rather, they constructed "economies," in which production and exchange appeared to operate autonomously, free from overt political control, through the "purely economic" mechanism of "supply-and-demand." What underlay that construction was a new legal order, which enshrined the supremacy of contract, private property, price-setting markets, and the associated subjective rights of "free individuals," viewed as utility-maximizing, arm's-length transactors. The effect was to institutionalize, at the national level, a seemingly sharp division between the public power of states, on the one hand, and the private power of capital, on the other. But, of course, states were all the while using repressive power to sanctify the land expropriations that transformed rural populations into "doubly free" proletarians. In this way, they established the class preconditions for the large-scale exploitation of wage labor, which, when combined with fossilized energy, powered a massive take-off of industrial manufacturing. In the periphery, meanwhile, European colonial powers dropped every pretense of political abstinence. Marshaling military might to underwrite wholesale looting of subjugated populations, they consolidated colonial rule on the basis of "free-trade imperialism" under British hegemony – all of which raises doubts about the expression "liberal capitalism." From virtually the start, moreover, this regime was wracked by instability, both economic and political. Its way of institutionalizing the economy/polity separation gave rise to periodic depressions, crashes, and panics, on the one hand, and to intense class conflicts, boundary struggles, and revolutions, on the other – all the while fueling international financial chaos, anti-colonial rebellions, and inter-imperialist wars. By the twentieth century, the multiple contradictions of "liberal" capitalism had metastasized into a protracted general crisis, which was finally resolved in the aftermath of World War II with the installation of a new regime.

Jaeggi: I assume you mean state-managed capitalism. How did that formation remake the relation between economy and polity?

Fraser: Well, in this regime, the states of the core began to use public power more proactively within their own territories, to forestall or mitigate crisis. Empowered by the Bretton Woods system of capital controls, which had been established under US hegemony, they invested in infrastructure, assumed some costs of social reproduction, promoted full employment and working-class consumerism, accepted labor unions as partners in trilateral corporatist bargaining, actively steered economic development, compensated for "market failures," and generally disciplined capital for its own good. All these efforts were aimed at securing the conditions for sustained private capital accumulation – and at pre-empting revolution. Although it stabilized things for a few decades, state-managed capitalism also ran up against its own contradictions – both economic and political. Rising wages and generalization of productivity gains combined to lower profit rates in manufacturing in the core, prompting new efforts on the part of capital to unshackle market forces from political regulation. And a global New Left erupted to challenge the oppressions, exclusions, and predations on which the whole edifice rested. In due course, the state-managed capitalist regime was replaced in turn by the present-day regime.

Jaeggi: And that regime is financialized capitalism.

Fraser: Right. The current regime has remade the economy/polity relation yet again. Whereas its predecessor empowered states to subordinate the short-term interests of private firms to the long-term objective of sustained accumulation, this one authorizes finance capital to discipline states and publics in the immediate interests of private investors. The dismantling of Bretton Woods, instigated by the United States, opened the way. Absent the capital controls of the previous era, states lost the ability to control their own currencies and steer their economies through deficit financing. They are now at the mercy of international lenders and bond rating agencies. Ironically, state capacity is used in this regime to construct transnational governance structures that empower capital to discipline the citizens and publics to whom public power is supposed to be accountable! Organizations like the IMF, the WTO, and the TRIPS (trade-related intellectual property regime) now establish many of the rules of the road, globalizing and liberalizing the world economy in the interests of capital. Moreover, debt plays a major role in the governance of financialized capitalism. In this regime, it is largely through debt that capital expropriates populations in core and periphery and imposes austerity on citizens, regardless of the policy preferences they express through elections. Nevertheless, this regime, too, is highly unstable. Having gutted the very public power on which accumulation

75

depends, financialized capitalism has now reached the point of crisis: not just the economic system crisis signaled by the near meltdown of the global financial order in 2007–8, but also the political-hegemonic crisis signaled by Brexit, Trump, etc.

Well, that's a rough sketch of the key shifts in the economy/polity nexus. It shows us that capitalism's general form as an institutionalized social order has undergone successive transformations in the course of its history. In each phase, the political conditions for the capitalist economy have assumed a different institutional form at both the state-territorial and geopolitical levels. In each case, the political contradiction of capitalist society has assumed a different guise and found expression in a different set of crisis phenomena. In each regime, finally, capitalism's political contradiction has incited different forms of social struggle.

Jaeggi: Another point is that the economy/polity relationship is not just about each state and its economy; it's also about how the entire international political order is organized in relation to the global capitalist economy.

Fraser: Exactly. In sketching these transformations, I have tried to highlight geopolitical arrangements, in addition to political processes within state borders. The international level is important, I think, because capital is inherently expansionist, driven to transgress borders. And that puts its economic logic, which is intrinsically trans-territorial, into potential conflict with the dominant modern logic of political rule, which is territorial. Each regime of accumulation had to manage that contradiction – usually by empowering a hegemonic power to construct trans- or inter-national political space. This is why, incidentally, I prefer to speak not of state–market relations, but rather about the relation between the *private power* of capital and *public power*. That formulation is better because it includes not only states but also the geopolitical hegemonies and trans-state governance structures that have always shaped capitalist development throughout history. It is important to note, for instance, that the shift from liberal to state-organized capitalism included a shift from British to American hegemony, and from the gold-standard, free-trade imperialism of the nineteenth and early twentieth century to Bretton Woods capital controls of the post-World War II era, while the most recent shift to financialized capitalism appears, at least for now, to have preserved US hegemony, albeit in a weakened form without much moral authority.

The trans-state level of governance is especially important in the current regime. Financialized capitalism is not at all about simple deregulation. On the contrary, it involves the erection of a new layer of governance above the level of states, which consists largely of global financial institutions, such as the ones I mentioned earlier: the IMF, the World Bank, the WTO, and TRIPS. To these we should add the central banks and bond rating agencies. None of these institutions is politically accountable. Yet all are actively engaged in authoritative rule-making on a pervasive scale. The rules they have made entrench distinctive neoliberal interpretations of private property and free trade, which now govern wide swathes of social interaction across the globe. Pitched at a level superior to, and able to override, domestic laws, they set strict limits on what states can and cannot do with respect to matters like labor rights and environmental protections; and they cannot be changed by political action at the state level. This is why Stephen Gill speaks of a "new constitutionalism."[8] A similar, de-democratizing logic is at work on the regional level, paradigmatically in the European Union. Imperatives emanating from the Commission and the ECB assume the weight and authority of unimpeachable "constitutional" provisions, as we saw in the case of Greece. In 2015, as you know, the Greek people elected a government pledged to reject austerity only to see that pledge rendered meaningless in the face of transnationally imposed imperatives, which are immune to political accountability and can simply invalidate official practices of political will formation. This, in a nutshell, is the new relation of economy/polity in financialized capitalism.

Rise of neoliberalism

Jaeggi: This is not the absence of politics, then, but a new form that politics has taken. A lot of people would say that neoliberalism just means that we finally got rid of the state, of any kind of political influence. Which is obviously not true.

Fraser: Right. First of all, it was states – above all powerful states, and particularly the US – that constructed this order. Much of it was built through the mechanism of interstate treaties. Some states benefit greatly from this. But even those that are on the losing end are quite active in devising strategies for establishing niches within it. Far from behaving as passive victims, some peripheral states set up export processing zones to attract foreign direct investment, while others encouraged labor emigration for the sake of remittances. Obviously, not all states are equally powerful in financialized capitalism, but when have they ever been? In every phase of capitalism's history, we have to distinguish those states that can push others around from those on the receiving end.

So I agree with you: financialized capitalism has not dispensed with, but reconfigured, political regulation of its economy. It has established a new international political/financial architecture, which constrains and channels the actions of states differently from the way that the previous Bretton Woods regime did. In general, what states can and cannot do always depends in part on the established international order. It is crucial, as Immanuel Wallerstein has long insisted, that capitalism developed in the absence of a world state. In it, a *world economic system* became conjoined with an *international state system*.[9] The latter has always comprised a multiplicity of territorial states more or less loosely organized by a succession of hegemonic powers. Each hegemon has had to manage its colonies and clients, as well as its rivals and allies, in the context of historically specific balances (and imbalances!) of power. Each has also taken the lead in organizing geopolitical space in a way that could foster expanded capital accumulation. Here we see a point that David Harvey has stressed: the political logic of capitalism differs from its economic logic.[10] The economic logic, if left to itself, would simply go everywhere, blithely transgressing and ignoring borders, as if they did not exist. But borders *do* exist, and the transnational space in which capital operates must be politically constructed.

Jaeggi: Let me ask one more question about the transition from stage three to stage four, from state-managed to financialized capitalism. What was the problem that couldn't be solved within state capitalism? What was the crisis? In which sense was neoliberal, financialized capitalism a reaction to or even some kind of a solution to problems that came out of state-managed capitalism?

Fraser: That formation entered into its crisis period in the 1970s and was replaced bit by bit, almost by stealth, by neoliberal financialized global capitalism. This makes for a striking contrast with earlier transformations. As we saw, the shift from mercantile capitalism to liberal capitalism transpired through dramatic events, like the English and French revolutions. And the shift from that regime to state-managed capitalism was equally dramatic, involving two world wars, Communist revolution, the rise of fascism, and a worldwide struggle to produce a new form of democratic capitalism. By contrast, the transition of our time is far murkier. Certainly, there have been economic recessions, and most recently, the 2007–8 financial crisis. And there were dramatic electoral shifts that brought Thatcher and Reagan to power in the UK and the US. But still, many of the structural changes were instituted imperceptibly and below the radar. Thanks to Nancy MacLean, we are now becoming aware of the little-known but highly consequential role of "the Virginia School" of public choice theory, led by James Buchanan and funded largely by the Koch Brothers, in conceiving, spreading, and installing economistic logics in the heart of US government bodies, all aimed at disabling democratic oversight and control.[11] Colin Crouch has disclosed related stealth transformations in the UK.[12]

Our understanding of this transition is fragmentary – it's very much a work in progress. The most widely circulated accounts are economistic and so are, from the perspective that we've been outlining here, not sufficient. They invoke a crisis of profitability, of falling rates of profit, in some cases due to rising labor costs in the capitalist core. They also talk about the over-accumulation of capital, the saturation of markets in the core, the search for new markets and investment outlets elsewhere. Accounts of this sort aim to explain why manufacturing was relocated from the core to the semi-periphery. All of this is relevant, of course, but it remains highly partial, focused exclusively on economic considerations, conceived in systemic terms, abstracted from politics and social action.

Jaeggi: Streeck's thesis in *Buying Time* suggests that the phase of state-run capitalism was inherently unstable, because from the very beginning it borrowed resources that it couldn't replace.[13]

Fraser: Streeck's approach is very interesting, because he rejects the standard view that democracy and capitalism go together, by some sort of elective affinity. For him, on the contrary, they are inherently in tension with each other. They appeared to be compatible only briefly, in the exceptional period following World War II. And that appearance could be maintained only so long as the state-capitalist regime of accumulation succeeded in papering over its own internal contradiction, which was a contradiction between two intrinsically incompatible principles of distribution: "market justice" and "social justice." For Streeck, it was only a matter of time before the tensions came out. He recounts a whole series of policy fixes, beginning in the 1960s, which aimed to keep them under wraps: for example, wage-driven inflation, sovereign debt, and "private Keynesianism" (which is to say, the promotion of consumer debt). But each fix only created new, more difficult problems, until the whole regime entered into overt crisis, came apart, and was replaced by financialized capitalism.

What I admire about this approach is that it holds the economic and political aspects together, in a single frame. This is an advance over the usual economistic accounts, which locate the source of the trouble exclusively inside "the economy." But I believe that we can and should go further than Streeck has done in developing the specifically political strand of the crisis of state-managed capitalism. I would stress not just policy dilemmas, but also social movement struggles, which posed serious and sharpening challenges to that regime from at least the 1960s. I am thinking of the New Left, of struggles for decolonization and "racial equality," and of the movement for women's liberation – all of which articulated expectations and aspirations that burst the bounds of social-democratic commonsense. Over time, their challenges converged, not only with one another, but also with those of a rising "neoliberal" party, determined to liberate "market forces" from state control and to globalize the capitalist economy. It was this one–two punch of emancipatory social movements plus neoliberalism that destroyed social democracy's hegemony and eventually the state-capitalist regime.

Jaeggi: One might also include the left-wing critique of the welfare state as a factor in this transformation. A critique of the disciplinary society, of administrative power, has always focused on the normalizing tendencies of the welfare state, on bureaucratization, and so on. But you also see a version of this critique in Habermas, in his account of the "juridification" and "colonization of the lifeworld."[14] So wasn't it the case that at a certain moment left-wing criticism and neoliberalism somehow went hand in hand, or converged? The green party, the idea of subsidiarity, even the idea of civil society at a certain point might have been part of delegitimizing the welfare state, saying as they did, "Let's organize in social movements; let's take care of our own issues." Twenty years after this movement, one can also see the downside to it, the downside of the state-criticism that was in place here.

Fraser: Yes, I agree. Those developments did indeed play a role in delegitimizing the welfare state. Their net effect was to cast the use and organization of public power in a negative light, especially since many of the actors you mentioned were relatively silent on the matter of *private* power. By concentrating their fire exclusively on the state, they let the power of capital and of corporations off the hook. And neoliberals were quick to spot the opening and to exploit it.

What is especially interesting to me, however, is the sociological dimension of this process. I would say, paraphrasing Marx, that social democracy created its own gravediggers, that it ended up disabling the very social forces that historically supported it. That was certainly the case in the United States, where the GI Bill promoted a wave of postwar suburbanization by subsidizing home ownership for returning veterans, at least for "Whites." The effect was to break up the immigrant working-class neighborhoods, which had been New Deal strongholds. As urban "White ethnics" moved to single-family suburban homes, their lives became more consumerist and less solidaristic. Many later became "Reagan Democrats." That is just one example, from the United States, of how the welfare state helped to destroy its own basis of support; there are many others.

But we should also consider the rise of new political subjects, whose concerns breached the limits of social-democratic political culture. For example, "youth" emerged as a political subject for the first time in history, thanks in part to the dramatic expansion of universities and the new centrality of science and technology in Cold War capitalism. The end of World War II also saw a renewal of the struggle against Jim Crow, as emboldened Black veterans and (especially) college students pioneered new forms of militant direct action to claim long-denied civil and political rights that state-managed capitalism, too, had failed to deliver. Likewise, college-educated women rebelled against the isolation of suburban housewifery, on the one hand, and against subservience to men in "the movement," on the other. All of this dovetailed with a new mass culture and a counterculture (TV, rock and roll, protest music), which fashioned a new understanding of what it meant to be a modern person. And this churned up the political universe. A social-democratic political imaginary centered on questions of wages and work could no longer contain these new energies and structures of feeling, many of which became situated later within the emerging new imaginary of "recognition." Eventually, the politics of recognition cross-fertilized with what remained of the New Left critique of bureaucratic paternalism and with rising neoliberal critiques of the nanny state.

Jaeggi: A nice cunning of history.

81

Fraser: Yes. And if we think about it in those terms we can construct an account that brings together the action side with the structural side.

Regimes of production-cum-reproduction

Jaeggi: Let's return to our central question of historicizing capitalism with respect to different spheres. How would you conceive of the changes that we observe within the sphere of social reproduction across these four regimes of accumulation?

Fraser: If we want to track historical shifts in this area, we must ask how social reproduction activities are situated in relation to capitalism's constitutive institutional separations. In which institutional arenas of society are these activities located? Are they situated primarily in households or neighborhoods or extended kinship networks? Are they commodified or organized or regulated by states? And how are the people who engage in social-reproductive activities positioned: as family members, as paid domestics working in private households, as employees of profit-making firms, as community activists or "volunteers" in civil-society associations, as salaried civil servants? For each phase of capitalism, these questions receive different answers, and the boundary between social reproduction and production is differently drawn. And because of that, the social contradiction of capitalist society takes a different form in each phase, as do the struggles surrounding it.

We can see the differences if we look again at our four major historical regimes of accumulation, taking care to distinguish here, as we did before, between developments in the core and in the periphery. Here's the story in a nutshell: in the capitalist core, mercantile capitalism left the business of creating and maintaining social bonds pretty much as it had been before – sited in villages, households, and extended kin networks, regulated locally by custom and church, far removed from national state action and relatively untouched by the law of value. At the same time, however, this regime violently upended precapitalist social bonds in the periphery – looting peasantries, enslaving Africans, dispossessing indigenous peoples, all with callous disregard for niceties of family, community, and kin.

The massive assault on peripheral sociality continued under so-called liberal capitalism, as European states consolidated colonial rule. But things in the metropole changed dramatically. There, "economic production" was split off from "social reproduction," which were now constituted as two distinct "spheres," separated spatially from one another: "the factory" versus "the home." As a result of this split, and of the all-out push to extract as much surplus as possible in commodity production, capitalism's inherent social-reproductive contradiction assumed a particularly acute form, becoming a flashpoint of crisis and stake of struggle. The process took an iconic form in the early manufacturing centers – think of Engels's Manchester, where industrialists dragooned newly urbanized and proletarianized people, including women and children, into grueling, ill-paid, and unsafe work in the factories and mines. Notoriously, this form of capital housed workers in fetid, overcrowded tenements in heavily polluted districts. Altogether, it trashed the social conditions for sustaining families and replenishing labor. And states merely looked on from the sidelines, offering no support, as working-class people suffered, coped, and began to organize. But it was chiefly middle-class reformers who took the lead in addressing this crisis, which they understood to be destroying "the family" and "de-sexing" proletarian women. Victorians advocated "protective legislation," which limited women's and children's exploitation in paid labor, but provided no material aid or compensation for lost wages.[15] Hardly a viable solution to social-reproductive crisis! Nevertheless, this form of capitalism was culturally generative. Detaching social reproduction from broader forms of community life and recasting it as the province of women within the private family, the liberal regime invented a new, bourgeois imaginary, centered on intensified gender difference and the new ideal of "separate spheres." But, of course, it deprived the overwhelming majority of people of the conditions needed to realize that ideal!

All told, the liberal regime incarnated the social contradiction of capitalism in a very sharp form: it posed a head-on conflict between the economic imperatives of production and the social requirements of reproduction. Far from ensuring stability, this arrangement sparked ongoing struggles over social reproduction. These were boundary struggles in the sense I've explained here, but simultaneously inflected as class and gender struggles, all of which eventually converged with struggles over production and political power. The end result was a general crisis, which first paralyzed and then dissolved the liberal regime.

Jaeggi: And the result, I suppose, was state-managed capitalism.

Fraser: Yes, and this regime addressed the production–reproduction contradiction in a different way, by enlisting state power on the

83

side of reproduction. It is widely understood that state-managed capitalism was based on mass production and mass consumption: the Fordist assembly line plus the Model T. But we should add that this regime partially socialized reproduction through state and corporate provision of "social welfare": old-age pensions plus family allowances. This was a major shift, as the state now assumed some responsibility for replenishing labor and sustaining family life in the countries of the core. In effect, it internalized social functions that had been previously left outside the officially managed domains of capitalist society. The "welfare state" was a historic achievement, won in many cases through broad-based democratic struggle spearheaded by organized working-class strata. At the same time, however, public responsibility for reproduction also served to bolster accumulation and shore up capitalism's legitimacy. Meanwhile, the gender imaginary shifted as well. Liberal capitalism's ideal of "separate spheres" now seemed increasingly quaint and soon gave way to the new, more "modern," "democratic" norm of the "family wage." According to that ideal, which had the strong support of labor movements and of most working-class women, the industrial working man should be paid enough to support his whole family, enabling his wife to devote herself full-time to her children and household. Again, only a relatively privileged minority was able to achieve this ideal; but it was aspirational for many more – at least, in the wealthy North Atlantic states of the capitalist core. Needless to say, peripheral populations were excluded from these arrangements, which rested on continuing predation of the Global South. And there were built-in racial asymmetries in the United States and elsewhere, as domestic and agricultural workers were excluded from Social Security and other forms of public provision. By definition, finally, the family wage institutionalized women's dependency and heteronormativity. So state-managed capitalism was no golden age. And yet it succeeded, at least for some and at least for a while, in defusing capitalism's inherent tension between production and reproduction.

Jaeggi: I'd like to hear more about what was happening in the periphery during this phase. Obviously, people there had no entitlement to the benefits that flowed to citizens of national welfare states in the capitalist core. But how was *their* reproduction socially organized? And how was it impacted when colonized countries achieved independence? Did postcolonial states also internalize social reproduction as a public and/or corporate responsibility? And what was the effect on social reproduction of imperialism, both before and after independence?

Fraser: Good question. As we already said, state-managed capitalism was also the era of decolonization. And, of course, independence movements hoped to transform peripheral societies root and branch. In the event, however, postcolonial states devoted far more of their straitened resources to production than to reproduction. Caught in the crosshairs of the Cold War, they focused chiefly on "development," which they equated with import-substitution industrialization to be achieved through large-scale projects. These projects, like the colonial enterprises that preceded them, utilized labor that had been produced "externally," in the countryside, where traditional kinship arrangements persisted. For the vast majority, therefore, social reproduction remained outside the purview of the state action; rural populations were left to fend for themselves. In the cities, by contrast, some regimes undertook to modernize family structures and gender orders, while others claimed to restore traditional pre-colonial orders, which usually meant enforcing gender difference and male domination. There are excellent accounts of this in Paul Ginsborg's fascinating book, *Family Politics*.[16]

Jaeggi: I see. And the state-managed regime unraveled, in any case. What role did social reproduction play in its crisis?

Fraser: Yes, it did unravel. Although the state-managed regime succeeded in pacifying capitalism's crisis tendencies in the core for several decades, it could not definitively master them. From the 1960s onwards, cracks in the edifice began to appear: the "productivity crisis," "the fiscal crisis of the state," and a full-scale crisis of legitimation. We already discussed the emergence of new political subjects, including middle-class women, to whom the family wage appeared outdated and to whom employment beckoned as a route to self-realization. In addition, as Streeck has argued, a new ethos of consumerist individualism cast public provision in an unflattering light – as clunky, standardized, conformist.[17] Under the cover of that "artistic critique," as Boltanski and Chiapello have named it,[18] capital also rebelled – against the corporate and capital gains taxes that had helped to finance the welfare state. In the end, as I just explained, a counterintuitive convergence of forces prevailed: on the one hand, movements descended from the global New Left, which mobilized youth, women, people of color, peripheral subjects,

85

and immigrants, all seeking emancipation – not only from racism, imperialism, and sexism, but also from consumerism, familialism, and bureaucratic paternalism; on the other hand, an ascending "neo-liberal" party of free-marketeers, intent on unshackling market forces from government "red tape," liberating entrepreneurial creativity, and globalizing the capitalist economy. When those two unlikely bedfellows joined forces under the banner of emancipation, the result was to shatter the social-democratic alliance of marketization and social protection. What emerged in its place was what I've called "progressive neoliberalism," a new alliance in which the proponents of marketization recuperated the dominant currents of movements for emancipation to double-team and eventually outgun the adherents of social protection.[19]

Jaeggi: And the result was financialized capitalism . . . How did the gender order change under that regime, and to what kind of crisis was it meant to be a solution?

Fraser: The gender order of financialized capitalism was built on the ruins of the family wage in the historic core. That arrangement succumbed to a double whammy: first, a steep drop in real wages, rooted in the shift from unionized manufacturing work to McJobs, which has made it virtually impossible for all but a privileged few to support a family on a single salary; and, second, the charisma of feminism, which delegitimized women's dependency upon a male breadwinner. What emerged in its place was another, more modern ideal: the "two-earner family." Sounds lovely, doesn't it? Like the family wage ideal, however, this one, too, is a mystification. What it obfuscates is the steep rise in the number of hours of paid work now required to support a household. This is, by definition, problematic for families with only one potential wage earner. But it is unworkable for most others as well. Given the contemporaneous retrenchment of public provision, virtually no working- and middle-class households whose members include children, elderly, sick, or disabled people can survive on the pay from one job. Nearly all are obliged to shift time and energies once devoted to reproduction to "productive" (i.e., paid) work. Between increased working hours and public service cutbacks, the financialized capitalist regime is squeezing social reproduction to the breaking point.

We see the effects of the squeeze in a whole set of convoluted strategies aimed at shifting carework onto others. There are, for example, the widely discussed "global care chains," through which struggling workers in the core countries offload reproductive work onto migrants from poor regions (often racialized women), who leave their own families in the care of other still poorer women, who must in turn do the same, and on and on.[20] Far from solving "the crisis of care," this arrangement merely displaces it, from the Global North to the Global South (including the ex-Communist countries). And it introduces a dualized organization of carework, commodified for those who can pay for it and privatized for those who cannot, with some in the second category performing reproductive labor for those in the first in return for (low) wages. Other coping mechanisms widely used by time-poor women in the US include egg-freezing (offered as a fringe benefit by the Army and by corporations in the IT sector), and mechanical pumps for expressing breast milk (furnished gratis by some employment-based health plans and by the Affordable Care Act).[21] These are the "fixes" of choice in a country with a high rate of female labor force participation, no mandated paid maternity or parental leave, and a love affair with technology. In the absence of a sustainable institutionalization of the production/reproduction division, they simply shoehorn social reproduction responsibilities into the interstices and crevices of lives that capital insists must be dedicated first and foremost to accumulation.

"Haven in a heartless world"

Jaeggi: OK. You've now sketched four orders of social reproduction-cum-economic production in the history of capitalism: the extended kinship order under mercantile capitalism, the "separate spheres" order under liberal competitive capitalism, the "family wage" order under state-managed capitalism, and now the "two-earner family" under neoliberal or financialized capitalism. This is clarifying. But before we move on, I want to get a little clearer about the role of the one-wage household – or, rather, of the middle-class ideal that a decent family is one in which the woman stayed home. It seems to me that this ideal underlies both liberal and state-managed capitalism, even if it takes different forms in each. And I suspect it still has some resonance now, under neoliberalism, despite the proliferation of two-earner families. If so, what should we make of the persistence of this male-breadwinner/female-homemaker ideal over the *longue durée* of capitalism's history? What role does the view of the family as a "haven in a heartless world" play within capitalism? And what is the relation between middle-class family ideology and the actual reality of working-class life? Do you think this family ideology has played a functional role within the development of capitalism? Has it served to stabilize and legitimate capitalist society? Or has it provided a point of critique?

Fraser: Well, I'm not sure that the male-breadwinner/female-homemaker ideal has proved as durable as you suggest. Of course, there *do* exist some continuities that subtend capitalism's varied history. There is the trend, over the *longue durée*, to reduce household size, to nuclearize the family, to construct it as a unit specializing in social reproduction, to emphasize gender difference, and to cast reproduction as women's work. All of that flows from capitalism's institutional separation of production from reproduction. Insofar as it constitutes reproduction as a female-centered hidden abode that enables accumulation by replenishing labor, capitalism creates "the family" as the complementary counterpart to "the market."

But the parameters set by that general framework are relatively broad, and they allow for some striking differences. In the core regions, capitalist development went hand in hand with the process that Maria Mies called "housewifization."[22] Originally a bourgeois invention, which served as a strategy of class distinction, the "separate spheres" ideal soon permeated the middle classes, while also exerting a pull on working-class people in the capitalist core. But the latter group did not simply swallow it whole. On the contrary, the laboring classes used it for their own purposes, as an argument for higher wages and as a strategy for political incorporation and democratization. They creatively transformed the Victorian bourgeois norm of "separate spheres" into the social-democratic ideal of "the family wage." But even that adaptation was not universal. In the US, African-Americans elaborated alternative gender imaginaries, which validated Black women's practice of combining waged work with unpaid domestic and community activities. Equally important, as Mies insisted, and as I noted earlier, developments in the periphery diverged sharply from those in the core. Far from creating housewives in the Global South, capitalism's advent turned some women into enslaved breeders and beasts of burden and others into rural farmers living separately from husbands employed in urban wage work, while leaving still others in communities based on extended kinship. Moreover, "housewifization" has come to a halt today, even for the middle and working classes of the core, thanks to the combined force of the feminist critique of women's dependency and of the neoliberal transformation of labor markets. Whatever support for it persists now is either a counter-historical expression of nostalgia or a residue of guilt on the part of women who lack the necessary time, energy, and resources to perform reproductive activities for which they still feel responsible.

Jaeggi: But I was asking whether "housewifization" as a reality and as an ideal has been functional for capitalism, and if so, whether it still is now.

Fraser: Right. Got it. My answer is yes and no. On the "yes" side, housewifization in its family-wage form emerged as a response to capitalism's built-in tendency to social-reproductive crisis. Unlike its bourgeois predecessor, the working-class variant of that ideal was the spearhead of a serious effort to mitigate or overcome the cruel and destabilizing effects of the structural imperative to endless accumulation, which otherwise simply chewed people up and spat them out. And in that sense, by sustaining families and replenishing labor, it permitted accumulation to continue – and indeed, to expand. On the "no" side, however, both middle- and working-class variants elaborated "extra-economic" values that harbored a "normative surplus" and could serve, under favorable circumstances, as a force for critique. But that "no" needs to be carefully qualified. Critique based on social-reproductive norms of solidarity and care is a double-edged sword: potentially transformative, yet easily recuperated into essentialist gender stereotypes. At its best, the ideal of a protected domestic sphere was an assertion of non-market values, a push-back against capital's demand for maximum profits. Yet it was also defined in terms of what it was opposing, as the flip side of "free" market rationality and as the rationale for women's dependency. In the end, its critical force was more often system-conforming than system-transforming.

Jaeggi: Yes, it's the flip side, but couldn't it also be seen as potentially creating some contradictory attitudes and emotional needs? And might not that be happening today?

Fraser: Reproductive norms are definitely contradictory, as are the experiences to which they are tied. Both the norms and the experiences are expressions of capitalism's deep-seated tendency to reproductive crisis. So it is not surprising that they incarnate all the tensions and ambivalences of the production/reproduction contradiction. The question is, under what conditions is it likely that their critical-transformative side will come to the fore? As for today,

89

I'd say that the prospects are mixed. On the plus side, it might be possible now, as it was not before, when feminist ideas were not so widely espoused, to detach the values of solidarity and care from the gendered ideal of the domestic sphere and the stay-at-home mother. In principle, a new type of feminist anti-capitalism could allow us to vindicate those values while rejecting the institutionalized forms that have hitherto embodied them, forms in which they were entangled with male domination. Such a perspective could inspire us to imagine alternative ways of institutionalizing those values, by reinventing the production/reproduction nexus. But that possibility is by no means guaranteed. It is also possible that today's acute strains on social reproduction will bring out the worst in people. Many may respond by hunkering down and building walls, both emotional and physical. The circle of solidarity may contract, and the lines separating "us" from "them" may harden. That, at least, is the impulse behind current forms of reactionary populism, which so far represent the main alternative to progressive neoliberalism. Clearly, that is not the alternative we want or need. The analysis I'm developing here points in a different direction, to the project of progressive populism, at least transitionally, as a way station en route to democratic socialism.

Jaeggi: That's an interesting diagnosis of the present political fault-lines in financialized capitalism. But I think we should defer discussion of this to chapter 4, when we discuss "Contesting Capitalism."

Capitalism's historical natures

Jaeggi: Now, by contrast, we should turn to "nature." I see some interesting parallels between that third "hidden abode" and the one we've just been considering. Discussing social reproduction from a feminist perspective makes us highly aware of its historical and socially malleable nature. Marxists and Marx himself have been blind to the systematic role of reproductive labor, and their own sexism made them embrace far too narrow an idea of class struggle culminating around one major contradiction. However, we might also say that in certain ways a Marxist or historical-materialist methodology already starts out from anti-essentialist concerns very similar to the feminist ones. Human beings, if we think of *The German Ideology* for instance, are those animals that produce the conditions of their own life.[23] Everything about who we are, what skills we have, is materialized past labor. And the same holds for the environments we inhabit: they are materialized labor too – they have a history. Thus, we might say that a Marxist methodology comes close to denaturalizing even nature – except that Marx throughout his work seems never to call into question the function of nature as a free bounty. Benjamin has this great line to the effect that the idea of nature "existing gratis" serves as "a complement to the corrupted conception of labor."[24] We have discussed in chapter 1 how you counter this taking-for-granted of nature by describing it as a necessary background condition of capitalism, but would you also historicize this relation? Or is this something that remains constant?

Fraser: Without question, we must "denaturalize nature." And you are right: Marxism's historicizing orientation is helpful here, even if it was not used systematically to that end until recently, with the emergence of a new generation of ecological Marxists. But I want to defend Marx against the charge that he took nature for granted as an infinitely available resource that could be drawn upon freely, without any regard for replenishment. Thanks to the research of John Bellamy Foster, we now know that Marx did not really hold the view that human labor is the sole source of wealth. On the contrary, he distinguished "wealth," understood as the general form of bounty created jointly by nature and labor, from "value," a term he reserved for the limited, historically distorted form that wealth assumes within capitalism. It was not Marx, in other words, but capitalist society that institutionalized "the labor theory *of value*" (not of wealth!) and thereby occluded nature's contribution. We also know, thanks again to Bellamy Foster, that Marx had a critical grasp of capitalism's penchant for ecological predation. In his time, that penchant was manifest in the disruption of the soil-nutrient cycle, as theorized by the German chemist Justus Liebig. Marx followed Liebig's work closely and related the scientist's account of the chemistry of soil depletion to his own sociohistorical analysis of industrial capitalism. This system introduced unsustainable, profit-driven farming to feed the proletarian masses in the cities, but failed to return the plundered nutrients to the soil, instead discharging organic waste into urban waterways. So it exhausted farmlands and polluted cities in a single stroke.[25] Marx explicitly noted these consequences of the "metabolic rift" between town and country in the nineteenth century. Far from being ecologically oblivious, he was grappling with capitalism's environmental contradiction *avant la lettre*.

Jaeggi: Fair enough. I'm willing to grant Marx the benefit of the doubt on both of those points. Nevertheless, as you pointed out, he did not develop a systematic critique of capitalism's "ecological contradiction" in the sense that you elaborated in chapter 1. So, tell me now, from your own perspective, how would you historicize that contradiction? And does your approach require that we historicize nature itself?

Fraser: Yes, it absolutely requires historicizing nature. Remember how you worried before that I was assuming a romantic view of pristine, unsullied nature, which capitalism despoiled? And remember how I replied, by giving a historical interpretation of capitalism's ecological contradiction? I said that capital free-rides on the *historically specific form of* nature that supplies its background conditions of possibility *in a given era and a given region*; and that in failing to replenish that specific form of nature, it destabilizes it, potentially jeopardizing its own conditions of possibility as they exist at that point in time and space. My point was that capitalism's ecological contradiction is always expressed historically: as a specific set of tensions between a given economic regime and the forms of historical nature associated with it. So I agree with thinkers, such as Jason W. Moore, who insist that we should speak not of Nature with a capital "N," but rather of "historical natures" in the plural, and with lower case "n."

Jaeggi: I suppose the idea is that each form of "historical nature" is already marked by previous human activity, which has given it a certain historical shape. But what follows from that? If "Nature" as such does not exist, then is everything reduced in the end to "society" or "human history?"

Fraser: No, not exactly. The ontology I want to defend is more complex. It eschews the metaphysical dualism, implicit in your question, which casts "Nature" (viewed as inert, objective, ahistorical) as the antithesis of "Humanity" (viewed as dynamic, "geistig," historical). That dichotomy is an artifact of capitalism, which developed in a relation of elective affinity with the seventeenth-century scientific revolution. Hardening distinctions inherited from Greek philosophy and Christianity, the mechanical view of nature replaced earlier suppositions of socio-natural proximity with a deep ontological chasm. In effect, it expelled "Nature" from the universe of "Human Subjectivity and Sociality," which it simultaneously constructed as Nature's stark antithesis. The resulting worldview *externalized* nature and was

92

sometimes seen as licensing its "rape."[26] But the problem is not only that the nature/society dichotomy has facilitated brutal extractivism. It is also conceptually misleading, in two respects: not only are human beings part of nature, but non-human nature is historical – thoroughly inter-imbricated with the social life-processes of human and non-human animals.

Jaeggi: But in saying that, don't you risk collapsing the distinction between human beings and nature? And if so, don't you end up with another, equally dubious metaphysics? And one that is just as politically problematic as the one you oppose? If the latter licenses extractivism, yours could legitimate what Heidegger called *Gelassenheit,* the attitude of standing by passively as disease ravages human populations.

Fraser: No, that's not my view. To reject the Nature/Humanity dichotomy is not to collapse the distinction between human and non-human animals. Nor is it to merge human societies into the ecosystems of which they're a part. The point is rather to relativize and historicize such distinctions. Both human society and non-human nature are historical. And the two terms are internally related. Each of them constrains, adapts to, shapes, and destabilizes the other over time. I like the phrase "socioecological relations," because it suggests the depth of the nature/society entanglement, while still enabling us to distinguish between them contextually.

Let me illustrate the point by referring to the work of William Cronon, who brilliantly deconstructs the ontological chasm that purportedly separates "external nature" from "human history." In *Nature's Metropolis*, Cronon shows how the small, early nineteenth-century, mixed Euro-Amerindian settlement of Chicago was transformed in a few short decades into the single most important US entrepôt for trade in lumber, grain, and livestock; how the city reconstructed the entire landscape to the West as *its* hinterland as it went about supplying the East; how the pull of its markets transformed biodiverse prairies into monocultural farm and grazing lands; how their produce became standardized and subject to abstraction in the buying and selling of futures; how fortunes were made and lost; how town/country relations, political power, class relations, and regional ecosystems were transformed together in an integrated symbiosis.[27] In Cronon's account, "nature" and "society" are inextricably entangled with one another. Yet neither is reduced to the other. What we get, rather, is a precise, dialectical, and thoroughly historical account of

93

the socioecology of US capitalism in the nineteenth century. To my mind, this is the right ontological starting point for an eco-critical theory of capitalist society.

Jaeggi: How would you apply that ontology to your view of capitalism's inherent tendency to ecological crisis? How, in other words, would you historicize the society/nature division of capitalist society?

Fraser: My thinking on this matter owes a great deal to James O'Connor, who pioneered the quasi-Polanyian approach I've elaborated here. Famously, O'Connor theorized the "second contradiction of capitalism," by which he meant capital's tendency to undermine its own "natural conditions of production" – especially by depleting resources and spewing waste in ways that threaten the profitability of ongoing production.[28] My approach builds on that idea, but, unlike O'Connor, I don't focus exclusively on harms to capital. Nor do I assume a fixed sum of "natural resources" that are progressively depleted. In that last respect my thinking has some affinities with the more recent eco-crisis theory of Jason W. Moore. Moore locates the nub of the contradiction in the fact that capital's demand for "cheap natures" rises faster than it can secure them.[29] By "cheap natures" he means "raw materials" for whose reproduction capital does not pay. That idea parallels what I have been saying about capital's free-riding on social reproduction and racialized expropriation. And it holds as well – indeed in spades – for "nature": capital virtually never pays the full ecological reproduction costs its activities generate. But Moore has something more specific in mind. He is focused above all on historical natures that have not yet been "capitalized" and can be "appropriated" gratis or well below cost. To the extent that it can commandeer such "new" natures and funnel them into production, capital profits from an "ecological surplus" over and above the surplus it extracts from exploited wage labor. The resulting bonanza provides a strong incentive to locate, map, and appropriate new natures on the far side of the given historical "frontier" that separates already capitalized natures from the still uncharted territories that could become subject to appropriation. But here's the catch. Once some chunk of "cheap nature" has been appropriated, it enters the capitalized zone, becomes a commodity, is subject to the law of value, and before long is no longer cheap.[30] This is like the fate of technological innovations in capitalist production: after generating windfall profits initially, they become generalized throughout a given industry, part of the normal cost of doing business, causing profit rates to resume their decline – until the outbreak of crisis opens the way to a new regime of accumulation and a new burst of innovation.

Moore adapts that familiar Marxian scenario to theorize the historicity of capitalism's ecological contradiction. He too understands capitalism's history as a sequence of historically specific regimes of accumulation, each of which resolves a crisis of the previous regime, before succumbing to one of its own. But, coming as he does from the Binghamton School, he follows Immanuel Wallerstein and Giovanni Arrighi in dividing each regime into an expansive, ascending "A" phase and a stagnating, declining "B" phase. In the "A" phase, new cheap natures are located and appropriated, thereby expanding the ecological surplus; as capital draws on that surplus, its productivity increases and its profits rise. In the "B" phase, however, the appropriated natures are capitalized, brought within the official, monetized sphere of the capitalist economy, and effectively normalized. The ecological surplus dwindles and is eventually exhausted – a process that might, but need not, coincide with the physical depletion of the no-longer-cheap natures on which the regime was based. What follows, in either case, is a crisis of the regime. And that sets the stage for the emergence of a new regime, based on new cheap natures.

Jaeggi: This still sounds economistic. In your account of it, everything appears to depend on questions of profitability for capital. So it's a functionalist or "systems-theoretical" view of crisis, to use your term. I don't see any reference to hegemonic crisis or social struggle. Where is the action-theoretical dimension?

Fraser: Yes, you've hit on a major weakness of Moore's theory – and one that my own framework is designed to avoid. Let me explain my strategy by contrasting his notion of a *frontier* separating uncapitalized from capitalized nature with my view of the nature/society *boundary*. Both conceptions posit an institutionalized division that is constitutive of capitalist society, a division that harbors a crisis tendency and is subject to historical shifts. But that's where the similarity ends. Moore's idea pertains exclusively to the system level, as you just said. Exactly where the frontier lies and when it moves is dictated by the law of value, not by social action. Nor is it understood as a moral and cultural question. For me, in contrast, capitalism's ecological boundaries are not only nodes of system crisis but also constellations of meaning and value, which are experienced and disputed as such in interaction. How and where "nature" is separated from, or incorporated into, "the economy" has as much to do with conflicts

95

over commonsense as with the rate of profit. Like capitalism's other boundaries, the one separating those domains is a stake of *social struggle*. It is contested by a wide array of actors, who mobilize variously to preserve, abolish, or relocate it. Of course, I would never deny that path-dependent logics of accumulation set the parameters within which firms devise their strategies for investing in, developing, acquiring, and using sources of energy and raw materials. But they must also contend with those who act from entirely different motives, such as defending community habitats or halting global warming. These latter actors run the gamut from social movements opposing drilling, mining, agribusiness, and industrial fishing, to civil society associations such as the scientists who formed the IPCC, to governments that set energy and environmental policies in response to cross-pressures from corporate lobbyists and public opinion, and finally to international agencies that purport to regulate carbon emissions and biotechnology through trading schemes and patent laws that generate new forms of property and rent. When such actors face off with capital, they turn the nature/society boundary into a major site and stake of struggle in capitalist societies. That boundary becomes especially fraught in times of crisis, when system impasses appear intractable and established hegemonies are coming undone. In such times, when the basic contours of social existence are up for grabs, environmental struggles may converge with political and reproductive struggles, all inflected by class, race, and gender, to redraw the nature/society boundary. If we hope to clarify such situations, critical theorists must conceive that boundary as operating simultaneously on two levels, not only the level of system, as conceived by Moore, but also the level of social action.

Socioecological regimes of accumulation

Jaeggi: That's helpful in clarifying the conceptual issues. But I still want to hear your account of the historical sequence of eco-social regimes and of the systemic and social crises that form the transitional moments between them. Could you say something about how all that looks for each of our four phases – for mercantile, liberal, state-managed, and financialized capitalism?

Fraser: Sure. Let's begin, once again, with mercantile capitalism – and with the question of energy. In this era, agriculture and manufacturing still ran almost entirely on animal muscle, both human and otherwise

96

(oxen, horses, etc.). So this was what J. R. McNeill calls a "somatic" regime: conversion of chemical into mechanical energy occurred *inside the bodies* of living beings as they digested food, which originated from biomass.[31] And that meant that, as in earlier epochs, the only way to augment available energy was through conquest. Only by annexing land and commandeering additional supplies of labor could mercantile-capitalist powers increase their forces of production. And, as we already saw, they made ample use of those time-tested methods, but on a vastly expanded scale that encompassed the "New World" as well as the "old." From the silver mines of Potosí to the slave plantations of Saint-Domingue, mercantile-capitalist powers worked land and labor to the point of exhaustion, making no effort to replenish what they expended.[32] In England, meanwhile, capital scaled up by other means: forcible land enclosures facilitated conversion of farmland to sheep pasture, enabling expanded manufacture of textiles even in the absence of mechanization. It was during the mercantilist era, too, as I mentioned earlier, that the scientific revolution incubated a new, mechanical view of nature as radically other than human society and external to it. We could say, with the benefit of hindsight, that in this era capital was amassing epistemic and biotic forces whose larger productive potential would only become apparent later, with the advent of a new socioecological regime of accumulation.

That regime began to take shape in early nineteenth-century England, which pioneered the world-historic shift to fossil energy. Watt's invention of the coal-fired steam engine opened the way to the world's first "exosomatic" regime: the first to take carbonized solar energy from beneath the crust of the earth and convert it to mechanical energy *outside of living bodies*. Tied only indirectly to biomass, this regime appeared to liberate the forces of production from the constraints of land and labor. At the same time, it called into being a new historical nature. Coal, previously of interest only locally, as a substance to burn for heat, now became an internationally traded commodity. Extracted from confiscated lands and transported in bulk across long distances, energy deposits formed over hundreds of millions of years were consumed in the blink of an eye in order to power mechanized industry – without regard for replenishment or pollution. Equally important, fossilized energy provided capitalists with a means to reshape the relations of production to their advantage. In the 1820s and 1830s, British textile manufacturers, reeling from strikes in the mills, shifted the bulk of their operations from place-bound hydropower to mobile steam – which also meant from country to city. In that way, they were able to tap concentrated supplies of proletarianized labor – workers with less access to means of subsistence and more tolerance for factory discipline than their rural counterparts.[33] Apparently, the cost of coal (which, unlike water, had to be bought) was outweighed by gains from intensified exploitation.

Fossil-fueled production in the capitalist core expanded throughout the liberal capitalist era. But the appearance of liberation from land and animal muscle was an illusion. Exosomatic industrialization in Europe and North America rested on a hidden abode of somatic-based extractivism in the periphery. What made Manchester's factories hum was the massive import of "cheap natures" wrested from colonized lands by masses of unfree and dependent labor: cheap cotton to feed the mills; cheap sugar, tobacco, coffee, and tea to stimulate the "hands" who operated them. Thus, the apparent saving of labor and land was actually a form of "environmental load displacement" – a shift in the demands placed on biomass from core to periphery.[34] Colonial powers ramped up the process through calculated efforts to wipe out manufacturing in their colonies. Deliberately destroying textile production in Egypt and India, Britain reduced those lands to suppliers of cotton for its mills and captive markets for their products. Theorists and historians of eco-imperialism are only now reckoning the full extent of this cost shifting,[35] while also revealing the close connection of anti-colonialism with proto-environmentalism. Rural struggles against colonial predation were also "environmentalisms of the poor," struggles for "environmental justice" *avant la lettre*.[36] They were struggles, too, over the meaning and value of nature, as European imperialists raised on distanced "scientific" conceptions sought to subjugate communities that did not distinguish sharply between nature and culture. In fact, "liberal" capitalism periodically redrew that boundary, as it first conjured and then appropriated a slew of new historical natures. In effect, the "Nature" that the mercantilist regime had externalized epistemologically, as Humanity's Other, was now internalized practically – commodified and brought "inside" the capitalist economy.

Glimmers of another kind of internalization appeared in the following era of state-managed capitalism. In this case, the idea was to bring nature "inside" the domain of the political, where it would become an object of state regulation. The leader here was none other than today's premier environmental laggard and climate-change denier: the United States. Having replaced Britain as global hegemon, the US pioneered Fordism, creating a new exosomatic-energic-industrial complex around the internal combustion engine, which was powered by refined oil. The result was the age of the automobile: icon of

98

consumerist freedom, catalyst of highway construction, enabler of suburbanization, spewer of carbon emissions, and reshaper of geopolitics. Thus, coal-fired "carbon democracy"[37] gave way to a distinctive oil-fueled variant in the United States.

At the same time, the US also begat a powerful environmental movement, centered originally on wilderness protection (the environmentalism of the rich) and later on issues of pollution and toxic dumping (the environmentalism of state regulation of capitalist industry). A parallel of sorts to New Deal agencies that supported social reproduction, the Environmental Protection Agency (EPA), founded in 1970, at the tail end of the regime, was its last major effort to defuse systemic crisis by turning "externalities" into objects of state regulation. The jewel in the EPA's crown was the Superfund, tasked with cleaning up toxic waste sites on capital's dime. Financed chiefly by taxes on the petroleum and chemical industries, the Fund realized the principle of "polluter pays" through the coercive agency of the capitalist state, not through market schemes like present-day carbon trading. And yet, however progressive in that respect, state-managed capitalist regulation of nature (like that of social reproduction) was built on some not-so-nice hidden abodes: environmental racism in the core (the unloading of eco-"externalities" disproportionately onto poor communities of color), and ongoing somatic extractivism and environmental load displacement in the periphery. Also integral to this regime were a raft of US-sponsored *coups d'état* in Latin America and the Persian Gulf, which secured the profits and position of Big Fruit and Big Oil. Clearly, oil-fueled social democracy at home rested on top of militarily imposed oligarchy abroad.[38] And, last but not least, the state-managed regime was all the while cranking out carbon emissions, which it increased exponentially.

All of those "bads" continue on steroids today, in the era of financialized capitalism – but on an altered basis. Relocation of manufacturing to the Global South has scrambled the previous energic geography. Somatic and exosomatic formations now coexist side-by-side throughout Asia, Latin America, and some areas of southern Africa. The Global North, meanwhile, increasingly specializes in the "post-material" triad of IT, services, and finance – in effect, Google, Amazon, and Goldman Sachs. But, once again, the appearance of liberation from nature is misleading. Northern "post-materialism" rests upon southern materialism (mining, agriculture, industry), and its consumption is energy-intensive, still powered by coal and oil, now supplemented by fracking and natural gas, while the addition of renewables here and there does little to reduce the overall carbon footprint. The general effect is to saddle the South with a still more disproportionate share of the global environmental load: extreme pollution in cities, hyper-extractivism in the countryside, and vulnerability to increasingly lethal impacts of global warming, such as rising seas and extreme weather, which create climate-induced migrations and environmental refugees on a growing scale.

These asymmetries are compounded by new, financialized modes of regulation, premised on new, neoliberal imaginaries of nature. With the delegitimation of public power comes the new/old idea that the market itself can serve as the principal mechanism of effective governance, now tasked with saving the planet by curtailing carbon emissions. *Ecce* carbon trading. In reality, however, such schemes only draw capital away from the sort of massive coordinated investment needed to de-fossilize the global economy and transform its energic basis. Money flows instead into speculative trade in "emissions permits," "ecosystem services," "carbon offsets," and "environmental derivatives."[39] What enables such "regulation," and is also fostered by it, is a new ontology of nature. Financialized capitalism economizes nature, even when it does not directly commodify it. The idea that a coal-belching factory here can be "offset" by a tree plantation there assumes a "nature" composed of fungible, commensurable units, whose place-specificity, qualitative traits, and experienced meanings are of little import and can be disregarded.[40] The same is true for the hypothetical auction scenarios, beloved of environmental economists, that purport to assign value to a "natural asset" according to how much various actors would pay to realize their competing "preferences" regarding it: are indigenous communities sufficiently "invested" in preserving their local fishing stocks to outbid the multinational corporate fleets that threaten to deplete them? If not, the rational use of the "asset" is to allow its commercial exploitation.[41] These "green-capitalist" scenarios represent yet another way of internalizing nature. Produced by epistemic abstraction, financialized nature is at the same time an instrument of expropriation.

Under these conditions, the grammar of environmental struggle is also shifting. The state-oriented currents of the previous era have lost much, though not all, of their punch, thanks to the market's charisma and the vogue for transnational governance. At the same time, the older, wilderness protection current has split, with one portion gravitating to "green capitalism" and the other to "environmental justice." Then, too, southern "environmentalisms of the poor" are themselves transnationalizing – linking up not only with one another but also with northern currents that target "environmental racism." Some of these activists set themselves in opposition to corporate and finance capital, and to the states that do its bidding, while others square off against "labor" – which is to say, against those working-class strata whose livelihoods depend on "development." But in every case, present-day struggles over "nature" proceed simultaneously in two dimensions: both as contests over the meaning of "nature" and as conflicts over the material bases of life.

Regimes of racialized accumulation

Jaeggi: Well, that's a very interesting sketch of the sequence of socio-ecological regimes in capitalism's history. But let's return, finally, to the hidden abode of expropriation. You argued in the previous chapter that capitalism's front-story of exploitation depended on a disavowed back-story of expropriation; and you also said that that structural division between those two "exes" underlay capitalism's persistent entanglement with imperialism and racial oppression throughout its history. I got the impression, too, that you think that entanglement has taken different forms in different periods. So don't you now want to historicize the relation between exploitation and expropriation? And if so, how exactly would you do that? How would you describe the distinctive forms those relations take in our four regimes of accumulation?

Fraser: I do indeed want to historicize this. In some of capitalism's phases, the two "exes" were clearly separated from one another, both geographically and demographically, with exploitation centered in the European core and reserved for the (White male) "labor aristocracy," while expropriation was sited chiefly in the periphery and imposed on people of color. More recently, however, those separations have blurred: some dependent subjects have appeared to advance from expropriation to exploitation, and yet their expropriation hasn't fully disappeared; meanwhile, free persons who formerly enjoyed the status of being "only" exploited have found themselves increasingly subject to expropriation. That's how I would describe the situation we face today.

To understand these variations, I propose to re-describe capitalism's history as a sequence of *regimes of racialized accumulation*. This means highlighting the historically specific relations between expropriation and exploitation within each of our four phases. For

101

"a sequence of regimes of racialized accumulation"

each regime, we need to specify the geography and demography of the two "exes." To what extent are they separated from one another, sited in different regions and assigned to distinct populations? How exactly are they inter-imbricated, and what is the relative weight of each in the overall configuration? What forms of political subjectivation characterize a given phase? And how does status hierarchy interact with other features to generate regime-specific dynamics of racialization?

Jaeggi: Okay, so let's run through the sequence of regimes one more time, beginning with mercantile capitalism.

Fraser: Mercantile capitalism was the phase that Marx had in mind when he coined the phrase "primitive accumulation." What he was registering, it seems to me, was the fact that the principal driver of accumulation in this phase of capitalism was not exploitation, but expropriation. Confiscation was the name of the game, manifested both in the land enclosures in the core and in the conquest, plunder, and "commercial hunting of black skins" throughout the periphery.[42] All of that long preceded the rise of modern industry. Prior to large-scale exploitation of factory workers came massive expropriation of bodies, labor, land, and mineral wealth, in Europe and Asia, but especially in Africa and the "New World." Expropriation literally dwarfed exploitation in commercial capitalism – and that had major implications for status hierarchy. On the one hand, this regime generated precursors of the racializing subjectivations that became so consequential in later phases: "Europeans" versus "natives," free individuals versus chattel slaves, "Whites" versus "Blacks." On the other hand, these distinctions were far less sharp in an era when virtually *all* non-propertied people had the status of subjects, not that of rights-bearing citizens. In this context, virtually *all* lacked political protection from expropriation, and the majority condition was not freedom, but dependency. As a result, that status did not carry the special stigma it acquired in subsequent phases of capitalism, when majority-ethnicity male workers in the core won liberal rights through political struggle. It was only later, with the (partial) democratization of metropolitan states and the rise of large-scale factory-based exploitation of *free* wage labor, that the contrast between "free and subject races" sharpened, giving rise to the characteristic racial orders of modern capitalism.

The shift from mercantile capitalism to liberal capitalism in the nineteenth century brought a new configuration: the two "exes" became more balanced and interconnected. As we saw, the confiscation of land and labor continued apace, as European states consolidated colonial rule, while the US perpetuated its "internal colony," first, through the extension of racialized slavery and then, after abolition, by transforming freedmen into debt peons through the sharecropping system. Now, however, ongoing expropriation in the periphery entwined with highly profitable exploitation in the core. What was new was the rise of large-scale factory-based manufacturing, which forged the proletariat imagined by Marx, upending traditional forms of life, and sparking class conflict. Eventually, struggles to democratize metropolitan states delivered a system-conforming version of citizenship to exploited (male) workers. At the same time, however, brutal repression of anti-colonial struggles ensured continuing subjection in the periphery. Thus, the contrast between dependency and freedom was sharpened and increasingly racialized. In the US, for example, the status of the citizen-worker acquired much of the aura of freedom that legitimates exploitation by contrast to the dependent, degraded condition of chattel slaves and indigenous peoples, whose persons and lands could be repeatedly confiscated with impunity.[43] In effect, those two statuses, the *free exploitable citizen-worker*, on the one hand, and the *dependent expropriable subject*, on the other, were mutually constituted; they co-defined one another.

Racialization was further strengthened by the apparent *separation* of exploitation from expropriation in liberal capitalism. In this regime, the two "exes" appeared to be sited in different regions and assigned to different populations – one colonized, the other "free." In fact, however, the division was never so cut and dried, as some extractive industries employed colonial subjects in wage labor, and only a minority of exploited workers in the capitalist core succeeded in escaping ongoing expropriation altogether. Despite their appearance as separate, moreover, the two mechanisms of accumulation were systemically imbricated, forming an *exploitation–expropriation nexus*. In this nexus, as we have already seen, it was the expropriation of populations in the periphery (including in the periphery within the core) that supplied the cheap food, textiles, mineral ore, and energy, without which the exploitation of metropolitan industrial workers would not have been profitable. In the liberal era, therefore, the two "exes" were distinct but mutually calibrated engines of accumulation within a single world capitalist system.

This brings us then to state-managed capitalism. In this phase, the separation between the two "exes" began to soften, although it was not abolished. And its softening brought something new. It now appeared that expropriation no longer precluded exploitation but could combine directly with it. I am thinking of the development of segmented labor markets in the capitalist core; in those contexts, capital exacted a confiscatory premium from racialized wage workers, paying them less than "Whites" – and less than the socially necessary costs of their reproduction. In this case, expropriation articulated directly with exploitation, entering into the internal constitution of wage labor. This was the case in the United States in the twentieth century, when African-Americans displaced by agricultural mechanization flocked to northern cities, where many joined the industrial proletariat, but chiefly as second-class workers, paid less than "Whites" and consigned to the dirtiest, most menial jobs. In this era, their exploitation was overlaid by expropriation, as capital failed to pay the full costs of their reproduction. And that condition was undergirded by their continuing political subjection under Jim Crow. Throughout the era of state-managed capitalism, African-Americans were deprived of political protection, as segregation, disfranchisement, and countless other institutionalized humiliations continued to deny them full citizenship. Even when employed in factories, they were still not fully free rights-bearing individuals. They were expropriated and exploited simultaneously.

Jaeggi: I would grant that African-Americans were relegated to a lower status, but I was wondering if you could clarify precisely why this should still be classified as expropriation as opposed to, say, a more extreme version of exploitation? Is it a result of the segregation regime and the fact that they were systematically denied civil and political rights? Or does it have to do with enduring, path-dependent consequences stemming from the history of slavery? I am not objecting to the thesis, but we should be aware that one danger with the concept of dispossession or expropriation is that it can become too broad. Harvey, for example, tends to overextend the concept to the point that it's not entirely clear how all of the things he describes as "dispossession" go together or what characteristic they share. To put the question another way, how precisely do you determine the point at which exploitation becomes expropriation?

Fraser: For me, the two "exes" are distinguished in two respects – one "economic," the other "political." The first, "economic" point is that in exploitation, capital assumes the costs of replenishing the labor it employs in production, whereas in expropriation it does not. The second, "political" difference is that exploited workers are free individuals and rights-bearing citizens with access to state protection, whereas expropriated subjects are dependent beings, who cannot call on public power to shield them from predation and violence. What distinguishes the situation of African-Americans is that it straddles the line on both of those counts. First, racialized labor in state-managed capitalism was paid a wage, but one that was less than the average socially necessary cost of its reproduction. And, second, African-Americans in that regime had the formal status of free persons and US citizens, but they could not call on public powers to vindicate their rights; on the contrary, those who were supposed to protect them from violence were often perpetrators of it. On both points, therefore, the situation of the US Black working class combined elements of expropriation with elements of exploitation. It is better understood in this way, as an amalgam or hybrid of the two "exes," than via the more familiar concept of "super-exploitation."[44] Although that term is undeniably evocative, it focuses exclusively on the economics of the racial wage gap, while ignoring the status differential. My approach, in contrast, aims to disclose the entwinement of *economic predation* with *political subjection*. And in so doing, it tries to grasp both the structural features of a given regime of racial accumulation and the path dependencies linking those structural features to prior regimes.

Jaeggi: We've talked before about core and periphery, and this relation was a big part of how you describe dispossession and expropriation under the first two regimes of accumulation. Of course, what we've been calling state-managed capitalism is also the period when we had a large wave of colonial liberation struggles. But obviously this was not the end of Western imperialism over these regions. Would you describe the postcolonial situation in these same terms, as a kind of "hybrid" where exploitation is shadowed by expropriation?

Fraser: Yes, I would describe it in exactly those terms. As you said, struggles for decolonization exploded throughout the era of state-managed capitalism, intensifying in the years following World War II. The effect was further to alter the configuration of the two "exes." With the advent of political independence, some postcolonials succeeded in raising their status from expropriable subject to exploitable citizen-worker – but precariously and on inferior terms. In a global economy premised on "unequal exchange," their exploitation, too, was suffused with expropriation, as trade regimes tilted against them siphoned value away to the core, notwithstanding the overthrow of colonial rule. But, of course, even that limited progress did not hold for all. Many more peripheral subjects remained outside the wage nexus and subject to overt confiscation. Now, however, the expropriators were not only foreign governments and transnational firms, but also postcolonial states. Centered largely on import-substitution industrialization, the latter's "development" strategies often entailed expropriation of "their own" indigenous populations. And even those developmental states that made serious efforts to improve the condition of peasants and workers could not fully succeed. The combination of straitened state resources, neo-imperial regimes of investment and trade, and ongoing land dispossession ensured that the line between the two "exes" would remain fuzzy in the postcolony.

And that's the point I want to stress here. Exploitation in state-managed capitalism no longer appeared so separate from expropriation. In this regime, rather, the two mechanisms of accumulation became internally articulated – in racialized industrial labor, on the one hand, and in compromised postcolonial citizenship, on the other. Nevertheless, the distinction between the two "exes" did not disappear, and "pure" variants of each persisted in core and periphery. Substantial populations were still expropriated pure and simple, and they were almost invariably people of color; others were "merely" exploited, and they were overwhelmingly European and "White." What was new, however, was the emergence of hybrid cases in which some people were subject simultaneously to both expropriation and exploitation. Such people remained a minority under state-managed capitalism, but they were the heralds of a world to come. When we turn to the present period, we see a vast expansion of the expropriation/exploitation hybrid.

Jaeggi: So what you're saying is that the distinction between expropriation and exploitation is gradually breaking down somehow, first under state-managed capitalism, but even more so today. How central is this to the current regime of financialized capitalism? In which respects does the current regime still rely on racism and race relations?

Fraser: Financialized capitalism rests on a new nexus of expropriation and exploitation, which is distinguished by two main features. The first is a dramatic shift in the geography and demography of the two "exes." Much large-scale industrial exploitation now occurs outside the historic core, in the BRICS countries of the semi-periphery. At the same time – and this is the second difference – expropriation is on the rise – so much so, in fact, that it threatens to outpace exploitation once again as a source of value and driver of capital accumulation. These two aspects are closely connected. Expropriation is becoming universalized, afflicting not only its traditional subjects but also those who were previously shielded by their status as citizen-workers. In the historic core, where low-waged precarious service work is replacing unionized industrial labor and governments are cutting public goods and social services at the behest of investors, capital is now routinely paying the vast majority of workers less than the socially necessary costs of their reproduction. The effect is to force them to rely on consumer debt in order to live, which means they are being expropriated coming and going. The financial sector markets a dizzying array of loans designed to fatten investors and expropriate citizen-workers of every color. But this dynamic is especially damaging to racialized borrowers, who are steered to hyper-expropriative "subprime" and payday loans.

Meanwhile, the relocation of industrial manufacturing to the BRICS has brought intense exploitation there, including in specially designated "export processing zones." But this combines with expropriation, as capital mobilizes new supplies of labor produced outside its official economy, for whose reproduction it does not pay. At the same time, global financial institutions, such as the IMF, press indebted postcolonial states to impose austerity. Demanding cutbacks in public services, privatization of public assets, and opening of markets to foreign competition, they condition loans on policies that transfer wealth from vulnerable populations to international corporate capital and global finance. This, too, represents accumulation via expropriation, as do intensified peasant dispossession and corporate land grabs. Debt is truly a major driver of accumulation by expropriation in financialized capitalism.

In financialized capitalism, then, we encounter a new entwinement of exploitation and expropriation – and with it, a new dynamic of political subjectivation. Instead of a sharp divide between the forcibly expropriated and the "merely" exploited, we now encounter a continuum: at one end lies a growing mass of defenseless expropriable subjects; at the other, the dwindling ranks of protected exploited citizen-workers; and in the middle sits a new hybrid figure, formally free and acutely vulnerable: the *expropriable-and-exploitable citizen-worker*. This hybrid figure made a brief appearance in the prior regime, as we just saw. But now it is becoming the norm. And yet the expropriation/exploitation continuum remains racialized, with people of color still disproportionately represented at the expropriative end. Throughout the world, they remain far more likely to be poor, unemployed, homeless, hungry, and sick; to be victimized by crime and predatory loans; to be harassed and murdered by police; to be incarcerated and sentenced to death; to be used as cannon fodder or sex slaves and turned into refugees or "collateral damage" in endless wars.

Intersections: prospects for a postracist, postsexist capitalism

Jaeggi: Your expanded conception of capitalism brings together a lot of structures of domination and oppression in an impressive way, but it also carries certain risks. One danger that comes to mind is the temptation to hierarchize different forms of domination. We can recall those past debates between feminists and Marxists over "dual-systems theory." Some Marxists held on to the idea that the "primary contradiction" is always capitalism and capitalist class struggle, while gender domination is only a secondary contradiction, the idea being that once we resolve the contradiction of capitalism all these secondary problems will follow. Feminists fought hard against this kind of argument.

So one might worry that the picture you're giving us comes too close to this kind of hierarchical way of theorizing, and one might also worry that it falls short of giving a convincing functionalist explanation concerning the dependencies between the different forms of domination. One might argue, for example, that gender domination is no longer a functional necessity for capitalism – if it ever was – and thus gender domination can be overcome without overcoming capitalism. More importantly, one could also argue the converse: gender domination might not disappear with capitalism. We do see these glass ceiling campaigns in feminism and this kind of "united colors of Benetton" ideal on the rise. Employers might consider it a waste of human capital to neglect talent based on race or gender. So there does seem to be a way in which racism and sexism come to be viewed as obstacles to efficiency and to capitalist accumulation. Take the need for immigrant labor, for example. There was a recent effort to attract IT specialists from India to Germany, which has a shortage of qualified labor. This was met with a right-wing campaign whose motto was "Kinder statt Inder!" – by which they meant that Germans should produce more children instead of admitting foreigners. So this would be an example in which a type of deep-seated, culturally embedded racism is actually becoming an obstacle to capitalist accumulation. It suggests that there can arise circumstances under which sexism and racism might conflict with capitalist imperatives.

So my question is: How do these instances of domination and oppression work together? How close do you come to the renewal of a primary/secondary contradiction picture, as opposed to the intersectionality picture?

Fraser: There are a number of important issues here. Let me say, first, that I emphatically reject the primary/secondary contradiction view. The whole point of disclosing additional "hidden abodes," beyond the one Marx focused on, is to show that the forms of oppression they harbor (gender and racial subordination, imperialism and political domination, ecological depredation) are built-in structural features of capitalist society – as deep-seated as exploitation and class domination. The entire thrust of my argument is to rebut the view that class alone is structural. And I would make the same case against anyone who sought to install some other single instance in that privileged position as the "primary contradiction."

Nevertheless – and here's my second point – I also reject pluralistic or additive approaches, such as dual (or triple) systems theory. Far from conceiving capitalism, patriarchy, and White supremacy as separate "systems," which somehow mysteriously articulate, I am proposing a *unified* theory, in which all three modes of oppression (gender, "race," class) are structurally grounded in a single social formation – in capitalism broadly conceived, as an institutionalized social order. And, unlike theories of intersectionality, which tend to be descriptive, focused on the ways in which extant subject positions crosscut one another, my account is explanatory. Looking behind those subject positions, to the social order that generates them, I identify the institutional mechanisms through which capitalist society produces gender, race, and class as transecting axes of domination.

There is also a third point. Contrary to what you just said, I reject the view that any of these modes of domination are simply "functional" for capital accumulation. In my framework, all of them occupy contradictory positions: on the one hand, all are enabling conditions for accumulation; but on the other hand, all are also sites of contradiction, potential crisis, social struggle, and "non-economic" normativity. This point holds for class, as Marx insisted, but equally for gender, race, and imperialism – indeed, also for democracy and ecology.

Finally, nothing I've said here rules out the possibility that (some fractions of) capital might (under certain historical circumstances) come to view (certain received forms of) racism and/or sexism as obstacles to its (historically specific) accumulation strategies (in a

109

given conjuncture). But notice how many qualifications I had to introduce into that sentence in order to state the idea in a valid way. The point is that your question must be addressed *historically*. Everything depends on the regime of accumulation in force, on how and where its constitutive boundaries have been drawn, on the extent to which its institutional matrix is unraveling and alternatives are being explored. So, yes, I agree with you that any given racial or sexual order could prove inimical to at least some sectors of capital, especially in moments of crisis, when established accumulation strategies appear exhausted and a search for alternative configurations is underway. Something like this may well be happening today, as you suggest. But that is a far cry from the general categorical claim that capitalism can, in principle, do without gender or racial hierarchy *simpliciter*.

Jaeggi: That brings me to the question that's been nagging me throughout this whole discussion. Our discussion in this chapter has been about how to historicize capitalism. At the same time, this master framework you've elaborated does not itself appear historicized; it remains more or less stable across historical periods. In what sense is capitalism really "historical" and in what sense is it subject to a "fixed" logic? And how do you interpret the relation between these historical and fixed aspects of your master framework?

For example, you say capitalism always needs subjects of exploitation and of expropriation. If this is the case, isn't it also possible to speak of what some sociologists call "functional equivalents?" In other words, as you just said, the exploited and the expropriated don't always have to be the same group. There is no reason they absolutely must be defined along gendered lines or racialized lines. And if this is true, perhaps one could radicalize the attempt to historicize capitalism a bit further and say that the gender order and the racial order merely describe empirical ways in which expropriation and exploitation came to be organized.

Fraser: My view is that every form of capitalism divides production from reproduction, exploitation from expropriation. Those divisions are not historically contingent; they are constitutive of capitalist society. But you rightly ask: does it follow that gender and racial domination are also *constitutive of capitalism*? Or might they be historically contingent? Could there exist a form of capitalist society that divides production from reproduction on some basis other than gender? Could there be a historical form of capitalism in which the

110

distinction between expropriation and exploitation is organized on some grounds other than race?

These are deep and important questions, but they are also tricky. We would go wrong, I think, if we began by assuming that people simply *are* divided by race and gender as a matter of fact, independent of social processes and relations of power, and then went on to ask whether capitalist society might not assign those already gendered and racialized people randomly to production or reproduction, exploitation or expropriation. That initial assumption turns matters upside-down. Far from being simply given as matters of fact, gender and racial "difference" are products of the power dynamics that assign individuals to structural positions in capitalist society. Gender division may be older than capitalism, but it assumed its modern male-supremacist form only in and through capitalism's separation of production from reproduction. And the analogous point holds for race. Although "racial difference" as we understand it now may have some affinities with earlier forms of color prejudice, it only took on its modern imperialist White-supremacist guise in and through capitalism's separation of exploitation from expropriation. Absent those two divides and the subjectivations that accompanied them, neither racial nor gender domination would exist in anything like their present forms.

By the same token, however, those forms of domination *must* exist wherever social arrangements split off production and exploitation from reproduction and expropriation and assign responsibility for those two hidden abodes to specially designated populations. This would be the case even if the people slotted for reproduction and/or expropriation were not disproportionately biologically female and/or of African descent. Whoever they were, those people would be feminized and/or racialized, subjected to gender and/or racial domination. And this casts the matter in a different light. Once gender and race are understood right side up, in a pragmatic, de-substantialized way, as outcomes rather than givens, the conclusion appears inescapable: if capitalism requires that production and exploitation be hived off from reproduction and expropriation, respectively, and if it requires that the latter functions be assigned to separate and distinct classes of persons, designated expressly for that purpose, then capitalism cannot be detached from gender and racial oppression.

Jaeggi: Your answer raises an interesting social-theoretical point. You say that, by definition, capitalism separates the front-story of exploitation and commodity production from the back-story of expropriation and social reproduction. You also say that racism and sexism are inherent in capitalism insofar as it assigns the back-story functions to specially designated populations, who will be racialized and feminized as a result. But you leave open another possibility. What if capitalism does not require that second condition? What if it were to expropriate and "reproductivize" nearly everyone, requiring work in those hidden abodes from the entire non-capital-owning population, over and above what it requires from them in exploited wage labor? Isn't that a possible scenario? And if it is, wouldn't the result be a non-racist, non-sexist capitalism? Finally, might we be moving in that direction today, given what you said about the universalization of expropriation in contemporary financialized capitalism?

Fraser: Well, you've certainly gone straight to the heart of the matter! So let me try to do the same. The scenario you just sketched is logically possible, to be sure. But I believe we can rule it out for all practical purposes. To see why, let's look again at the present conjuncture. You are right: today's financialized capitalism *is* a regime of universalized expropriation. Not just racialized populations but also most "Whites" now earn wages that fail to cover the full costs of their reproduction. No longer shielded by public provision, bankruptcy protections, union power, and labor rights, they too are at the mercy of "austerity," predatory lenders, and precarious employment. By the same token, exploitation is also being universalized. Not just men but also most women must sell their labor power full-time in order to feed their families. Able neither to access a generous "mother's pension" nor to lay claim to a "breadwinner wage," they too must clock in long hours of waged work, often in excess of the once standard 40-hour week. And yet, present-day capitalism is anything but post-racist or post-sexist. As I said, the burdens of expropriation still fall disproportionately on people of color, who remain far more likely than others to be subjected to poverty, homelessness, illness, violence, incarceration, and predation by capital and the state. Likewise, the onus of reproductive labor still falls overwhelmingly on the shoulders of women, who remain far more likely than men to be single heads of households, with primary care responsibilities, and far more likely, too, even when they have male partners, to work the "double shift," returning home from a long day of paid work to cook, clean, do laundry, and care for kids and parents.

In general, then, racial and gender-based domination persists – even within the fuzzier contours of the present regime. In fact, the new configuration may actually aggravate racial animosity and gender resentment. When centuries of stigma and violation meet finance capital's voracious need for subjects to exploit and expropriate, the result is intense insecurity and paranoia – hence, a desperate scramble for safety – and exacerbated racism and sexism. Certainly, those who were previously shielded from much predation are less than eager to share the burden of it now – and not simply because they are sexists or racists, although some of them are. It is also that they, too, have legitimate grievances, which come out in one way or another – as well they should. In the absence of a cross-racial, cross-gender movement to abolish a social system that imposes near-universal expropriation while cannibalizing social reproduction, their grievances find expression in the growing ranks of right-wing authoritarian populism. Those movements, which flourish in virtually every country of capitalism's historic core, represent the entirely predictable response to the hegemonic "progressive neoliberalism" of the present era. The latter cynically deploys appeals to "fairness" while extending expropriation and gutting public support for social reproduction. In effect, it asks those who were once protected from the worst by their standing as men, "Whites," and/or "Europeans" to give up that favored status, embrace their growing precarity, and surrender to violation, even while it funnels their assets to private investors and offers them nothing in return beyond moral approval. In the dog-eat-dog world of financialized capitalism, it is practically impossible to envision a "democratic" path to non-racial, non-sexist capitalism.

Jaeggi: But do you really think it is easy to envision a path to a non-racist, non-sexist social order that is *post*capitalist?

Fraser: No, of course not. But the kernel of that project is clear. *Contra* traditional understandings of socialism, an exclusive focus on exploitation and production cannot emancipate working people of any color or gender; it is also necessary to target expropriation and reproduction, to which exploitation and production are in any case tied. By the same token, *contra* liberal feminists and anti-racists, an exclusive focus on discrimination, ideology, and law is not the royal road to overcoming racism or sexism; it is also necessary to challenge capitalism's stubborn nexus of expropriation and exploitation, reproduction and production. Both projects require a deeper radicalism – one aimed at structural transformation of the overall social matrix. This means overcoming both of capitalism's "exes" and its production/reproduction divide by abolishing the larger system that generates their symbiosis.

Jaeggi: That's a bold and inspiring stance. But whether the argument is fully persuasive remains to be seen. We will return to it, and to your *Zeitdiagnose*, in our final chapter, "Contesting Capitalism." But first, we need to take up another matter that has shadowed our entire discussion without being explicitly broached: having conceptualized and historicized capitalism, how exactly should we go about criticizing it?

3

Criticizing Capitalism

Ways to criticize capitalism

Jaeggi: We should now turn to the question of *what is wrong with capitalism*, and, therefore, to the matter of *criticizing capitalism*. On what grounds is it possible to criticize capitalism? And what kinds of critiques are appropriate for the institutionalized social order that we call capitalism?

There have been various critiques of capitalism for as long as capitalism has existed. But not all critiques are equally insightful, and not every critique is something we would want to endorse. Some claim to be taking aim at capitalism when what they're really criticizing is modern society; some draw tenuous links to trace everything they find wrong in the world back to capitalism; and some blame capitalism for problems we find in virtually every form of social organization. Some tend to be too nostalgic or have a conservative tenor; some are diffuse or simplistic; and not all of them have aims we would describe as "emancipatory." Some are downright regressive or even fascist.

So it's important that we specify our standards of critique and, moreover, that we do so in a way that is tailored to thinking about capitalism. We should have an idea of *what exactly* we are criticizing when we take up a viewpoint on what is undesirable about our global capitalist order. We can agree there is something problematic about capitalism and the way our societies are organized, but it is not always obvious when a particular malady in the world can be traced back to it specifically.

Fraser: Agreed. We don't want to trace every conceivable social ill to some all-powerful, but under-specified thing called "capitalism."

115

That would turn the concept into a catch-all, another "black box," as it were. Nor do we want to imply that the solution is to return to a supposedly pristine precapitalist way of life. But that still leaves open many possible paths for developing critique. How exactly do you want to proceed?

Jaeggi: I always liked the way Philippe Van Parijs framed the question in the 1980s: What, if anything, is *intrinsically* wrong with capitalism?[1] What is it we find fundamentally problematic about it, which is not just a side-effect or a chance particularity, but which occurs systematically in conjunction with capitalism? If what we are looking at – the object of our critique – is something that happens in all conceivable societies, or if it is something that happens just incidentally in capitalist society, then it is not really a critique of capitalism. If something in the social systems we're considering is supposed to be wrong or problematic, is it in fact *capitalism* that is to blame, or is it something else?

I suggest we begin by distinguishing three models of argumentation or three strategies of critique: a *functionalist* critique, a *moral* critique, and an *ethical* critique. The functionalist argumentative strategy holds that capitalism is intrinsically dysfunctional and crisis-prone; the moral or justice-oriented mode of argument asserts that capitalism is morally wrong, unjust, or based on exploitation; finally, the ethical critique contends that a life shaped by capitalism is a bad, impoverished, meaningless, or alienated life.

Fraser: Fine, let's start by considering these three critical genres, even if it might turn out that this is not a complete set of options.

Jaeggi: And even if we find that there are unresolved problems with respect to each.

Functionalist critique

Jaeggi: Simply put, the functionalist strategy of argumentation is that capitalism cannot function as a social and economic system. It is intrinsically dysfunctional and necessarily crisis-prone. The theoretically simplest version of this kind of critique is pauperization theory – the diagnosis that capitalism, in the long run, will not produce enough for people's subsistence, and this will lead to the breakdown of the system. There are more complex versions of this idea, involv-

116

ing systemic theories of market and production crises, and the most sophisticated of these is probably the Marxist theorem of the tendential fall of the rate of profit: the capitalist dynamic undermines itself through changes in the ratio of living labor to machinery, or what he called the "organic composition of capital."[2]

Note that the functionalist mode of critique is not restricted to dysfunctions *within* the economic system. There are also functionalist critiques of capitalism that home in on relations between the economy and other social spheres and resources. Some focus more on the so-called "culture of capitalism" and its motivational resources. Daniel Bell argued that capitalism systematically undermines psychic and cognitive dispositions that are necessary for its own development and conservation.[3] Joseph Schumpeter said something similar.[4]

Now, there are noticeable advantages to this kind of strategy. Most importantly, as a framework of critique, it doesn't seem to need independent standards of justification, and this relieves it of a number of philosophical entanglements. The object of critique is simply ineffectual; it just doesn't work. It undermines its own capacity to function on the basis of the grounds it lays for itself, and so it refutes itself entirely and patently. In some versions, this intrinsic dysfunction provides grounds for the proposition that the problem in the long run will dispose of itself, will finish itself off.

But there are noticeable disadvantages to this kind of strategy as well. The functionalist mode of critique is not as freestanding as it seems to be. Whether or not something is functioning – or functioning correctly – depends on how we define what the function of that thing is supposed to be and what it means to fulfill that function successfully. For example, we might say a knife functions (or doesn't function) in relation to cutting, since it's generally safe to attribute this function to the knife without question. But it is not nearly as clear what the "function" of a social formation like capitalism is. "Function" and "functionality" are not uncontested givens in relation to social facts. They require interpretation. Is it really so clear what capitalism's purpose, aim, or proper function is, let alone under what circumstances we can say it is falling short? Can we really say that capitalism even *has* a particular function? In what sense can we say that capitalism is dysfunctional when it systematically produces poverty, devastation, and ecological disaster? Just to be clear, I don't deny this is the case. But I do question whether we can make a critical argument on purely functionalist grounds. We have to ask: dysfunctional with respect to what? And here we are already confronted with the possibility of disagreements.

117

Fraser: Fair enough. If we treat capitalism as a form of economic organization, and if we assume that we already know what an economy is and what it's "for," then we might persuade ourselves that we need only invoke that "economic function" as the indisputable standard by which to evaluate it. But this would be self-deluding, even apart from the fact that capitalism is much more than "an economy."

The problem is that the very concept of "an economy" is itself an artifact of capitalism and it can't be neatly separated from it. It is not a neutral idea that we can bring in from "outside" of capitalism in order to judge it. It's not possible to say what an economy "is" and what it's "for" in a way that isn't always already caught up in a tangle of disagreements that are colored by the history of capitalism and the conflicts surrounding it. So, for example, some people would say an economic system's function is to satisfy human needs; others that it aims more fundamentally at generating growth; and still others that its deeper thrust is to develop the forces of production. These various claims express major *political* conflicts over how we should evaluate capitalism. There is no way to rise above them and arrive at a "true," non-ideological view of capitalism's "inherent function." And yet we shouldn't conclude that any view as to whether or not capitalism is "working" today is as good as any other. Rather, when someone says that it is or is not working, we should look at the broader context from which they are speaking. We should ask, what underlies the judgment? Whose perspective does it express? What expectations are in play? What is being assumed about what it means for capitalism to "work?"

Jaeggi: Exactly! And this is where I would say normativity comes in. If the question of what kind of function we should attribute to this system is itself an object of political and social struggle, then this becomes even more obvious. If capitalism creates wealth for some and poverty for others, saying this is a "failure" requires some set of assumptions about what capitalism *should* be creating and *for whom*. Even with respect to ecological depletion, we could ask what makes it a problem. If we want to claim that capitalism destroys its own preconditions of existence, such as natural resources or social bonds, then we are already implicitly presupposing a picture of what society *should* be like or what an economic system *should* be like. Institutions don't last forever, and it's a normative question in what sense a way of life should be sustainable or how concerned we should be about generations living after us. Wealth, poverty, depletion, sustainability – these are all things *we attribute* to social systems and their effects,

118

and it is we who judge whether and in what sense they are indications of success or failure. In the social world, the "functional" is always interwoven with normative components; there is no such thing as a "pure function" that is not already entangled with, and even constituted through, normative expectations.

Fraser: The need for a normative component is crystal clear. The purely functionalist image of a machine breaking down doesn't apply when we're talking about human societies. Nevertheless, it would be a mistake to leave matters there. If we simply dismiss the functionalist strategy for criticizing capitalism, we risk falling into a jejune, counterproductive form of skepticism. Granted, a skeptic could always say: "So what if the planet becomes unable to sustain life? So what if people are everywhere dying of hunger? This doesn't mean that capitalism isn't 'working!'" But this would be an external critique. In actuality, there is hardly anyone living under capitalism who wouldn't find the prospect of such developments horrifying. Critical theory should not adopt a stance of radical external skepticism, which simply dismisses people's intuitions about what is and isn't "working." Rather, we should be trying to clarify those intuitions. And this requires theorizing from a standpoint that is sensitive to the experience of capitalism's subjects, which is already laden with social interpretations and normative evaluations. We want to understand the sources of these interpretations and evaluations, whether and how they can be justified, and how to understand disagreements over them. Moreover, as you noted before, we want to understand how differently situated subjects within capitalist society arrive at different and at times incompatible judgments about whether or not the system is "working," and we want to understand what happens when they confront those disagreements directly, through social struggle. One possibility is to treat the struggles as themselves grist for functionalist critique. In that case, one would ask whether the system has entered into a legitimation crisis, by which I mean a situation in which it lacks sufficient popular support (and/or passive acceptance) to continue to "function." In other words, people's beliefs about how well capitalist society is functioning themselves play a role in determining how well it "functions."

In general, then, I am against any wholesale rejection of the functionalist strategy for criticizing capitalism. I would prefer, rather, to reconceive that strategy so as to link it to the interpreted and norm-laden social worlds in which capitalism's subjects actually live. I am pretty sure that you agree with this. I simply want to stress that it is a mistake to dismiss the project of functionalist critique on externalist-skeptical grounds. That would be to train all our ammunition on a very weak version of functionalist critique – a straw man, really – while overlooking subtler and better versions.

Jaeggi: Yes, it's true, we agree about that. Functionalist assessments can certainly form *part* of a strategy of critique, but a well-formed critique of capitalism would need to somehow get a hold on both the functional and the normative aspects.[5] To the extent that an object of critique fails to function, it fails against the measure of particular goals and associated value-judgments or norms. The non-functionality is always already normatively stamped. We find this nicely illustrated in Hegel's *Philosophy of Right*: the opposition between poverty and prosperity appears as a contradiction only when specific conditions obtain in civil society – only when it is interpreted as a scandal in a normatively charged way. So in Hegel's account of the "oppressive problem of poverty in civil society," the "rabble" produced by the dynamics of the bourgeois economy is not simply impoverished; it is outraged. And it is this outrage and its consequences that potentially threaten the cohesion of society.[6] Still, in order to identify the way in which the normative and the functional are intertwined here, we might need to do more than simply point out the link between the "objective" function and people's subjective attitudes. We need to show how something could be wrong with certain aspects of capitalism even when there is no outrage.

Moral critique

Jaeggi: Now, one straightforward response to the shortcomings of a purely functionalist critique is to turn directly to the normative questions involved. This brings us to our second mode of criticism, which argues directly from the point of view of morality or justice: capitalism is problematic because it produces results that are morally indefensible. This kind of argument has many different aspects. One strand says that capitalism destroys people's lives or ruins their means of subsistence in a way that, from a moral point of view, is wrong. One can also say capitalism is based on exploitation: it withholds from people the fruits of their labor in an unfair or unjust way, and it makes them subservient to a system that, in one way or another, cheats them out of what they are due. In short, capitalism is wrong either because it is based on an unfair social structure or because it produces a structure with all sorts of morally unacceptable consequences.

But my fear is that simply pointing out certain moral wrongs is, in its own way, insufficient for the kind of critique we want. If our question is not just about what happens in capitalism that is wrong but what is *specifically* wrong with capitalism, this mode of argumentation doesn't take us very far. The moral or justice-theoretic critique, with its focus on "distribution," has a relation toward its object, which, from the start, amounts to a kind of "black box" approach. It is oriented to the *effects* of a system or social structure, but it does not immediately engage with the particular dynamics and constitution of the economic and social institutions that bring about these effects. It doesn't tell us whether these effects are an intrinsic part of capitalism or merely incidental to it, or whether capitalism is unique in the kinds of injustices it causes or if they are just another version of injustices we might find in any type of society. Even if we accept that the normative measures sketched out above are valid, this approach remains vulnerable to the famous Hegelian charge of the "impotence of the moral ought."

As a matter of fact, Marx didn't use these kinds of moral arguments – at least, not in a straightforward way – and there is a long-standing debate among Marxists over whether or not Marxism implies normative standards at all. But the really interesting point is not *whether* his critique is normatively laden or purely technical; rather, it is *how* his normative argument works. Marx had good reasons not to criticize capitalism primarily on account of its moral wrongs, but it also seems clear that these obviously immoral aspects are what move most people to participate in social movements and social struggle. No small number of the riots, revolts, and conflicts we see seem to be triggered by moral outrage.

Fraser: It's true that a freestanding moral critique is not adequate to the enterprise of critical theory. And yet it's completely understandable and appropriate that social actors (including us!) respond with moral indignation when confronted with events like the collapse of Bangladeshi factories due to substandard construction, killing many hundreds of workers. That we (and others) react that way is not at all problematic. But we should distinguish the moral critiques that *social actors* develop from the perspective that a *critical theory* must develop. There's no problem with moral reactions as such. But they are not the final word. As you know, people can also be outraged in ways we would find troubling. They may mobilize, for example,

121

against immigrants getting things they think they shouldn't be getting. This would not be the kind of moral reaction we want to endorse, so we need some basis for distinguishing acceptable from unacceptable moral reactions.

As you noted, most philosophers look to freestanding moral theory to provide that basis, but that is not sufficient for a critical theory. The problem is that moral philosophy is too thin. Theories of distributive justice can show that end-state distributions under capitalism are unfair: some people enjoy absurdly lavish lifestyles while others die from malnutrition. But critical theory must go beyond such outcomes to problematize the processes that produce them. It must eschew the "black box" approach that underpins the freestanding moral critique preferred by egalitarian liberalism. We are concerned not only with distributive inequities but also, and more fundamentally, with the structural mechanisms and institutional arrangements that generate them. We aim, in other words, to connect the normative aspect of critique with the social-theoretical. That's the hallmark of critical theory.

Jaeggi: One could also make the case that freestanding moral critique is never really able to pin the injustices it identifies *on capitalism*. Of course, capitalism is exploitative and unfair. But so was ancient slave society, and so was feudalism. Unless one says more about the specific ways in which capitalism exploits and is unfair, we can't be sure that what is being claimed is really about capitalism at all. We can't know whether it's really a critique of capitalism per se.

That's one reason freestanding moral critique is not enough, but perhaps there are others. Why do you think it is important to distinguish the moral wrongs of capitalist exploitation from the moral wrongs of other societies? Why is it important to distinguish wrongs that are incidental from wrongs that are intrinsic?

Fraser: In addition to the conceptual reasons you just gave, which I find fully convincing, I would offer some practical reasons, which flow from the "action-guiding" character of critique. From a practical standpoint, it makes all the difference whether the inequities condemned by egalitarian liberalisms are accidental or systemic. If they are accidental, it makes sense to try to correct them by pursuing reforms that do not alter the basic framework of capitalist society. If they are systemic, however, structural change is needed. Likewise, there are good practical reasons for figuring out whether the injustices in question are inherent in all modern forms of social organization or specific to capitalism. If the former, overthrowing capitalism will not do the trick; if the latter, it conceivably could. Putting the two points together, I would say that a critical theory of capitalist society needs to identify a set of "bads" that arise systemically and non-accidentally from the deep structure of that society and are in that sense specific to it. That's a good part of what distinguishes it from egalitarian ⁓ liberalism.

Jaeggi: I want to get clearer about what's lacking in philosophical liberalism. Let's imagine a political philosopher who writes from within this liberal tradition, but who also understands how capitalism works institutionally, to some extent. Suppose this philosopher even has some very specific institutional suggestions. So what is the real difference between someone like this and a critical theorist? Is it that our hypothetical liberal still relies on the "empty ought?" Is she still using the "black box" approach, even though she is more institutionally nuanced?

Fraser: Your question makes me realize that we need to add another element to what we've said so far. We've said that critical theory should have a normative dimension, and that this should connect with an analysis of the structures and processes that create systemic injustices in capitalist society. Now, as you described her, your hypothetical egalitarian liberal philosopher has both of those bases covered. Whether she handles them adequately is an open question, but she has a conception of justice and an account of how the workings of the international financial order and interstate system systematically violate it. Yet she is nevertheless missing one essential ingredient of a critical theory: namely, an interest in and a way of approaching the standpoint of situated agents who are potential participants in social struggle aimed at transforming the system. In place of such an account, which is crucial for clarifying the prospects for social transformation, she offers policy prescriptions, from a position outside of and above the terrain of social struggle. Although she identifies moral fault lines (between haves and have-nots, as it were), she fails to map social and political fault lines. What's missing is an account of how differently situated agents understand themselves, what they consider their due, what they expect from their bosses and rulers, and what spurs them to act politically. That's the sort of account that a critical theory needs in order to fulfill the task of clarifying the grammar of social struggle and the prospects for social transformation. This doesn't mean accepting the outrage of social actors uncritically. I'd

123

endorse a line from Thomas McCarthy: critical theory doesn't give participants in social struggles the last word, but it does give them the *first* word.[7] I think this is absolutely crucial for a critical theory.

Jaeggi: I agree. Critical theory must situate its theoretical analysis historically, in relation to contextually specific potentials for emancipatory social transformation. Horkheimer called critical theory the "intellectual side" of emancipation.[8] But when he wrote that in 1937, he still equated "emancipation" with the victory of the proletariat. He had a very clear historical-materialist criterion for which historical subject to bet on, as it were. Moreover, the specific "historical subject of emancipation" he had in mind already brought along its own normative justification – it was realizing the "course of history." Of course, this framework unravels once we are faced with not only a multiplicity of social movements, but also a number of regressive, problematic ones, which then returns us to the question of how to assess their – or our own – normative claims. So the reference to social movements and actors is important, but not as far-reaching as we might think.

I think it is informative to examine Marx's own critique of morality and his nevertheless normative critique of capitalism in some detail. He used the strongly normative term "exploitation," but his critique of capitalism is not ultimately moral. Rather, it is normative only in a *broader* sense – one related to a Hegelian notion of "ethical life" or *Sittlichkeit*. Just think about his astonishing claim that there is no injustice involved in exploitation. He says that the fact that labor is that commodity, which, when purchased, produces surplus is simply "good luck" for the capitalist.[9] In the *Critique of the Gotha Program*, he makes it very clear that his critique of capitalism is not that it robs workers of the surplus of their labor.[10] These transfers are not straightforwardly illegitimate. I take him to be saying that there's nothing wrong from a standpoint within the system – there is contractual agreement and compensation, after all – and thus there is no injustice involved in the narrow sense. But that doesn't mean there is no injustice in a broader sense. Marx wants to explain the ongoing relations of domination and exploitation beneath the cover of the contractual relations of civil society. If the "real" institutional innovation of the capitalist economy is the existence of a free labor market, based on free entry into contracts and the idea of equivalence – labor power is exchanged for equivalent compensation in the form of wages – then it is not easy to see at first glance in what sense these relations are exploitative. And this is exactly what Marx is trying to figure out. Again, it is not unfair in the sense that most contemporary theories of distributive justice would evoke. It is still injustice – but it is injustice in a broader sense.

I'd say that we can only grasp the normative-critical character of the Marxist theory of exploitation, and its apparent dismissal of moral implications, if we comprehend the Marxist critique not as a moral or justice-theoretic critique but as an *ethically* inspired critique, one which applies to capitalism in its entirety as a distorted mode of ethical life (*Sittlichkeit*) or, as I would put it, as a form of life. It uses this lens to examine the kinds of relations responsible for structures of emotionless domination and invisible coercion, which facilitate a quite specific mode of exploitation. So the problem is not that the mode of production in itself generates exploitation: this is simply how it functions, it is part and parcel of the rationality of the system, and it is unassailable according to its own internal standards of justice. *That* it functions in this way, however, is nevertheless a problem, because the mode of production is itself a problem. And this is the deeper reason why a narrowly moral or justice-theoretic critique is insufficient for the critique of capitalism.

Georg Lohmann makes what I take to be a similar point when he says there are two conceptions of justice in Marx. The internal issue of distributive justice is there, but there is also a more comprehensive conception of justice that has to do with the foundations – or what he calls the "proto values" – of a comprehensive form of life.[11] It's not just about the equivalence or non-equivalence of wages but a *qualitative inadequacy of world- and self-relations* that emerges when labor is exchanged as abstract labor on a free market.[12] So it makes sense that the moral dimension of the evil of capitalism is not "freestanding" but needs to be situated in the *sittliche* or "ethical" dimension of its expanding problematic. The injustice of capitalism is "comprehensive" in the same sense as the discussion of "right" in Hegel's philosophy of right is comprehensive, where "right" encompasses in its entirety the rationality and being-good of a social order.

In other words, the problem is not that labor contracts – the purchase of wage labor and promotion of productivity – are unjust or unfair. This does happen frequently without doubt. But the disputes over wages, working conditions, and the length of the working day are simply "part of the game." It doesn't belong to the game to enforce any other standpoint than those exemplified by the profit interests of those involved. If we want to criticize something here, we have to criticize "the game itself." But then we are criticizing the fact that here we generally negotiate and treat labor power as a

125

commodity, and this requires us to transcend the narrow limits of a justice-theoretic or moral critique.

Fraser: I agree that Marx's thinking is informed by an idea of justice and that this idea is deeper than the distributive conception of justice in egalitarian liberalism. What I'm less sure about, however, is whether we should call the Marxian idea of justice ethical or moral. Let's return to the *Critique of the Gotha Program*. We agree that, in that text, Marx argues that the wages of workers in capitalist society do not cover the full value of the commodities they produce, but that this is not simple robbery, at least not in the ordinary sense. It's not robbery because workers have no "right" to be compensated for the portion of the social surplus produced by their own individual labor. (And they would not be compensated for that under socialism either, by the way.) Nevertheless, the way in which capitalism disposes of social surplus *is* unjust, because another individual (the capitalist) appropriates the workers' surplus labor. After all, if the individual worker doesn't "deserve" it, then neither does the capitalist. And if the capitalist nevertheless appropriates it, that's an injustice – it's morally wrong. The reason is not that the individual worker is robbed of what's rightfully hers, but that the capitalist takes as his own private property what is really the collectively produced wealth of society. And I'd say that *is* a form of stealing, albeit at a different level. It's not stealing from individuals but from society as such.

Jaeggi: But does it still make sense to point to this as a kind of moral injustice for Marx?

Fraser: Yes, I think it does. There is an ineliminable "moral" strand in Marx's critique, despite the fact that he sometimes disavows it. And I think the term "justice" captures it well. But in saying that, I am reinterpreting the meaning of justice. Instead of allowing liberal moral philosophers to define it in narrow distributive terms, I'm suggesting we take it back and give a more expansive meaning – just as social movements all over the world have been doing for hundreds of years.

Still, it doesn't follow that the moral perspective (however defined) is by itself adequate or sufficient for critical theory. Nor is it adequate for radical social movements. And yet we cannot deny that moral judgments and intuitions provide the starting points for mobilization. When people see bankers getting multi-million-dollar bonuses while they are themselves working four jobs and losing their homes, they rightly discern an injustice.

Jaeggi: This is an interesting point because it means that, although you shouldn't restrict yourself to this kind of critique, on the other hand you shouldn't simply deride it either, as many radical leftists do.

Fraser: Yes, let's not be "too sophisticated!" I feel the same outrage that lots of people do, and I don't want to "correct" that reaction by dissolving it into some "objective," affect-free intellectual analysis. I want, rather, to channel it into a deeper understanding of why things happen as they do and what we can do about it. I want to keep my intuitions about injustice, not negate them. And I think critical theory needs to do that as well.

Jaeggi: Of course, Marx said the same thing: that people were struggling and that his role was to bring in a deeper and broader picture. So maybe he wouldn't even deny that there is a sense of moral impulse. I very much like the way you discuss this – that a two-level approach to critical theory should have different standards from those of social movement actors.

Ethical critique

Jaeggi: There is another mode of critique that is widespread and has been around since the very beginning of capitalism. This is the "ethical" critique of capitalism, which I would distinguish from the moral critique we just discussed. This critique refers to the dramatic changes capitalism has effected with respect to our way of life. There are many variations of this line of argument, but the basic claim is that life under capitalism is a "bad" or an alienated life. It's impoverished and meaningless; capitalism destroys essential components of the good life. Such critiques target the way capitalism changes our everyday life and the value things have for us, along with the way we relate to them, to the world, and even to ourselves. Many today talk about emptiness and often refer to the loss of personal connection. Such ethical critiques have been around as long as capitalism has, but not all of them are necessarily progressive or formulated with emancipatory intent, and some are quite conservative, nostalgic, or even reactionary.

Many point to the objectification and qualitative impoverishment of social relations or to the social indifference that comes along with money. But I also think of Simmel's and Sombart's accounts of modern capitalism, both of which contrast the personal relations of precapitalism to the calculating relations of capitalism.[13] Sometimes these are traced to commodification and marketization, and at other times to other things, as in Max Weber's account of rationalization.[14] Hartmut Rosa's critique of social acceleration might to a certain degree also be an ethical mode of critique.[15] Although I take Marx's critique to be different, he also makes mention of these features when he discusses the implications of alienated labor, its abstractness, and the way things are torn apart or lose a certain kind of meaning.[16]

So, what is to be said about this kind of critique – what's right or wrong with it? As with the functionalist and moral strategies for critique, we might not want to reject it entirely, even if it has its own flaws. I would say the ethical perspective is certainly thought-provoking and informative; even the culturally conservative and nostalgic variants make a compelling case that capitalism leaves its stamp on our forms of life, and that the way we treat things and ourselves and how we conceive of these relations is not neutral. That we have come to conceptualize things, skills, and relationships as "commodities" indicates a notably peculiar relationship to the world. So whatever else might be said about the particular ethical claims and counter-visions evoked by these critiques, they convincingly de-naturalize the seemingly self-evident character of the capitalist form of life.

But there are still some serious philosophical problems associated with this way of criticizing capitalism. First, it is not always clear which of the symptoms taken up by an ethical critique are in fact specifically the product of capitalism. Do they really have to do with capitalism, or would they be better characterized as features of modernity in general? Second, it's very hard to establish well-grounded ethical standards. Some of these critiques rely on dubious accounts of precapitalist virtues, looking back to some former era when life was supposedly richer, often overlooking the ways these more "meaningful" relations espoused their own forms of oppression and deprivation. They also tend to disregard the ways in which the indifference and impersonality that accompany money, commodification, and marketization can also be interpreted as a kind of freedom. The fact that you can just buy what you need without sharing ethical commitment does have a liberating dimension that we shouldn't lightly discard.

I know you share many of these criticisms, but since it is clear that capitalism does deeply affect our form of life, modes of thinking, and ways of relating to ourselves, don't we still need to take these kinds of ethical arguments into account? Shouldn't we be able to integrate them into a critical theory of capitalism? And if so, how?

Fraser: It certainly *is* difficult to establish appropriate ethical standards – and all too easy to lapse into romantic communitarian thinking that airbrushes domination from precapitalist society. Here I would endorse Marx's insight about how liberating capitalism actually is. It provides freedom from having to establish thick ethical relations and from at least some traditional forms of domination. Granted, this is "negative" freedom, and we can still say that capitalism denies us a sufficient measure of "positive" freedom. But, even so, an ethical critique that doesn't acknowledge the emancipatory moment of capitalism is deeply flawed.

On the other hand, even "emancipatory" forms of ethical critique raise difficulties. One can read Marx's own alienation critique as a kind of ethical critique, wherein alienated labor creates a bad life because people are divided from themselves, from nature, from their fellow producers, and from the product of their labor.[17] But as you know, that common reading of the *1844 Manuscripts* has been criticized as "expressivist." If the critique is right, then we can't cite Marx's "youthful" alienation argument as a case of "good" ethical critique. Perhaps we can get closer to such a case by recalling that a different sort of alienation critique can be found in the "mature" Marx, in the *Grundrisse* and in *Das Kapital*. The core idea there is that the producers actually *create* the very force that usurps their freedom. As I put it in chapter 1, capital becomes the subject, and they become its servants, even though it is they who have created capital. Now, is that an ethical critique? It certainly isn't nostalgic or communitarian. At the same time, it does say there is something perverse about capitalist society, in that it turns the subject into the object and the object into the subject.

Jaeggi: This is how I suggest we should read Marx, and I think this is already the point in the early manuscripts: we produce as communal beings, but not for each other as communal beings. It already hints at some kind of collective self-determination and freedom. And we shouldn't forget that Marx was not the first to come up with the problem of alienation; similar diagnoses had already become ubiquitous by then, as a reaction to the "malaise of modernity." What he did was to connect these complaints to capitalism by exposing its structurally and systematically alienating features.

Fraser: That helps to specify what a non-essentialist ethical critique should do. It should connect the "bads" that capitalism generates to its constitutive institutional divisions – the separations of production from social reproduction, of economy from polity, and society from nature. I've already shown that these divisions have moral injustices built right into them, but we could also say that they harbor an "ethical aspect" that is itself normatively wrong: they structure the capitalist form of life as one that sharply divides "work" from home, "economics" from "politics," human from non-human nature. And it's definitely worth asking whether that sort of divided form of life permits us to live well – and whether we would be better off living in other, less divided ways. But, whatever we say about that, there's also another problem: capitalism's institutional structure predefines some fundamental contours of our form of life, and it does so in a way that deprives us of our collective capacity to design the modes of living we want. So we might well criticize it for that and for blocking our chances to live in more fulfilling ways. Again, I don't know if this sort of critique should really be called "ethical." But if so, I'd suggest we call it a *structural-ethical* critique, as opposed to, say, a substantializing-ethical critique.

Freedom

Jaeggi: So now that we have this tableau of some variants to justify a critique of capitalism – and a first idea of how philosophically tricky the enterprise can get – let's look at what strategy of critique we would advocate.

Fraser: Well, I would start, once again, by referring to Marx. What I find so powerful about *Das Kapital* is the way it weaves together all three genres of critique that we've been discussing: functional, moral, ethical. At the deepest level, the critical focus of the work is on the question of whether society's surplus should be privately appropriated. And that question involves all three of our critical genres. It has a functionalist aspect because the private appropriation of surplus installs a "contradiction" (a self-destabilizing imperative to endless accumulation) at the very heart of capitalist society. It has a moral aspect because the arrangement entrenches deep-seated relations of domination along lines of class, gender, "race," and empire, while also allowing a small group of private individuals and firms to usurp what is actually the collective wealth of society. Finally, it has a structural-ethical aspect because the private appropriation of surplus establishes a class monopoly on the power to determine the whole direction of the society, a power that can only rightly inhere in the collective.

Jaeggi: I want to follow up on that last point about collective self-determination. I'm wondering if this might not turn out to be yet another way of criticizing capitalism. If the surplus of society is privately appropriated, then we can't be part of the most important decisions that affect our individual and collective lives.

Fraser: Exactly. Under capitalism, we are denied the capacity to participate in fundamental decisions about who we are or want to be, and about what our form of life is and should be. So our democracy is severely compromised, because decisions of that sort and that magnitude should be organized democratically. Capitalism truncates democracy by restricting the political agenda. It treats what should be major political matters as "economic" and hands them over to "market forces." But that's not all. Private appropriation of social surplus also restricts our *autonomy*, our collective ability to take up an active role as the joint authors of our collective life process. Capitalism prevents our doing that with respect to society's surplus. So at least three ideas are implicated here: participation, democracy, autonomy.

Jaeggi: From what I understand you to be saying, it sounds like you connect autonomy with participation and collective self-determination. This would already be a break with liberalism and liberal philosophy, which tends to prioritize "negative freedom" above all else. For the sake of argument, why wouldn't it be enough to be master of my own life in the private sense? Why would you say autonomy requires this kind of collective self-determination?

Fraser: Genuine self-determination requires both personal and collective freedom. The two are internally connected. Neither can be assured in the absence of the other. Personal autonomy is in part about being able to choose among a set of alternatives in matters of career, residence, marriage – you name it. But this assumes an already established grammar of life and a pre-formed "menu" of options. And that's where public autonomy comes in: the design of the grammar and the menu. This is the argument Habermas makes in *Between Facts and Norms*: you can't really have personal autonomy in a meaningful sense without public autonomy, and vice versa.[18] I am fully on board with that argument, and I think a version of it is implied in Marx's objection to the private appropriation of surplus in capitalist society. Unfortunately, Habermas did not develop his autonomy argument in this Marxian way. But we should. In that case, we would end up with an argument centered on participation, democracy, and autonomy. What's ultimately at stake in this argument is the *meaning* of freedom.

Jaeggi: Would you consider this freedom and democracy account of normative critique to be a version of the moral critique, or would you characterize it as something distinct – a fourth category of sorts?

Fraser: One could classify the "freedom/democracy" argument as moral, as a claim about what is required for "political justice." If democracy requires the chance to participate with others in consequential decision-making about the design of one's social order, and if one's chance to do that is usurped by some class or social force, then one is deprived of something to which one is rightfully entitled. That's a straightforward justice argument – and it holds, I think, regardless of whether the depriving force is another individual, a social class, or a whole social system.

We are especially interested here in the third case: where the deep structure of capitalist society necessarily (non-accidentally) compromises democratic participation and collective decision-making. Precisely through its separation of economy and polity, that structure limits the political agenda by treating many fundamental questions, including the disposition of the social surplus, as if they were subject to "natural economic laws" that we simply cannot interfere with. We need only look at recent cases in which central banks and bond markets have informed peoples who voted overwhelmingly to reject austerity that they can't spend public money on schools or hospitals. That's a dramatic example, but the same result is also and more often achieved in subtler, less visible ways. Whatever the means, the effect is to thwart freedom and impoverish democracy. Capitalism is not only a system of exploitation and expropriation but also a system of political injustice. One could argue that this has something to do with ethical critique, suitably redefined. But it also resonates strongly with the moral register of critique, albeit in a way that exceeds the bounds of distributive justice.

Historicity

Jaeggi: I wouldn't necessarily characterize this line of thought as ethical in the problematic sense we discussed above; however, I would say it is also an argument about history and *Sittlichkeit*. (I

132

should make it clear that I don't interpret *Sittlichkeit* or "ethical life" in Hegel's sense as being *merely* ethical, but something more encompassing that includes moral and even functionalist aspects.) So, even beyond these functionalist, moral, and ethical criteria – at least taken individually – capitalism denies our access to what society has produced *in a historical sense* – what Hegel called the inheritance of humankind – including not only the means and products of production in the narrow economic sense but the entire history of our technological progress and of everything humanity has achieved.

There is a certain normative dimension that has to do with our ability to appropriate and build upon our own achievements as individuals and as societies. I'm convinced Marx had something like this in mind when he was talking about alienation from species being. Regarded in this way, the argument about alienation does not simply identify an ethical problem or an isolated pathology in capitalism. It maintains that we as human beings are being expelled from our species being, meaning we don't participate in certain decisions that affect our lives and, more broadly, we are not inheriting what is our common history in the sense that we can fully understand it as our own, take responsibility for it, and contribute to carrying it further.[19]

Fraser: I like the temporal, historical way in which you just elaborated this point. In fact, I would generalize it by saying that capitalism disrupts the relation between past, present, and future. Marx actually says this explicitly – in the *Grundrisse*, if I'm not mistaken.[20] And the idea is already implied in his definition of capital as the domination of dead labor over living labor. According to that definition, capital is nothing but congealed past labor, which has been transformed into a hostile power that dominates living labor. "Living" human beings are the producers not only of commodities, but also of capital itself, the very force by which they are subjugated. And that means that the past dominates the present. So there are really three points here: first, your point that capitalist society robs its subjects of their historical inheritance – in effect, distorting their relation to their past; second, the point I just made, that it robs them, too, of their current activity, which is not their "own" because it is dictated by the dead hand of capital – thus distorting their relation to the present; and finally, as we said before, the private appropriation of social surplus usurps their ability to determine their future collectively – thereby stunting their relation to that temporal moment as well.[21]

Perhaps this idea of historicity affords a non- or post-metaphysical interpretation of the idea of "species being" – one that is neither conservative nor essentialist but open-ended. In any case, whether we call it ethical or moral or historical, it's at the core of my understanding of the basic normative argument in Volume I of *Das Kapital*. That argument is not about distributive shares in the usual liberal sense, nor is it an ethical argument in the usual communitarian sense. It's an argument about historicity and freedom.

Jaeggi: Freedom from domination?

Fraser: Well, why not? After all, capitalism really does entrench domination – in at least two different senses. First, its constitutive institutional divisions entrench social relations of domination among classes, genders, "races." And second, those same divisions also entrench a form of generalized domination, which stunts the freedom of everyone. In both cases, the domination is hard-wired into capitalist society and cannot be redressed by the redistribution of divisible goods. There is no way to overcome it definitively short of deep-structural transformation.

Alienation

Jaeggi: We might also consider a way of reconstructing Marx's theory of alienation as a critique of the loss or blockage of freedom, a very rich notion of social freedom not yet realized in history. This is exactly how I understand alienation – not in a substantial ethical way, as some kind of falling away from an anthropological given, but as an obstacle to freedom and a form of domination.[22] If we take alienation as the inability to establish a relation to other human beings, to things, to social institutions, and thereby also to oneself, then we can reconstruct these moments as "relations of relationlessness" and, as such, a distorted mode of appropriation. These moments then prevent us from realizing, as well as shaping, the relations that we are already in and our life as a whole. It creates a specific kind of powerlessness, such that we are then turned into passive objects at the mercy of unknown forces. My argument is that, by reconstructing the critique of alienation, we gain insight into how demanding the preconditions for being the subject of one's own life really are, and this is a perspective we can use to see the shortcomings of the liberal idea of freedom. An alienation perspective allows us to see what kind of social preconditions we need in order to be free. Alienation, in other words, is an obstacle to social freedom.[23]

134

I think the prospects for this kind of an alienation critique are good, but they require turning away from substantial accounts toward what I call formal accounts. These involve how we form certain attachments and the way we conceive of and relate to our own deeds. It's not about the essence of who we "really are" or what we as human beings are meant to be, but about distorted and non-distorted modes of appropriation of our own wishes and deeds.

Fraser: You've developed a very sophisticated analysis of alienation, which I find both interesting and promising. But I still want to mention one worry. Do you think that the account you've just sketched is vulnerable to the criticism of Prometheanism? Does the idea that alienation blocks our capacity to shape our relations and our life as a whole presume the possibility and desirability of complete transparency and human mastery of contingency? That's a familiar charge made by poststructuralists who've been influenced by Heidegger. And it's also implied by some strands of ecological thought, which warn that we aren't actually separated from nature, but remain part of it to the very end. Recall the account in *Dialectic of Enlightenment* of the process by which we split ourselves into two: on the one hand, a master and subject, apart from nature; on the other hand, nature as the object which we seek to master and which we rush to leave behind, but which "bites back."[24] Granted, Horkheimer and Adorno ran a bit wild with this idea, but there might still be something worth salvaging from it.

Jaeggi: As I understand it, Horkheimer and Adorno, as mournfully as they present it at times, do also affirm the need for such a split or separation as the precondition for emancipation.[25] Would you read that differently and highlight the potential for reconciliation or harmony one can also sense at certain moments of their writing?

Fraser: I doubt that human and non-human nature can ever harmonize perfectly; and I also doubt that that's even a good way to frame our aspirations. But capitalism poses them against one another in an unnecessarily sharp and dangerous way. I would paraphrase Marcuse: Capitalist society entrenches not merely necessary but surplus tensions, tensions exacerbated beyond what civilization itself requires.[26] And I would say that whatever tensions are inherent in the relation between "society" and "nature" could (and should!) be lived in a less antagonistic way.

135

Jaeggi: Yes, the idea that we are masters of the universe is not even valid regarding the social world. In that sense, you don't even have to bring in the ecological aspect, though this is not to discount its importance. We were discussing the aspect of alienation that makes us slaves to a world which we ourselves created, but which then takes on a life of its own such that we lose control of it. But this reconstruction of alienation and its relation to the critique of unfreedom has to be spelled out very clearly; we need to be very careful not to buy into the idea of a fully transparent world. This is not the case with nature, which is obviously not of our own creation, but it isn't the case with society either.

On a very deep level, it always holds true that we can't get hold of everything we are doing. There is finitude. We can't always predict what happens to our own actions, as Hannah Arendt so brilliantly shows.[27] Sometimes we create something that becomes alien to us, in the sense that we couldn't have expected what the outcome would be. This is even true in the realm of production – we have to take into account all kinds of unexpected results and situations of non-transparency. We also have to accept that we are not even transparent to ourselves, and what we understand to be our own motives are not always a faithful mirror of our real intentions. This goes not only against substantialism but also against the ideas of mastery and self-transparency.

This is not, in principle, an obstacle to our freedom. If one turns away from a productivist Promethean conceit and toward human action and praxis, then it may be possible to integrate the fact that we're not able to account for everything and that even the results of our own actions might still become "alien" to us.

Strategies of integration and forms of life

Jaeggi: We both agree that a freedom perspective should be in the background of an ethical critique, or should replace its substantial, traditionalist, or communitarian versions. But even if we were to succeed, there might still be domination as such, injustice, exploitation, or moral wrongs. How are the moral wrongs or injustices of capitalism integrated in this renewed ethical perspective?

Fraser: For me it's quite simple. I already said that the constitutive institutional separations of capitalist society institutionalize all three types of wrongs simultaneously: first, morally unjust relations

136

of domination, both hierarchical and generalized; second, structural-ethically bad obstacles to freedom and distortions of our historicity; and third, contradictory dynamics of destabilization that produce crises. So all three strands of critique – functionalist, moral, and structural-ethical – are already grounded in my "expanded" view of capitalism as an institutionalized order; and all three are related to one another. The structural transformation of that order is a necessary condition for overcoming each of them individually and all of them together.

Jaeggi: I also think we need to connect these strands of critique. It is not just that these three modes of the critique of capitalism have strengths and weaknesses, but that these weaknesses can be overcome by putting all three "dimensions" together. A critique of capitalism as a "form of life" would relate all three dimensions: the functional, the moral, and the ethical. In other words, it would encompass the ethical without restricting itself to "cultural" issues of capitalism, while also accommodating a strong structural dimension. By "form of life," I mean social formations constituted through what I call "ensembles" of practices, and these include economic practices as well as social and cultural ones. The whole point of a "form of life" approach in this context is to understand economic practices as social practices – in a continuum with the other practices together and in connection to each other. If we can understand forms of life as more or less inert and more or less robust aggregate ensembles of social practices of different kinds, economic practices also belong within the scope of this context of practices. Economic practices are therefore not "the other," but rather a part of the socio-cultural fabric of society.

To understand capitalism as a form of life is to treat it, thus, as an ensemble of social practices and institutions that links together social, economic, and cultural dimensions. Moreover, this ensemble is also constituted by normative criteria of appropriateness. To criticize capitalism as a form of life means examining it with regard to its ability to solve normatively pre-defined problems, and to enable appropriate processes of learning and experience. It would then no longer be the invasion of the economy into the social but defects in the shape and content of economic practices and institutions themselves that come into view. It is the intertwining of functional disturbances – both practical crises and normative deficits – which sheds light on the irrationality and wrongness of capitalism as a form of life. This does justice to the functionalist aspect criticized above. Surely a form of life such as capitalism has always failed normatively. However, that

137

we do not want to live in this way is not simply an ethical value-judgment descended from the heavens or out of tradition; rather, it is inseparable from functional deficits and the practical convulsions and crises that come with them. As against an ethical critique, narrowly understood, and against both a functionalist and a moral critique, what is at stake here is the prospect of a renewal of a critique of capitalism as an *irrational social order* in a certain sense: it is irrational in as much as it blocks social experiences and learning processes of some sorts, and it therefore represents a distorted way to react to crises. The critique of capitalism then would be an immanent crisis critique.

Immanent critique and social contradictions

Fraser: I am quite intrigued by your idea of capitalism as a form of life. But where exactly does it leave us with respect to critique? We agree that a critical theory of capitalist society has to encompass all three genres of critique. We also agree that a vital task is to integrate them – to build a normative moment directly into functionalist critique. But how? We've rejected approaches that appeal to a God's-eye-view standard of judgment. Now, it seems that you are suggesting a strategy of immanent critique. I want to know more about how you understand that. Is it a matter of taking free-market ideology at its word and then going on to show that it cannot fulfill its promise to produce good lives for everyone? That, for reasons that are non-accidental, it *must* betray the very goals it sets for itself?

Jaeggi: My understanding of immanent criticism, or, let's say, a crisis-oriented version of immanent critique, locates the contradictions a bit "deeper." If a social order doesn't live up to the standards and promises that it purportedly represents, this might be a contradiction, but it's not a very deep one. I prefer to describe this as "internal" rather than "immanent" critique, and there are some real shortcomings to this way of conceiving critique. One problem is how we decide whether the "standards and promises" in question are even worth living up to. They could set a rather low bar to begin with or even be objectionable in their own right, in which case we're already looking elsewhere for normative standards. Internal critique also presupposes that we can identify, in an uncontroversial way, the promises of an entire social order, whereas in fact this matter is essentially contested and open to interpretation. If one isn't careful, an internal critique of this kind could end up being ideological in its own right, because it points to an overly broad and static view of what a social order should be about.

I would say that Marx has a more demanding and interesting version of immanent critique. A simple example might be the idea that a "free labor market" presupposes that participants are "free" and that workers and employers contract as "equals." This isn't just a normative standard – it's a functional condition of a capitalist labor market, and, as we said before, of the capitalist mode of production in general. And yet, of course, the worker is free and equal "only formally" and is in reality unfree and unequal. It's not just that the free labor market fails to live up to certain promises or standards it set for itself; it is utterly *incapable* of meeting the standards through which it *defines* itself. The most important thing to understand, then, is that this is a systematic feature that drives the social formation in question beyond itself. Conceived as a systematic contradiction, it is the source for crises.

But beyond this, immanent critique is also about deep potentials that have evolved within history. The contradiction between forces of production and relations of production is not in the end a story about false promises; it is about there being actual capacities and possibilities for us to do something and live up to something, which we are not fulfilling. As I understand Marx, certain relations of production actually become hindrances to a certain kind of productivity, and in this sense to its own functionality as well as normativity.

But then, the idea of a contradictory social reality, of "practical contradictions," itself is not unproblematic. For example, take this idea that there is a contradiction in the fact that the process of production requires social cooperation, and yet the materials of production and the things produced are privately owned. Now, this is not strictly speaking a contradiction – at least, it's not a logical contradiction – but you can see that there is more in play here. Capitalism is predicated on this idea of growth and productivity, and yet making the most of our collective productive capacities points to conditions that the relations of production systematically deny. It suggests that, beyond the normative questions, there is something fundamentally and even functionally inconsistent about our social practices that simply cannot be reconciled in their current form.[28]

Fraser: I like the idea that immanent critique is about spelling out the deep-seated contradictions of a social order. But I would distinguish different types of contradiction. There is, first of all, the orthodox Marxian idea of a contradiction internal to the capitalist economy – for example, the rising organic composition of capital implies at least a tendential fall in the rate of profit. That's what I would call an "intra-realm" contradiction at the "system level." And I do not under any circumstances want to throw this idea out. What makes it plausible is the fact that the capitalist economic system really does have a machine-like quality. The normal functioning of the system really does produce wild swings between booms and busts. Historically, moreover, the normatively interpreted experience of these "contradictions" has inspired social action – on the part of unions, labor parties, and socialist movements.

But there are also other sorts of contradictions. In previous chapters, I've stressed what I would call "inter-realm" contradictions – between the requirements of production and those of social reproduction, between the imperatives of accumulation and the need for robust public powers, between the need for "cheap natures" and the requirements of ecological sustainability. I don't want to belabor all that again. But I should add that inter-realm contradictions don't operate exclusively at the "system" level. They also appear as "social" or "lifeworld" contradictions, in the form of clashes between the various normative ideals associated with the different realms that together compose the institutionalized social order that is capitalism. This is a point we should return to later, when the time is right.

Finally, there are contradictions that arise historically, when normative expectations that people developed in an earlier time are at odds with present-day pressures and realities. For example, working-class people who lived through the Great Depression, World War II, and the postwar welfare state internalized the expectation that it's the role of government to protect their standard of living, to provide full employment, and to insure their social security in the face of market convulsions. Today, however, those expectations conflict head-on with neoliberal commonsense, which attributes economic downturns to excessive state regulation and holds that the solution is to let the market work its magic, unmolested. Under the right conditions, conflicts like these (between historically sedimented expectations and contemporary commonsense) can rise to the level of a *political contradiction*. I mean the sort of contradiction that Marx had in mind when he claimed that sharpening class struggle was the political expression of a systemic crisis tendency.

Normative functionalism

Jaeggi: It goes without question that there are internalized sets of normative expectations. The problem is that those normative expectations might be poorly formulated or misleading. Those who supported fascism had normative expectations as well, a certain kind of cultural-communitarian "embeddedness" that we would reject out of hand. So pointing to internalized expectations only moves the problem of the normative criteria around. We still have to evaluate them: some might be wrong, some might be understandable but not feasible, and so on.

Now, the important point here is to shift the place where we look for "the normative," and to connect the normative and the functional aspect on an even deeper level. You might call this a "materialist" move, or an attempt to figure out what is valid in materialism.

We have spent a lot of time lately spelling out how social norms are contingent. But in a certain way they are not: they are directed toward societal reproduction. I don't mean this in the sense of a philosophical anthropology, but in a historical sense. We can't simply impute any set of normative functions we like to a social order that emerges and develops historically. At the same time, they are also not immediately obvious or given. They lay somewhere in between the poles of deliberately formulated and already implied, and this is how we might think about the formation and interpretation of these internalized expectations. They develop historically over time.

So these normative expectations might be justified by examining how they came to be formed in the context of the relations between society and economy – and how they developed. Feudalism provided people with an expectation that, even though they were dominated in the cruelest way, they would be somehow cared for insofar as they "belonged" to the feudal lord in a broad sense. Feudal labor then is unfree labor also in a double sense, at least so long as a certain kind of feudal paternalism is in place. Bourgeois civil society, in contrast, set people free (in the double sense mentioned) while promoting the expectation that everyone would be able to care for themselves. They would be free and equal, and they would gain their subsistence and self-worth through participating in the labor market. In one sense, bourgeois society did provide these means of achieving subsistence and self-worth – the free labor market – while in another sense it denied them through the disintegrating forces of the same set of institutions. I mentioned this earlier, but I think Hegel analyzes this with real insight when he said that the rabble is not only starving but outraged: they were not only complaining about their deprivation, but they also had a right to be upset – and to a certain sense of entitlement – since the expectations they formed vis-à-vis what he called "the system of needs" (i.e. bourgeois society) were justified.[29]

141

In other words, we could develop an account of how these expectations emerged throughout processes of historical experience. The frustration of the poor is not the same frustration at all times; it is not caused by the brute fact of a lack of resources but the lack of resources as it is conceived of through these normative expectations and as it has evolved historically. This is nicely illustrated in Polanyi's Speenhamland example.[30] Charitably administering to the poor in a world where at the same time they are pushed to sell their labor power for starvation wages is more disgraceful than it would have been under feudal relations. The market treats them as individual contractors, yet, despite their contributions to the generation of wealth, they cannot sustain themselves. If, as the Speenhamland legislation did, society reacts in a way that treats the paupers like beggars, we can analyze that as functionally counterproductive and normatively problematic. This is the strategy I would recommend regarding these normative expectations. It's still about class conflict and why people would struggle for certain normative ideals, but it's not freestanding: these expectations are rooted in the way society is and has developed, as well as in the way a society reproduces itself at a certain historical stage. The entanglement of the normative and the functional, then, comes down to the fact that poverty in bourgeois society is not only wrong, but at the same time disintegrative, and thus dysfunctional.

Fraser: I'm very sympathetic to what you just said. You've assuaged my worries about the "straw man" criticism of functionalist critique, which threatened to land us in external skepticism. And you've also overcome the shortcomings of freestanding normative critique that isn't connected to historical experience and social learning. But I still have one question. As I understand it, you propose to ground a critical theory of capitalist crisis on narratives: on historical accounts of how people came to acquire a sense of entitlement with respect to social protection, social rights, individual freedom from status hierarchy, and so forth; how those historically acquired expectations encounter difficulties, for example, when the regime of accumulation shifts; how they become subject to contestation and modification in times of crisis; and how they give way to new expectations. All of that is congenial to me. But we still need to face the crucial question: how do we distinguish better from worse historical narratives?

Inter-realm contradictions

Jaeggi: That's exactly the question I wanted to pose to you! Let's see if we can't bring it into sharper focus through the idea of a crisis critique. We are both attracted to a concept of critique that shows how capitalism's instability is not accidental but built into its very structure, yet we both are aware of the advantages and disadvantages of this model, particularly when it is understood in an economistic and deterministic way.

The model you've been proposing seems to understand crisis tendencies not as economic per se, but grounded in contradictions between the economic foreground and the non-economic background – that is, the contradiction is not internal to the economy but encountered in relation to the non-economy. This certainly gets us beyond the economism problem, at least in the narrow sense. Then again, there have been other functionalist critiques that didn't confine themselves exclusively to the economic realm as such. I mentioned Daniel Bell's account earlier, which takes capitalism's motivational structure as a kind of cultural background condition.[31] Habermas, too, reframed the crisis tendencies of organized capitalism in terms of their relation to the non-economic background of the "lifeworld," with politics and bureaucracy wedged in between.[32]

So here is my question: This kind of analysis might provide us with useful diagnosis of capitalism's instabilities, but it's not clear to me whether this is enough to establish a sound critique. If a functionalist account needs some kind of normative back-up, wouldn't this then still be true for your background/foreground analysis?

Fraser: My idea, like yours, is that a crisis critique must disclose deep-seated contradictions or inherent tensions within a social formation. It is a historical question as to when and how these contradictions express themselves in more or less acute forms of crisis. And it is a political question as to what strategies are available, and politically feasible, for defusing, finessing, circumventing, or displacing these contradictions, at least temporarily. All of that matters tremendously, of course. But what I want to stress here is a point that you stressed as well: crisis is grounded in contradiction. And, as you rightly said, I don't assume that the only relevant contradiction is internal to the capitalist economy. Capitalism harbors equally fateful contradictions *between* its various "realms."

You mentioned two well-known examples of critical theories focused on such "inter-realm" contradictions: Daniel Bell's account

143

of the contradiction between economy and culture; and Habermas's account of the contradiction between economy and polity in *Legitimation Crisis*, and between system and lifeworld in *The Theory of Communicative Action*. Polanyi is another example. For him, the fundamental contradiction of capitalism is between economy and society: the ongoing drive to create self-regulating markets in all the major inputs to commodity production undermines the fabric of solidarity, community, and shared understandings upon which markets ultimately depend. We could also cite eco-Marxian thinkers, like James O'Connor, who posits a contradiction between the dynamics of capitalist production and its necessary "natural conditions," as well as feminist theorists, like Lise Vogel, who diagnoses a contradiction between commodity production and social reproduction.[33]

All of this is grist for my theoretical mill. My project is to integrate all of these "contradictions" (both the inter-realm ones just listed and the internal-economic ones posited by Marx) in a single critical theory of capitalism, viewed as an institutionalized social order. The foreground/background model I've outlined here affords a way of tying them together in a unified crisis critique of capitalist society. In the previous chapters, I focused on three constitutive institutional separations: production/reproduction, society/nature, economy/polity. Each of them harbors an "inter-realm" contradiction grounded in the fact that capitalism's economy simultaneously needs and destabilizes a "non-economic" background condition.

Jaeggi: It's an interesting diagnosis and there's a lot to be gained from it, but, again, is it enough for critique? In a way, capitalism works better than we think. It may eat up its own resources and its institutional preconditions, but it also seems able to create new resources for itself. We might think it's an evil system, yet somehow it always manages to persevere. Capitalism is functionally alive and it's not clear that it's on any certain trajectory to total breakdown. It may be a very dangerous system for human beings and the environment, and the societies that it generates might not be worth living in in the long run, but it does seem to "function." So why can't capitalism eat up its own resources, as long as it continues working? I am thus left to wonder whether the normative problem we discussed earlier still remains. In what sense is the problem "functionalist," and in what sense "normative?" And how do these two aspects tie together in your approach?

Normative contradictions

Fraser: I concede that, if we were to stop here, we would have something that looks very non-normative, leaving us without any evaluative standard for saying what is bad or wrong and what should be abolished, overcome, or changed. In that case, we would have simply a picture of instability that could be more or less acute. But, as I said earlier, there's no need to stop here. We also need to include an account of the way people live those instabilities. Have they internalized normative expectations from a previous era – for example, expectations of solidarity, government aid, a rising standard of living, and the expectation that their children should have a better life than they had? If so, crisis and instability may be lived as the violation or defeat of those expectations; and the situation takes on a normative character.

But I want to add another point, which I mentioned briefly a little while back. My idea is that each of capitalism's multiple institutional arenas is associated with a set of normative ideals with which it has an affinity. For example, ideals of growth, "market justice," and individual "choice" resonate with and predominate within its economy. Ideals of solidarity, care, and social security typically hold sway within the communities and families that sustain much of social reproduction. Ideals of democracy, citizenship, and "the public interest" are associated with capitalism's polity. And ideals of sustainability, stewardship, and just relations between generations find a foothold within contexts experienced as proximate to "nature." These ideals can live together, however uneasily, in "normal" times, when most people respect capitalism's institutional divisions and dutifully invoke a given ideal within its "rightful" sphere. But they can also conflict head-on, as they do in times of crisis, when people apply them "wrongly" in "the wrong sphere." In the latter case, we have yet another type of "capitalist contradiction" – I would call it "normative contradiction." The potential for normative contradiction is built into capitalism's deep structure as an order configured through institutional differentiation and foreground/background relations. Neither the normative ideals nor the conflicts among them are contingent or arbitrary. Rather, they are deeply entrenched in the very structure of capitalist society. And the same is true of the "boundary struggles" we spoke about in chapter 2. Such struggles congregate around the established institutional divisions of capitalist society. They often involve conflicts over which normative ideals are appropriate in a given situation. Should struggles over fishing rights be resolved by appealing to norms of economic growth or ecological sustainability or the imperatives of social reproduction in indigenous communities? That sort of contradiction is at once lifeworldy and systemic – simultaneously functional, moral, and structural-ethical.

Jaeggi: I was recently reading Upton Sinclair's novel *The Jungle*. Here, capitalism eats up its own preconditions to the extent that it makes social reproduction impossible. Workers couldn't even raise kids, millions were unemployed, and the result was to reveal that the process had limits, assuming one accepts that you can't just let people starve.

It is true that, whenever or wherever it has the chance, capitalism tends to threaten the very basis of social reproduction. But it also seems that, when things get really bad, capitalism is quite able to develop a solution, be it through some kind of protectionist strategy or facilitating new forms of solidarity to replace the ones that have been destroyed. In other words, we can ask about the relationship capitalism has to the maintenance and refurbishing of these resources – whether it is accurate to think of them as resources that exist externally to the system or whether capitalism has some ability to create new resources for itself and even readapt its own preconditions of existence. Capitalism has a tendency radically to throw these preconditions into question, but even unrestrained capitalism seems aware that it has to offer some means for social reproduction. So an argument can be made that the system has certain adaptive capacities built into it.

Fraser: If we're speaking of the capitalist economy, it is not and cannot be self-correcting. Such corrections and adaptive measures as are needed to assure its necessary background conditions can only come from outside the economy – which is not to say from outside of capitalist society. Historically, that "extra-economic but intra-capitalist outside" has been politics. It is true that there have been moments in capitalism's history when "farsighted" capitalists understood this and took a leading role in organizing state-sponsored forms of social protection – in large part to save the system from itself. The US New Deal is a case in point: most of the capitalist class fought FDR tooth and nail, but not all. Even capitalists have other lives, and some of them appreciate the "non-economic" precincts of social life, which they understand not only as functionally necessary but also as valuable in their own right. But still, the moments when they are willing to act collectively on that basis are relatively rare. Where, we

146

might ask, are those "enlightened" capitalists today, when we need them? And, in any case, the major social forces that have spearheaded politically organized social protection have come from elsewhere – from working-class movements, anti-racist movements, women's movements, movements for national liberation. At their best, those movements have pioneered expansive solidarities, which draw from but also transcend the given "resources" that already exist within capitalist society at any given moment of crisis. In "making" such new solidarities, social actors draw creatively on the sparks arising from the friction created by capitalism's "normative contradictions."

Jaeggi: But to return to your view of capitalism's foreground and background spheres: as you see it, these different spheres are linked together, but not in a tight functionalist way. They have a life of their own and they inspire their own kinds of normative attachments in people, even as they work together with, or against, one another. The background in one sense stands in relation to the foreground, but in another sense its components have some sort of independent life – a normative dynamics of their own.

Fraser: Right. Each of these spheres is permeated with normativity, and especially (though not exclusively) with its own characteristic normativity. So capitalism's normativity is multiple, not singular. All of its subjects live in more than one sphere, and all are in contact with more than one set of norms. When crisis tendencies erupt into view, what they experience is not simply material deprivation or sheer instability, but *normative conflict*. In some periods, such conflict is defused via "normative segregation": one is solidaristic at some times and in some "spheres," while being competitive at other times and in other spheres. In "normal" times, these divisions hold. But at other times, including times of overt crisis, the walls break down, and capitalism's multiple normativities clash head-on. This is how I would answer your criticism that functionalist analysis isn't critique unless it has a normative dimension. It's not that individuals bring in normative ideals from the "outside." On the contrary, their ideals emerge from deep within the institutional formation of capitalism itself, which is premised on the very divisions that constitute the foreground/background relation.

Jaeggi: I completely agree. If a functionalist account has some critical impact, it's because the functional and the normative are already intertwined within these social institutions. If institutions are already norm-laden, then it's critical to be able to spell out how they fail to live up to those standards. But why wouldn't this also hold for the economic practices themselves? I have started to become uneasy with the way we distinguish between the economic and the non-economic, which tends to bring with it assumptions that we find built into many of these approaches – that there is a "good," normatively rich lifeworld or society, and a "bad" or "norm-free" economic sphere, and when the latter intrudes upon the former there are these danger- ous effects.

Against Polanyian dualisms

Fraser: Well, I, for one, do not assume that that economic life is norm-free – I referred just now to normative ideals of growth, market justice, negative freedom, and individual choice, whose "natural home" is capitalism's economy. Nor do I assume that non-economic norms are always "good." I've argued that a major weakness of Polanyi's *The Great Transformation* is his failure to reckon with the possibility that the "society" he counterposes to "economy" might itself be a cesspool of domination, exclusion, and inequality. Nor does he appreciate that the introduction of economic norms can sometimes have emancipatory effects.

Jaeggi: You've criticized Polanyi before on this point – that he over-romanticizes the social resources he counterposes against the economy, without acknowledging how they harbor their own structures of domination. This is one reason you introduce an idea of "emancipation" alongside his ideas of "social protection" and "marketization."[34] At the same time, it seems a strength of Polanyi's approach that he combines normative and functionalist aspects to show how forms of life are destroyed when societies are commodified all the way down.

Fraser: As I understand him, Polanyi connects, in a fairly tight way, a quasi-functionalist crisis critique with a substantive ethical critique. But he's quite weak on moral critique, especially with regard to ques- tions of domination and fairness, which are largely absent from his account. It's scandalous, really, that he neglects to take them up. If he had, he would never have ended up counterposing a "good society" to a "bad economy." He would have understood that "society" is replete with domination, exclusion, hierarchy, and that "economy" can serve, at least in principle and on occasion, as a force of liberation from some forms of domination. I don't for a moment think that Polanyi's neglect of these obvious points was intentional, but its effect is to push his ethical-cum-crisis critique in a nostalgic and conservative communitarian direction. What I've done in reconstructing his project is, first, to reinterpret the ethical element structurally, in a non-substantial way; and second, to introduce the missing moral element. That is why, first, I proposed a "structural" interpretation of his idea of "fictitious commodification," as an alternative to his "ontological" interpretation;[35] and why, second, I replaced his idea of a double movement with that of a triple movement.[36] I should explain that the triple movement assumes that three leading values can clash and must be mediated: marketization, social protection, emancipation. None of the three is wholly good or wholly bad in its own right – not even emancipation. As I just said, the foreground harbors its own normative surplus centered on negative liberty and consent. But – and here's my concession to the ethical – there is also some value to social security, social stability, and social solidarity. People have a legitimate interest in not having their lives suddenly turned upside down because of a corporate merger. Still, this has to be corrected by the third, "emancipation," pole, which holds out the ideal of freedom as non-domination in a sense that goes well beyond liberal norms of negative liberty and equality of opportunity. All three poles, in other words, must receive their due. This picture is considerably more complicated than Polanyi's, which opposes the good pole of social protection to the bad pole of marketization. The model of a triple movement has at least three sets of norms. Once we factor in this more complicated, differentiated story about foreground and background, moreover, the contradiction is not just economy versus society, as Polanyi maintained, but economy versus society, polity, and nature – at the very least.

Internal resources for critique

Jaeggi: I nevertheless wonder if you share more of this dualistic aspect of Polanyi than you might like to admit in the way you formulate your foreground/background model, with these various background spheres providing these independent resources of normativity. Isn't the very idea that there is some pre-existing, "independent" resource already problematic? There are two possible problems here: one is the essentialist idea that there is some innocent arena of social life that the "bad" system invades or "colonizes," as Habermas would say. But even if we acknowledge that these resources are not "innocent" and have their own mixes of good and bad characteristics, there is also a question of whether they were ever really "independent" of the system in the first place. If they are not only prone to domination in their own right, but also from the start co-constructed by the same "outside" forces they seem to be resisting, then this account faces problems from the standpoint of standards of critique. This is a Marxian as well as Foucauldian point that it's not a simple matter of pointing to these background resources as an independent normative anchor for our critique, because they are already constitutively inter-twined with capitalism and influenced by what they stand against.

Fraser: You've helpfully distinguished between two different problems. The first is that the background may already be bad in its own different way and therefore cannot provide an innocent standard. In effect, we can't simply take the side of the background against the foreground. On this I fully agree!

The second problem, on which you're pressing me now, is whether the background really pre-exists the foreground or is actually produced by it, and what this means for critique. This is a very interesting question. I reject the strong Foucauldian thesis, which holds that the background is *nothing but* a creature of the foreground – as, for example, when Foucault insisted that the "deep self" is wholly illusory, with nothing whatsoever behind it, even though it has real performative effects. Applied to the questions we are discussing, that view strikes me as simply wrong. It's not that nature is pure or good, but it is definitely *there*. Giving birth and changing diapers are likewise real – they weren't just created by capitalism. Nevertheless, capitalism reorganized life, institutionalizing a much sharper and more radical distinction between reproduction and production than existed before it. In earlier social systems, they were not distinct "realms" at all, but were thoroughly entwined with one another and with other aspects of social life. Activities that we would call "reproductive" were not simply called into being out of thin air by capitalism. But they have nevertheless been deeply "stamped" (to use your word) by its institutional structure. And the stamping was not such as to make them into mere mirrors of what concurrently became the economic foreground. Rather, it made them appear to be the latter's opposite number and to provide a basis for anti-capitalist critique. That last appearance is deeply misleading, however. I reject the view, which is quite fashionable nowadays, that one can simply withdraw from capitalist society

150

and build a counter-society "in the (non-economic) background," as it were, without confronting the all-too-real power apparatus of the foreground and without transforming capitalism's fundamental ground rules and institutionalized separations. This "delinking" strategy is illusory because the background is not independent; nor is it a counter-power per se. But at the same time, as I said before, it has alternative normativities built into it. And these may be experienced by some people as worth defending, even as others see them rather as starting points to be transformed in the course of struggle. In general, then, the foreground/background dynamic is not simply a question of functionality. It also has normative and social-action dimensions.

Jaeggi: But couldn't one also argue that, today, under the neoliberal regime of capitalism, the independence of these normativities has been eroded in such a way that we can no longer really talk about these alternative normative bases as being semi-autonomous? In an earlier phase of capitalism, it was actually the artisanal workers who became the most militant wing of the workers' movement, in part because they had another set of traditions to draw upon – skills, ways to cooperate, and a certain kind of pride connected to them. Yet couldn't it also be the case that these earlier normative standards became subject to their own kinds of "great transformations," so that workers no longer have precapitalist normative resources to bring to their social struggles? How "durable" are these normativities as resources for resistance? It there a historical "time limit?" In a way, this brings back the whole debate around Lukács's thesis that there has been a *real* colonization of these other spheres, which undermines their ability to provide resources for critique.

Fraser: I don't agree with the diagnosis of total or near-total colonization. There is a new version of it circulating now, which uses Foucauldian governmentality theory to argue that we are now being subjectivated virtually exclusively as self-responsibilized managers of our own "human capital." This view mistakes a neoliberal project for a social reality. It illegitimately generalizes from the lifestyles of hipsters and other members or aspiring members of the professional–managerial stratum to everyone else. But this is not the self-understanding or social practice of working-class people, who are, after all, the overwhelming majority.

Nevertheless, you are right that nothing lasts forever. Historicity and change are fundamental here, but so is human creativity. People living in the interstices, even in the worst, most degraded favelas, still find ways to build some kind of a life, even if these aren't necessarily lives we want to hold up as models for how things should be. Some of them find or create resonances among different forms of resistance, survival, or criticism, and these can accumulate into movements, parties, or even governments that attempt to do something different.

We should also keep in mind that the foreground is itself a source of norms that cannot be entirely reduced to capitalism. Norms like negative freedom, equal exchange, and even the notion of getting ahead through work have their own normative surplus, whose realization is blocked in capitalist society. In some cases, they can even have a positive influence, introducing an "emancipatory solvent" of sorts that facilitates the renovation of traditional norms and communities. So even the normativity of the foreground has its own emancipatory surplus. As Marx would say, it gives rise to aspirations or ideals that could burst the integument of capitalist relations and create new ones.

Division, dependence, and disavowal

Jaeggi: I want to press you more on how you conceptualize these contradictions and crisis tendencies – between production and reproduction, between society and nature, and between economy and polity. I'm particularly interested in hearing more about exactly "how deep" these contradictions are supposed to be seated. At certain historical points, the regimes that we have been talking about achieve a certain shape, putting certain constraints on what we can do against them. But they also contain possibilities, as new dynamics and new lines of conflict emerge.

My first question is whether, looking at these different regimes within capitalism, one could simply claim that these apparent contradictions and conflicts are all just part of capitalism's dynamic as a modern social formation – which is to say, part of its ongoing dynamics but not actually a crisis. Capitalism, under the second, "liberal" regime, was faced with problems stabilizing and integrating the sphere of social reproduction, to which it then generated solutions under the third, state-managed regime. Thus, the arrangements we find in state-managed capitalism can be read as solutions to the problems that came up in liberal capitalism and so on, and one could conceive of these solutions as just part of capitalism's dynamic capacity to evolve and generate innovative solutions to deep-seated tasks. Where, then, is the deep-seated contradiction or the crisis? If we conceive of social formations and societies as being dynamic in themselves, confronting various sets of problems and going through certain kinds of transformation with respect to different ways to solve the problem, why would this be a crisis? Why would this be a contradiction?

One idea, of course, would be that it is a crisis because there are social struggles, because you see that people are unhappy with it, have been unhappy with it, and that capitalism cannot satisfy their demands. But this would locate the crisis tendencies on a rather superficial level. Another way would be to say there is a certain way to deal with these problems "adequately," meaning that unless we treat the sphere of social reproduction, for example, in a way that involves certain kinds of personal relationships that are concrete and direct, the solution is going to be wrong, because this sphere is of such a character that it can only be dealt with in a certain way. But this would come close to an essentialist view of these social spheres and how they should be shaped. And it would then go against your attempt to historicize society, or against the insight that human life is malleable – that it has changed and it will continue to change.

To put it in practical terms, the question I'm asking comes down to: how essentialist should we be with respect to these contradictions and crises, and what would an account that is not essentialist look like?

Fraser: You've outlined a dilemma and a challenge! In my view, capitalism's contradictions and crisis tendencies are not superficial but inherent and deep-seated. But this is not because the society's institutionalized domains have inherent natures that get violated when the activities that comprise them are not handled in the proper way. That understanding of contradiction is deep-seated, to be sure, but in the wrong way; it is essentialist and ahistorical. My conception of contradiction is entirely different – it is premised on a view of the *relations* among the domains, not on assumptions about their supposed essences or substantial characters.

As I see it, the tensions built into the capitalist social order are grounded in three distinctive features. I think of these as the three "Ds": division, dependence, and disavowal. Let me explain. By *division*, I mean capitalism's institutional separations of production from reproduction, economy from polity, and human society from non-human nature. As I have been saying throughout our discussions, these divisions did not exist in previous social formations. Far from being historical universals, they are artifacts of capitalism – as are the tensions between them. Nevertheless, capitalism not only divides its economy from polity, nature, and social reproduction, it also makes economy dependent on those "others," which it casts as economy's background conditions of possibility. As I've insisted throughout, there can be no capitalist economy in the absence of public power, social reproduction, and inputs from "nature." So the relation is not just division but also *dependence*, which is the second "D." And that is potentially a source of trouble if and when the necessary background conditions are jeopardized. The third "D" is *disavowal*. Capitalist societies do not only divide their economies from the latter's necessary background conditions; nor do they only make the former dependent on the latter. In addition – and here's the final *coup de grâce* – they disavow or deny the value that the capitalist economy siphons from these realms that capitalism constitutes as "non-economic." There's the nub of the contradiction: capitalist economies constantly siphon value from those realms while simultaneously denying that those realms have any value. The upshot is that capitalists assume the all-but-infinite availability of social reproduction, public power, and natural inputs. Treating these things as free gifts, they don't concern themselves about replenishing them. They undermine the very inputs on which they rely.

So those are my three Ds: *division, dependence, and disavowal.* When you put them together, you get a perfect storm of potential instability, which is deeply entrenched in capitalism's structure. We could sum it up in a fourth D: capitalist society harbors a built-in proclivity to (self-)*destabilization* along *all three* of its constitutive boundaries: production/reproduction, polity/economy, human society / non-human nature. All of which, I repeat, represent crisis tendencies specific to, and inherent in, capitalism. The result is a picture of capitalist society that allows us to understand its crisis tendencies in a way that is not "ethical" in the problematic sense (whereby a contradiction consists in failing to treat something in a way that it requires by virtue of its essential nature).

Now, contrast this with the argument Habermas made in *The Theory of Communicative Action* about the colonization of the lifeworld. His thesis rested on the idea that there exist designated lifeworld activities that must, by their very nature, be treated communicatively, and that these are necessarily deformed when state-managed capitalist society commodifies or juridifies them. In some cases, Habermas called the result a "crisis," but more often he referred to "pathologies." That terminology is telling. Pathology-talk implies the substantive–essentialist view that dysfunctions erupt when something is treated in a way that violates its inherent nature. Crisis-talk, by contrast, is structural. A social formation is crisis-prone, on

154

my view, when its inherent structure and dynamics are such as to destabilize its own conditions of possibility. This formulation avoids ethically deep claims about the essential nature of this or that. It is a far thinner and more structural idea.

As a final point, I also want to stress that at this point we are talking about crisis *tendencies* and not full-blown crises. This is a very important distinction, which we owe to Marx, who was careful to insist that crisis tendencies do not always or normally manifest themselves as actual acute and overt crises.

Universal theory of history

Jaeggi: I'm very sympathetic to your idea of "disavowal," which one could easily retell in a Hegelian–Marxian mode. After all, it was Hegel who spelled out how bourgeois society makes individuals independent of each other and frees them from certain traditional connections, but, at the same time, it makes certain dependencies even stronger. Being atomized, everyone depends on certain kinds of infrastructures such as the market, ironically leading to a condition where everyone depends on everyone *even more so* than in traditional communities. And then bourgeois society would be, to paraphrase Marx, a *"Zusammenhang der Zusammenhanglosigkeit"* – a connection of disconnectedness or a context of contextlessness. This idea that there is some kind of connection and dependency that at the same time is denied is central to my own approach as well. So I'm all for the formal account that you seem to be aiming at, because I don't think a thick ethical account will do the work, and I don't think an essentialist account of various spheres of social life will help us.

Still, I would like to push things a bit further: if the "disavowal" of the relations of dependency between institutionalized spheres is something that is so characteristic for institutions and social practices in capitalist societies, the next step would be to spell out why this disavowal is so problematic. You could say there's always something we deny or don't see, in one sense or another. There may even be reasons to claim that certain disavowals or invisibilities are "necessary." Why would this be problematic?

I was thinking about these different spheres and capitalism as a certain kind of *Gestalt* – that there is a certain kind of "shape" capitalism brings to these spheres. These separations are specific to capitalism; politics and economics were intertwined in a different way in precapitalist or pre-modern societies, as were family relations,

155

personal relations, and so on. But there is also a certain perspective from which you might claim that the kind of sphere differentiation capitalism institutionalized is itself a kind of solution to some pre-existing set of problems. There was a certain dynamic that came out of feudal societies, and at a certain point there was a need to institute a separation – for example, between polity and economy. Or, if not a "need," there were preconditions for further development that required a new set of relations among these various activities. After all, it's very hard to imagine an industrial society based on the feudal idea of the household or the "great chain of being." One could see these separations, such as the differentiation between spheres of polity and economy we find in capitalism, as a response to some previous set of problems or crises, just as you could see these regimes within capitalism coming up with solutions to the problems that come out of that separation. That would be my perspective.

Fraser: Two points: first, I'm not saying that disavowal is always necessarily problematic. But I do claim that when you put it together with the other two Ds (division and dependence), as capitalism does, then you are asking for trouble. The overall conjunction is what's problematic – because, as I said before, it is self-destabilizing. It installs a set of crisis tendencies in the deep structure of capitalist society.

Second, I'm sympathetic to your suggestion that capitalism's peculiar institutional topography can be viewed as a solution to a general crisis of a previous (precapitalist) society, at least in Europe. Some historians (Marxist and otherwise) have tried to spell out that idea. But I would say that that claim only makes sense as a retrospective reconstruction. And I'd be wary of efforts to generalize it into a universal history or grand narrative that purports to lay out, once and for all, the crisis tendencies of human society as such. There are social theorists who have tried to do that. But I'm not one of them.

Jaeggi: I'm not engaged in a substantial account of human history either. But I am interested in the conceptual and theoretical groundwork and the overall *theory* of history, society, and human action that is at stake. It seems to be a worthwhile enterprise to re-think historical materialism while rejecting its all too simple deterministic versions. This problem-solving approach I'm suggesting is meant to be a very general attempt to understand the dynamics of human societies – a kind of pragmatist version of historical materialism. The existence of crisis and an understanding of history in terms of crisis-driven dynamics would then apply to (human) history as such, not only to capitalism. Capitalism and its crises are then a special case and, maybe, an instance of a distorted dynamics.

For Marx's historical materialism, historical development is crisis-driven all the way down, but then it takes on a certain contradictory form once we reach capitalism. Understanding the broader historical dynamics as they are driven by the material needs of social reproduction – needs that at the same time are social needs, historically and normatively imbued – still seems to be crucial for understanding processes of social transformation. At the same time, getting back to the normative standards of critique, it seems a way to avoid normativistic approaches on the one hand and contextualistic or relativistic ones on the other.[37]

Fraser: Possibly. There is a strand in Marx that appears to posit a universalist philosophy of history, centered on the forces and relations of production and so on. I'm not so wild about that side of Marx. I think he is at his best as a critical theorist, analyst, and diagnostician, who's revealing to us the crisis tendencies built into *capitalism*. So I'm going to plead agnosticism about these other phases of history. It may be worthwhile, for a variety of reasons, to reconstruct a broader theory of history on a grander scale, but, even without such a theory, I still think we can say something very interesting about the ways in which capitalist societies have their own specific, deep-seated or inherent tendencies to crisis.

Every regime of accumulation within capitalism's history must deal in one way or another with the system's inherent tensions between economy and polity, production and reproduction, human society and non-human nature. If a regime has any staying power – any ability to sustain itself historically over a period of time – then that is because it has found ways to soften or finesse these contradictions. Maybe it's even at times found ways to make something positive out of these tensions – to "make lemonade out of the lemons." But these "solutions" are necessarily provisional. They don't definitively overcome the contradictions, which remain constitutive of capitalist society.

You said before that capitalism's inherent dynamism ensures that it doesn't simply reproduce itself in a static way over time. Rather, it regularly releases new energies and forms of life. I agree. But I would add that it does so in ways that tend in the course of time to create new tensions along the institutional fault lines that I've diagnosed. The effect is to create suffering for those who live in capitalist society and to incite them to engage in boundary struggles. Neither the suffering nor the struggles are wholly contingent. They are responses, rather, to deep-seated structural dynamics.

Blockages and learning processes

Jaeggi: I would, again, push things a bit further with respect to the normative but not normativistic foundations for our critique. I would say that what makes this kind of disavowal problematic is the way it leads to blockages of experience. It blocks learning processes – it hinders our ability to come up with adequate solutions to certain kinds of crises, because it blocks out the resources we need to experience our situation in a sufficiently rich way fully to grasp the problems we're confronting.[38] We both know Alistair MacIntyre's 1970s essay on "epistemological crises and narrative," where he talks about how the rationality of history is always constructed "retrospectively."[39] There is a certain, somewhat deflationary version of a materialist theory that we could recover through this idea of retrospective narratives of problem-solving, which might serve as the alternative between an ultra-essentialist account and a superficial one unable to locate deep-seated crisis. In other words, if you were to come up with a narrative and reconstruct the story of problem-solving with a view to these second-order questions about resources, as a way of conceptualizing and understanding these problems (as I suggested in my book on forms of life), then we could have criteria for judging whether certain solutions and certain ways to understand or react to a crisis are adequate or not. This would be something that is not ethical or about the good life in a decontextualized or Aristotelian sense regarding the character of these spheres, but it would also ground our normative judgments of the dynamics we observe – judgments, that is, of their rationality or irrationality. We could spell out, for example, how the regime of liberal competitive capitalism was a certain kind of answer to antecedent problems that stabilized the situation for a period of time, which it certainly did; and we should also be able to assess why, in retrospect, this was still a solution based on a characteristic blocking of experience, a characteristic disavowal of the kind of connectedness that these spheres in capitalism institutionalize. So this is the general outline of how this alternative mode of reasoning could come up with normative foundations for a critique, as well as criteria for how social struggles might be adequate or inadequate in the face of crisis.

Fraser: This is quite interesting. You've posed an important question: "Why is it problematic that capitalism characteristically disavows the dependency relations it institutionalizes?" And your answer puts a slightly different twist on this problematic of disavowal than I have given it – and than I would want to give it. It's not that I disagree with your answer, but I think it may be one-sided. The issue is not in the first place that disavowal blocks us from solving problems; it is that it *produces* problems. My answer to the question of why the disavowal of dependency is problematic is that it leads to structural problems. The disavowal is *itself* destabilizing: it leads to runaway climate change, it leads to insane time crunches that make people feel they have to do things like express breast milk while they're driving their car to work or freeze their eggs while they pursue a career. In other words, the triad of Ds (division, dependence, disavowal) is problematic because it's inherently destabilizing; it ensures that capitalism is always eating its own tail. That's "Part A" of my answer.

But there is also a "Part B," concerning your claim that the disavowal of dependencies blocks learning processes. I'm assuming that when the structural side gets severe enough, the chances increase that disavowal breaks down. In such moments, learning processes accelerate and get cranked up a notch or two, so that people begin to think that maybe the established paradigms are not up to the job. In short, I don't know whether capitalism blocks learning processes, but I am sure that it blocks implementing solutions once they're discovered.

Jaeggi: I would say that blocking learning processes or experiential processes does more than block solutions; it blocks us from even understanding what the problem is. Blocking learning and experience renders a whole realm of social experiences no longer accessible. I should also be clear that I'm not talking about individual learning processes or even just collective learning processes; I would put these processes on the structural or systemic level. This is about the systematic learning processes that a given society goes through or doesn't. Runaway climate change and denial, acquiescence to extreme time crunches – this all would be relevant to what I would call learning processes. You could also call it a dynamic version of understanding certain kinds of dysfunctionalities. It's about the capacities of a form of life to make sense of the contradictions posed by its own social practices and to transform itself accordingly.

Fraser: Well, if it's true that capitalism blocks us from learning, then we're in trouble. I would invoke the Marxian idea that the "new society is gestating with the old." That's a way of saying that "learning" is nevertheless going on, at least beneath the surface. And that in turn suggests to me that capitalist society may offer more openings for critique than meet the eye.

In any event, the story of disavowal in capitalism must have two parts. The first part should enlighten us as to how economy's disavowal of its dependence on non-economic background conditions generates objective blockages, such as climate change. The second should clarify how those disavowals affect our capacities to interpret and respond to those blockages – or rather, how they affect the problem-solving capacities of differently situated people in capitalist society – because some people understand very well what others deny.

Jaeggi: I'm all for the objective blockages; it was only an attempt to give an answer to why disavowal is problematic. If you want to bring this in as a formal standard, then you have to explain what's wrong with disavowal.

Fraser: I understand, but let me clarify an important point. Disavowal in its capitalist form is problematic because of its place in a larger complex that destabilizes its own conditions of possibility. Moreover, disavowal in capitalism is directly tied to "the law of value": to its economy's need for "inputs" to which it accords no economic value and for whose reproduction it does not pay. That's the *specific* form of *capitalist* disavowal (or disavowal-cum-division-and-dependence) that makes this form of life so crisis-prone. I believe we agree about that!

Latent crises and problem-solving /

Jaeggi: We both support a crisis approach and the idea of developing a crisis critique of capitalism. But one problem we have to deal with is that it's not so easy to spell out where a crisis starts and where the "normal" dynamics of every social formation in every society ends.

For me, one of the interesting things about a crisis approach is that you can come up with the idea of a "latent crisis," a "crisis in latency," or "crisis tendencies" without having to rely on the givenness of social struggles and conflicts that are already in the open. It's a way of theorizing about deep conflicts and deep crisis, and it allows us to make judgments about the social order that are not superficially reliant on a social movement showing up at a certain point or moment. This is a definite advantage of a crisis approach that distinguishes between latent crises and crises that are already articulated in social struggles and conflicts. The second advantage of a crisis critique is that, insofar as it is also a version of immanent critique, it transcends the distinction between a merely contextualist and a freestanding, context-transcending mode of critique. The moment of "crisis" disrupts a merely internal framework since what happens in a moment of crisis cannot be denied and cannot be integrated in a certain context or framework. We may agree or not about certain sets of norms, but the fact that at some point our social practices and institutions disintegrate, collapse, become dysfunctional, or don't make sense anymore – even if it's still a matter of interpretation that this is the case – cannot easily be dismissed. This is a moderately "realist" but also pragmatist point, referring to the Deweyan idea that problems and crises can neither be invented nor denied. There are real dysfunctionalities and hindrances in play, and disavowal here has real consequences. As with the birthgiving and diaper-changing example you gave earlier, there is a sense of facticity, of matter-of-factness involved. In some sense, then, "crisis" is located at the border between the external and the internal, between the subjective and the objective, and between the observer's perspective and the participant's perspective.

But the reference to crises also raises two questions. The first, which goes along with some of the questions we've already raised, is: "How 'latent' can a crisis be?" If a certain regime is stable for over 300 years, can we still talk about deep contradictions and crises? This relates to the question of what role social struggles still play in a crisis critique. My take on it would include a point Anthony Giddens once made on social crisis and conflict: that at a certain point a crisis has to become manifest; it has to be actualized as a social conflict.[40] Granted, one could allow for certain kinds of conflicts being "hidden" – not fully articulated because they are suppressed, hampered by collective action problems, or otherwise prevented from making themselves visible. But we still have to figure out how to distinguish the normal dynamics of capitalist society from its crisis dynamics. It's simply not credible to say, "Okay, superficially, everything seems to be fine – everyone is happy and the economy works well – it's just that *we* still see a deep conflict and underlying crisis." The second question is about the normative direction of the dynamics of crises. Even if a given crisis erupts into conflict and leads to some kind of radical transformation, not every transformation is a progressive or emancipatory one. We are back then to the question of the normative direction of social change.

161

Fraser: I sympathize with the motive behind your question, which I take to be the boy-who-cried-wolf problem. There's a kind of absurdity in the posture of those who repeatedly announce the imminent collapse of capitalism, and meanwhile everything carries on just as before. You're absolutely right to be wary of a crisis diagnosis that remains entirely theoretical and never manifests itself overtly in any way. So I agree with Giddens's idea that a crisis tendency must at some point actualize or express itself in an overt crisis, and in some form of social conflict.

On the other hand, I have to say that the objection is itself too "theoretical." After all, it's not as if the last 400 years of capitalism have been smooth and crisis-free. I would insist that there is plenty of empirical historical evidence that capitalism is inherently crisis-prone and has been experienced as such. So I would frame the problem differently: the question is not the actuality of capitalist crisis, but the capacity of capitalism to resolve its crises (at least temporarily) by reinventing itself in ever-new forms. That to me is a far more serious problem for critical theory than the worry that crisis tendencies will remain forever latent.

In any case, if we want to clarify the general grammar of the concept of crisis, I would return to the distinction you just mentioned between the *observer's* perspective and the *participant's* perspective. I'm very glad you brought up MacIntyre's essay. It played an important role in my doctoral dissertation many years ago because it gave me a way to think about the observer's perspective that is not itself outside of history and that can therefore be linked up with the participant's perspective. Applied to our problem, we can say that there is something inherently retrospective in the process of understanding crisis dynamics: looking back, with the benefit of hindsight, we see that there was a regime, that it entered a crisis, that a new regime developed and replaced the old one, that the successor regime provided a way of dealing more or less successfully with problems that its predecessor was unable to solve.

This MacIntyre-ish account fits well with an idea that we share, according to which a regime generates problems that it is unable to solve and that can cumulate to the point of crisis, both structural and lived. The question then arises as to whether and how the social struggles that arise in response to this crisis can in time develop sufficient breadth and vision to forge a counterhegemonic project capable both of transforming society and of successfully resolving extant problems. I agree with MacIntyre that we only discover the answer retrospectively, through our ability to narrate the historical transformation as a successful case of problem-solving. This is primarily a matter of according intelligibility to social transformations. We assume there is a possibility of retrospective intelligibility through this kind of narration, even if there is no way in advance to definitively "know." I suggest that we hit on a successful model of retrospective intelligibility in history in chapter 2, where we narrated the history of capitalism as a path-dependent sequence of regimes of accumulation. In that account, each regime ran into problems it couldn't solve, generating forms of social conflict that coalesced in such a way as to give rise to a new regime.

Of course, this is stylized history. As critical theorists, we are not interested in how the past "really was" – *wie es eigentlich gewesen.* What we want, rather, is a broader historical narrative, which orients us in the present – a narrative that clarifies how we got here, what we're facing, where we want to go, and how we might actually get there. We are situated, as Arendt famously put it, "between past and future." Here, accordingly, the observer's perspective shades into the participant's perspective and leads eventually to the question of social struggles. But we have to be careful in thinking about how participants invoke the term "crisis."[41] That term is available and widely used, largely thanks to Marx, but it is often used very loosely. We hear of a "crisis of doping" in international sports, for example, but that's not the concept of crisis we have in mind. We need to distinguish between loose crisis talk and the kind that interests us, which is when social actors come to believe not just that things are going badly, but that the current form of social organization is constitutionally incapable of fixing them – and that they themselves have the capacity and the responsibility to change it. There have been historical periods when many social actors came to that view. Those times were doubtless chaotic, roiling with competing diagnoses and conflicting programmatic ideas, including from those who sought to defend the faltering order. In situations like these we are no longer faced with "normal" dissatisfactions and "normal" conflicts, but with "crisis" in the emphatic sense.

We should also return to the idea of a "general crisis," which I introduced in chapter 2. When many different strands and interpretations of crisis converge, it makes sense to speak of a general crisis of the social order. In that case, what we face is neither "merely" an economic crisis nor an ecological crisis nor a political or social crisis, however serious each of these might be in and of itself. It's rather an overarching "crisis complex" in which all those strands come together.

But once again, we must qualify the point. It's entirely possible, after all, for people to think they're in this sort of crisis, while in reality the social order proves capable of resolving it. In that case, it turns out that social actors misjudged their situation. But the converse is also possible. People may not think they're in a crisis – believing, for example, that climate change can be staved off by carbon trading. And they too could turn out to be wrong, even if almost everyone believes it at the time.

Then, too, we need to problematize the terms "everyone" and "almost everyone," considering how widespread the belief in crisis is and which sectors of society hold it. Of course, there's always dissent in society, but the crucial question is whether the dissent cumulates, coalesces, and rises to the level of a *crisis of hegemony*. In that case, an objective system crisis is conjoined with a legitimation crisis in which the participants have come to believe that they cannot, will not, and/or don't want to go on in the same way – that they have no confidence in the normal patch-it-up mode of problem-solving and are seeking a deep-structural transformation.

Jaeggi: Again, with MacIntyre, there is the "normal" course of problem-solving and there is "epistemological crisis," a situation in which the framework itself collapses. The latter asks for more radical ways of transformation, but both cases involve dynamics of crisis and problem-solving. You, of course, make an analogous contrast using Rorty's distinction between "normal" and "abnormal."[42] But my point is that even the most radical revolution is a discontinuity *within* continuity, because even radical change doesn't come out of nowhere but is occasioned by a crisis *within* history. And with respect to the normative direction of these transformations, I would argue that emancipatory transformations are those that provide an adequate, and therefore non-regressive, answer to the problems posed and the crises undergone. I admit this sounds quite formalistic, and we would have to spell out criteria for adequate versus non-adequate solutions to a crisis. But this already brings us to our next chapter.

4

Contesting Capitalism

Class struggles and boundary struggles

Jaeggi: Let's talk about what follows from our broader view of capitalism for the question of social struggles. The traditional Marxist idea was that *class struggle* is the most characteristic and potentially emancipatory form of conflict in capitalist society. This was based on a certain conception of history and the way capitalism was organized. You've argued that what we are faced with today are *boundary struggles*, a view that is drawn from your broader account of capitalism as an institutionalized social order. How do boundary struggles relate to the idea of class struggle?

Fraser: It's true that my view of capitalism implies a different account of social struggle from the one widely associated with Marxism. By conceiving capitalism as something larger than an economic system, it renders visible, and intelligible, a broader spectrum of social contestation than orthodox paradigms do. Let me mention three specific ways in which the view of capitalism as an institutionalized social order enriches our understanding of social struggle.

First, this view discloses the structural bases in capitalist society of axes of domination other than class. We saw, for example, that gender domination is built into capitalism's institutional separation of production from reproduction; also, that domination along axes of race, nationality, and citizenship is inscribed in its separations of exploitation from expropriation and of core from periphery. This helps to explain why struggles along these axes arise so frequently in the course of capitalist development. That can only appear as a mystery to approaches that equate capitalism with its official economy

165

"excludes struggles over unwaged and expropriated work"

and identify its primary injustice with capital's exploitation of wage labor. The mystery dissolves, however, when capitalism is viewed as an institutionalized social order premised on foreground/background divisions. Seen that way, struggles against racism, imperialism, and sexism respond to forms of domination that are every bit as real, unjust, and deeply anchored in capitalist society as those that give rise to class struggles. Perfectly intelligible responses to structural harms, they are neither expressions of "secondary contradictions" nor embodiments of "false consciousness." So that's the first way in which my perspective expands our picture of social struggle in capitalist society: it discloses the salience of struggles along axes of domination other than class.

But that idea is complicated by a second one, which casts doubt on the standard definition of "class struggle." For orthodox Marxists, such struggle is centered on the conflict between labor and capital, where labor is defined narrowly as waged work, especially in industrial factory settings. Those who do this work appear, along with the capitalists who employ them, as the paradigmatic protagonists of class struggle. The iconic site of such struggle is "the point of production," where the two sides meet face to face. Struggles that originate there are thought to nurture the most advanced class consciousness and to be most likely to become revolutionary. They are supposed to pose the deepest challenge to capitalism and to have the greatest potential for emancipatory social transformation.

I find this view of class struggle problematic because it excludes struggles over unwaged and expropriated work. The latter are not counted as class struggles, just as those who perform such work are not counted as "workers." On my view, by contrast, the "hidden abodes" that support wage labor are domains of socially necessary work, while the propertyless people employed in those domains are "workers" whose struggles should count as class struggles. This holds for those who replenish and reproduce the labor power on which exploitation depends; for those who cultivate resources that are confiscated and funneled into accumulation; and for those who sustain the habitats and historical natures on which commodity production relies. Granted, their struggles often occur far from the point of production and are typically shaped by other axes of domination, including gender and race. But they are often directed against fractions of the capitalist class and its political agents; and they concern processes that contribute at least indirectly to the accumulation of surplus value. Capitalism, broadly conceived, entails an expanded view of "the working class" and an enlarged understanding of "class struggle."

"an enlarged understanding of "class struggle""

There is also a third way in which my view enlarges our view of social struggle in capitalist society. Inspired in part by the thought of Polanyi, it treats capitalism's constitutive institutional boundaries as likely sites and stakes of struggle. What I have called "boundary struggles" emerge not from "inside" the economy, but at the points where production meets reproduction, economy meets polity, and human society meets non-human nature. As nodes of contradiction and potential crisis, these boundaries are both sites and stakes of struggle: at once locations where conflict erupts and objects of contestation. No surprise, then, that struggles over nature, social reproduction, and public power arise so regularly in the course of capitalist development. Far from constituting a theoretical embarrassment, they are deeply grounded in the institutional structure of capitalist society – as deeply grounded as class struggles in the narrow sense. They cannot be dismissed as secondary or superstructural.

In all three of these respects, therefore, an expanded view of capitalism entails an expanded view of social struggle in capitalist society. This point is of very great practical significance. On the one hand, we should expect to encounter multiple forms of structurally grounded social conflict, all of which represent, at least in principle, pertinent responses to capitalist crisis and potential sources of transformation. On the other hand, the struggles in question are heterogeneous and do not automatically harmonize or converge on a single trajectory, as class struggle was supposed to do in the orthodox view. Practically speaking, therefore, my view of capitalism offers both expanded prospects and intensified challenges.

Jaeggi: The concept of "boundary struggles" strikes me as a productive one. And I find the whole tableau you are offering really fascinating. But I am still trying to figure out whether it amounts to an *addition to* or a *replacement of* class struggle. There were certain strands in early critical theory that suggested this latter notion – giving up on the proletariat as the motor of history, as it were – though who would take its place remained an open question (Marcuse, with his focus on new needs and marginalized groups, was the only one who had a new revolutionary subject in mind[1]). In any case, it's clear that you don't stand for that gesture, so what is the relation between boundary struggles and class struggle in your account? Is class struggle a form of boundary struggles? Are boundary struggles a form of class struggle?

Fraser: It follows from what I just said that boundary struggles are neither additions to nor replacements for class struggles in the narrow sense. Rather, this concept belongs in the same conceptual framework as the expanded view of class struggle I just outlined, which also includes struggles over unwaged and expropriated labor, including social reproduction, and over the natural and political conditions that support it. Boundary struggles overlap with and entwine with class struggles in this expanded sense, just as they overlap with and entwine with gender struggles and with struggles over racial oppression and imperial predation. In fact, I would say the distinction is in large part a matter of perspective. To use the expression "boundary struggles" is to focus on the way in which social conflict centers on and contests capitalism's constitutive institutional separations. To use the (expanded) concept of class struggle is, by contrast, to focus on the group divisions and power asymmetries that correlate with those separations. In many cases, if not all, one and the same social struggle can be usefully viewed from both perspectives. In fact, I would say that in such cases it *should* be viewed from both perspectives. To see it exclusively through the lens of class (or, for that matter, of gender or race) is to miss the underlying structural-institutional features of capitalist societies with which domination is entwined and through which it is organized. But the converse is also true. To view such a struggle exclusively from the boundary vantage is to miss the social fault lines and relations of domination to which those institutional divisions give rise.

What I'm saying is that the distinction between class and boundary struggles is analytical. In the real world, many social conflicts contain elements of both. To understand them adequately, critical theorists need to bring both perspectives to bear, asking for any case: Are both boundary and class (or gender or race) divisions in play? If so, do the participants recognize and thematize both aspects? Or do they focus exclusively on one – for example, by stressing the class (or gender or race) elements and glossing over the boundary elements, or vice versa? Are those two elements set in tension with one another or are they harmonized? When we look at struggles in this bi-perspectival way, we gain access to a whole new set of questions, which allow us to probe "the struggles and wishes of our age" in a deeper, more critical way.

Recall our discussion, in chapter 2, about struggles over social reproduction. We spoke there about the tendency of early capitalist industrialization to undermine possibilities for family life; about the provisional solution afforded by social democracy; and about the latter's unraveling in contemporary financialized capitalism. At each stage, the boundary dividing social reproduction from economic production emerged as a major site and central stake of social struggle. The contestation in every phase fits squarely within the category of boundary struggles. But those struggles intersected with and were overdetermined by the fault lines of race/ethnicity, gender, and class, now understood in a broader sense.

This is clearly the case today. In the present conjuncture, we encounter at least two distinct class responses to financialized capitalism's weakening of the boundary between social reproduction and economic production. At one end of the spectrum, we find the responses of the poor and working classes, who scramble as best they can to care for their families in the interstices, while working long hours at multiple low-wage McJobs. Some of them have joined populist movements that promise to protect them from a social machine that eats up their time, their energies, and their ability to sustain social connections and to reproduce a common life that they can recognize as good – or even human. At the other end, we find the responses of the professional–managerial strata, who embody the high-end variant of the two-earner family, in which qualified women pursue demanding professions, while subcontracting out their traditional carework to low-waged immigrants or racial/ethnic minorities. The result, as I said before, is a dualized organization of social reproduction: commodified for those who can pay for it, privatized for those who cannot, with some in the second group performing it for very low wages for those in the first. Those at the upper end move more of their lives onto the economy side of the boundary – the paid work side – while those at the lower end shift more of their responsibilities onto kin and community networks, which means to the unpaid side. At both ends, struggles erupt over and at the boundaries separating society, market, and state. And these struggles are overdetermined by questions of class. Under the right conditions, the class dimension could become explicit, disclosing the imbrication of class struggles with boundary struggles. And that is in principle how things should be. In fact, I would say there is something wrong if a struggle with a clear class dimension is not politicized in these terms. Important aspects of the situation are distorted or suppressed if the class dimension doesn't become explicit.

Jaeggi: This raises the possibility that social movements can emerge but fail to address these kinds of tensions and contradictions in a certain vocabulary. Would you say that all these conflicts and contradictions *must* be expressed as class struggles if they are to be rightfully expressed?

Fraser: My answer is "yes" and "no." When the class element of struggles is suppressed – say, by something in the prevailing political culture – and does not become an explicit focus of struggle, then something is wrong. Among other things, this opens the door to scapegoating and other regressive forms of political expression. But that doesn't mean that every social struggle must be expressed *only* or *above all* as a class struggle – at least not in the narrow, orthodox sense.

In the example we were just discussing, the class element is deeply intertwined with a strong gender element. As we know, the capitalist division between production and reproduction has historically been a gendered division, and the fallout from this initial gendering by no means disappeared, but has rather been remade, in different periods in capitalism's history. This division is also cross-cut by dimensions of race, ethnicity, and nationality as well, as it's largely immigrants and people of color who are saddled with the low-paid precarious carework that was previously the unpaid responsibility of middle-class White women. But to say that the problem has a crucial class element does not mean going back to some oversimplified view that class is the "real" issue, while race and gender are epiphenomenal. On the contrary, I would also insist on the converse of what I just said about class: when the gender and race/ethnicity/national dimensions are suppressed, something has gone deeply wrong.

Jaeggi: There seem to be dimensions of boundary struggles that can't be covered by the vocabulary of class, where it just wouldn't make sense to translate it into a class struggle.

Fraser: Well, as I just said, gender and racial/ethnic domination are just as pervasive and deeply entrenched in capitalist society as class domination is. So, we really should expand your question to encompass those social fault lines as well. In any case, I will respond by returning to our discussion in chapter 3 about the need to integrate several different genres of critique. The implication there was that there are multiple, overdetermined reasons for criticizing capitalism's major institutionalized separations, reasons embodying all the various strands of critique we discussed in that chapter. One of the reasons I stressed refers directly to class: capitalism entrenches normatively unjustifiable structures of domination along class lines – but, also, along other cross-cutting axes: gender, race/ethnicity, nationality. That was the "moral" critique of capitalism, which targets its inherent injustice or unfairness. But the two other reasons I gave don't refer directly to class – nor to any other relations of domination. First, capitalism's way of organizing social life is inherently prone to crisis in several respects: ecological, economic, political, social. That's the so-called functionalist critique. And, second, capitalism subjects everyone, not just the dominated, to the blind coercive force of the law of value and deprives all of us of our freedom to organize our life-activities and consciously to establish our connections to past and future generations and to non-human nature. That's the "freedom" critique.

As I said, neither the functionalist nor the freedom critique refers explicitly to class – nor, for that matter, to race and gender. Crisis and heteronomy affect everyone. And yet they nevertheless carry class subtexts – but also race and gender subtexts. The most acute expressions of crisis fall disproportionately on the poor and working classes, especially on women and people of color; and it is those populations who are most disadvantaged by the denial of collective autonomy. That suggests to me that, while the three critiques are analytically distinct, the conditions they target are thoroughly inter-imbricated in social reality. Practically speaking, then, the class injustice question cannot in the end be definitively separated from the crisis and freedom questions. All must be addressed together – as must capitalism's other major axes of injustice, including gender, race/ethnicity, and imperialism.

Jaeggi: We both reject giving an "essentialist" account of boundaries, whereby some given criteria such as "the conditions of human nature" can be used to dictate how various spheres should be separated or related to each other, and to delimit the proper domain of each. But if we've rejected the essentialist version, doesn't this mean that even a "classless society" (were we to get there) would still have to feature legitimate ongoing political conflicts about boundaries? These conflicts may take place under different conditions, but it seems there would still be one part of what it means to live in a democratic society that involves constantly having to negotiate and renegotiate these boundaries, even if the problem of class has been resolved.

Fraser: I fully agree that a classless, democratic society would not be a society without tensions, disagreements, or conflicts. And I would add that such a society would provide its members plenty to disagree about: for example, our relation to non-human nature, the organization of work, its relation to family and community life, as well as to political organization (local, national, regional, global). In fact, such

171

disagreements would be more explicit than they are now, because these matters would be treated as political questions, to be submitted to democratic resolution, instead of being stealthily devolved to capital and to "market forces" protected from challenge by pre-existing, non-negotiable boundaries. But that's the point. Capitalism's institutional structure removes all these issues from democratic contestation and resolution. And, even on those occasions when it does permit us to entertain them, the terms of debate are grossly lopsided – tainted by all the fault lines of domination we've been discussing, not to mention public spheres dominated by corporate for-profit media and by the penetration of private money into elections. So, while a postcapitalist alternative would not (indeed, should not!) eliminate such contention – and would probably in fact increase it – it would assure far fairer terms for processing and resolving disagreements.

Of course, that still leaves open the question of what a postcapitalist alternative should look like. It is often said – and I agree – that critical theory cannot fully pre-decide this. Many specific features of a "good society" must be left to the imagination and desires of the participants. But still, some things are clear. First, no acceptable "solution" can come off the backs of any given identifiable stratum of the population, whether defined by class, race/ethnicity, or gender, or by any other entrenched relation of domination.

Second, the economy/polity relation is especially crucial, and must be considered with nuance and care. On the one hand, we need to take on board Marx's famous critique of the way that division operates to protect capital in a bourgeois society. I am thinking especially of his essay "On the Jewish Question," where he criticized a "merely political" emancipation that expels the entire economic process from the precincts of political life, while also glossing the resulting domination as "democratic."[2] This critique is often reduced to the idea that Marx didn't value bourgeois rights and dismissed them as just another layer of ideology. Frankly, I find this reductionist reading irritating, because that wasn't his point at all. I think it is a very powerful and telling critique, which must inform our critical theory of capitalist society.

Nevertheless, our critique must also be informed by a counter-consideration, which I draw from the experience of "really existing socialism" of the Soviet type. Those regimes tried simply to "liquidate" the capitalist division between polity and economy, establishing command economies directed by the Party-State; and that proved truly disastrous in many senses. We might draw the lesson that we can't live with the existing capitalist form of the polity/economy division, but nor can we live by liquidating the latter entirely. We need to consider alternatives to both those extremes: for example, democratic planning, participatory budgeting, or market-socialism, combining "political" and "economic" forms of coordination. I recall a brilliant essay from 1988 by Diane Elson that outlined some extremely interesting ideas about this.[3]

The Left needs to devote much more attention to such questions. And the same is true for parallel questions concerning the production/ reproduction division and the human society / non-human nature division. Those divisions too cannot be simply liquidated. Rather, they need to be creatively re-imagined in ways that detach them from domination, enhance collective autonomy, and render the life-forms they structure less antagonistic vis-à-vis one another.

Boundary struggles and contemporary social movements

Jaeggi: Let's shift our focus to the nature of these boundary struggles on their own terms. What are these struggles about in relation to these institutionalized separations and spheres? We can understand the idea of a boundary struggle in a couple of ways. One account would come very close to Habermas's colonization thesis. We have these various institutionalized spheres – economic, political, reproductive, etc. – and boundary struggles occur when one sphere "invades" another and this other is trying to push back. But we could also envision a more radical kind of boundary struggle. On this account, the struggle wouldn't be just a matter of protecting the lifeworld from colonization or, say, the political sphere from the economic sphere (we've already discussed reasons to find this image problematic). Rather, it would be more pro-actively about the "shape" of these spheres, where to draw or re-draw the lines between them, or whether even to have a line at all. As we noted earlier, the feudal order did not have the same kind of separation between economy and polity, state and society. It's a specific feature of bourgeois-capitalist society that the economy is viewed as something distinct, and it is against the background of this initial boundary-drawing that certain disavowals are ideologically established to make the market economy appear as if it were fully independent.

So, which is it? Do boundary struggles have to do with fighting off invasion across an otherwise clear boundary, or is it a struggle over whether it would be reasonable to draw the line differently, to repoliticize the economy or to bring economics back into a richer mode of social life?

173

Fraser: All of the above. Boundary struggles come in many flavors, including the ones that you just elaborated. They can be *defensive*, aimed at repulsing an invasion, incursion, or slippage across a boundary, which is experienced as problematic. Defensive struggles arise in cases where people are more or less satisfied with an existing or past arrangement that's being eroded and find themselves "pushed too far into a corner." They want to shift the boundary back to where it was before. But that does not exhaust the concept. There are also *offensive* boundary struggles. The neoliberal project was precisely aimed at extending the domain of matters subjected to an economizing logic of market relations. And some anti-systemic movements have responded offensively, not by trying to defend the old boundary, but by trying to push it further in the other direction, so as to bring matters previously treated as "economic" into the domain of the "political."

But we could also distinguish boundary struggles in other terms. For example, I would distinguish between *affirmative* and *transformative* boundary struggles. I first introduced this distinction in another context,[4] but I think it is useful here as well. By an affirmative struggle, I mean one whose proponents assume that a given institutional boundary should exist in more or less its present form, while insisting that it is currently situated in the wrong place. They want only to shift its location. By contrast, those engaged in transformative struggle maintain that the problem is not just the boundary's location but its very existence, its character, or the process by which and by whom it was drawn. They want to change the arrangement's deep structure, if not to abolish the boundary altogether.

I should add that the affirmative/transformative distinction is more complicated than it first seems, because of the possibility of "non-reformist reforms." That was Andre Gorz's expression for struggles that are affirmative by any strict measure, but that nevertheless give rise to transformative effects because they alter relations of power and thereby open a path for further struggles that become increasingly radical over time.[5] Struggles over the economy/polity boundary are especially susceptible to this dynamic. Initially modest-seeming reforms aimed at conquering more ground for democratic politics can set in motion a democratizing logic that picks up speed as it goes along, leading eventually to a major transformation of capitalism's structural-institutional order.

I should also mention struggles over whether a given boundary should be "hard" or "soft," impenetrable or porous. Also "meta" struggles over the processes by which boundaries should be drawn. All of these questions could easily invite transformative answers.

174

But the point is that boundary struggles come in a variety of forms. Everything I have mentioned here (and more!) counts as an instance of boundary struggle.

Jaeggi: So, this seems to be a distinction about the radicalness of the struggles in question, which is simultaneously linked to their normative assessment. It is fair to say that Marxists have at times gone overboard in trying to label which movements were "on the right side of history" and keeping pace with the development of the means of production. Only these could be emancipatory, and all the others would be deemed regressive. Even Marx was not immune to this kind of thinking, even if he, later on, arrived at a more differentiated picture. You seem to start from a situation of greater ambivalence from the outset. So, would you say that, with an eye on boundaries, we will always encounter struggles that have multiple faces at once?

Fraser: Actually, I haven't yet said anything at all about how we should make normative assessments of boundary struggles. And in fact, as I shall explain later on, I would not recommend that we approve or disapprove of them according to how radical they are. Here, however, I am making a different point – which is that boundary struggles come in different kinds: they can be defensive or offensive, affirmative or transformative. But the same is true of class struggles. They too are all over the map: in some cases, defensive; in others, offensive; in some cases, affirmative – as, for example, when they seek shorter hours and higher wages; in other cases, transformative – as when they aim to transform property relations and the process by which surplus value is created and distributed. Both boundary struggles and class struggles admit of a variety of different forms and degrees of radicalism.

We could develop this point by returning to the previous discussion of "liquidationism," by which I mean projects aimed at eliminating a boundary altogether, such as the Soviet effort to liquidate the polity/economy division. We can see that as one extreme on a spectrum. The other extreme is "prohibitionism," in which social actors aim not only to establish a boundary but to make it virtually impenetrable. In US history, the term is associated with the Temperance Movement, which sought to prohibit the sale and consumption of alcohol. But we could also use the term for those feminists who seek to outlaw all commodification of sex, reproduction, and carework, or for those "deep" ecologists who oppose all buying and selling of land or mineral wealth and so on.

175

Jaeggi: So, the lesson is that the more transformative and "boundary-smashing" types of struggle are not automatically the more emancipatory ones. Where would you situate yourself between these extremes of liquidationism and prohibitionism?

Fraser: Right. Some transformative claims are quite unsavory. Fascist states sought to instrumentalize reproduction in ways that were at once deeply transformative of established boundaries and utterly regressive. Conversely, some affirmative claims are normatively justified – for example, campaign finance reform. What this shows is that normative assessments depend on other considerations – for example, on whether proposed boundary revisions would mitigate domination, enhance freedom, and promote the right kind of social security.

But you asked about liquidationism. I myself would not recommend complete liquidation of capitalism's constitutive boundaries, as I already explained. Nor would I support full-out prohibition, which is usually defensive and essentialist. I'd focus instead on the process of boundary-making, militating for a new, more democratic way of drawing boundaries. And I'd also support multiplication of possibilities. This entails thinking about what it might mean to soften, harden, or relocate institutional boundaries. It also requires weighing the pros and cons of doing things in one way versus another. Right now, capitalism already does all this for us. These questions have been taken out of our hands, and part of what it means to have a more radical or transformative way of thinking about the current crisis is to raise the question of boundaries to a higher level of conscious, collective self-determination. What exactly we decide upon is one thing, but that it should be a matter of collective self-determination is something else.

And the fact is, there are many useful ways in which we can think about boundaries and the struggles that can be waged over them. I'd say we have a lot to learn from social and political geographers who work on the dynamics of "spatialization." They distinguish "hard" from "soft" boundaries. They highlight not only what boundaries separate but also what they connect. Critical theorists should take such insights on board.

All of this is grist for my central argument. As an institutionalized social order, capitalism is centrally built on the construction and transgression of boundaries. It follows that any politics that seeks to reform, reject, or surpass capitalism must place the boundary question front and center.

Jaeggi: So, your model gives us a lot of possibilities, but it also leaves us with a rather messy picture. I want to press you further about the socio-theoretical and normative issues at stake. And perhaps we can use the Habermasian position as a foil. Habermas's colonization thesis revolves around a struggle over the boundary between lifeworld and system, and it is framed in such a way that the relevant boundary is, normatively speaking, already in place. For Habermas, there is a type of defensive boundary struggle that is normatively permissible, or even required, since there are parts of the lifeworld in which the system shouldn't intervene. By contrast, offensive struggles aimed at eliminating the functional differentiation of modern society would be pre-modern, regressive, potentially even bordering on fascism. In his view, we need both the lifeworld and the system, and we need the boundary to keep each in its proper place.

I've mentioned before why I find this account fundamentally flawed, on a number of grounds. At the same time, Habermas's framework is at least able to provide us with a clear-cut way to distinguish regressive from emancipatory boundary struggles. It is this feature that gives Habermas's thesis a certain normative impact, which I do not yet see in your account of boundary struggles. How might we derive a comparable standard from your account? This is what I mean when I say you leave us with a somewhat messy picture. We've agreed that we don't want to rely on an essentialist view of these spheres and boundaries, but how do we determine what kinds of radical boundary questioning are emancipatory and what kinds are not? You seem to imply there is no clear-cut distinction. Even struggles aimed at re-drawing the line between certain spheres can be legitimate from an emancipatory point of view – that is, they do not *have* to be pre-modern in a "bad" or regressive way. So how do we decide which are the regressive or emancipatory moments? How do we distinguish "progressive" from "regressive" struggles and social movements without some kind of a normative standard?

Fraser: I agree with the premises that underlie your question. I agree, first, that Habermas establishes a pre-given, a priori normative boundary, which can be breached from either of two directions: from the system side, as when administrative or market forces begin to colonize the lifeworld; or from the lifeworld side, as when radical socialists or anarchists seek to "de-differentiate" those institutions and thereby to "regress" and surrender the "achievements of modernity." Either way, a fundamental imperative, rooted in the very nature of things, is violated. Like you, I reject that approach. I also agree,

177

second, with the conclusion you draw from that point. Once we reject the Habermasian solution, we have to find an alternative basis for assessing the emancipatory potential of various movements, political programs, and ideas. So far, so good. Failing that, our critical theory lacks critical force. So, yes, I agree. Evaluative criteria are essential.

In fact, the view of capitalism I've offered here provides three normative criteria for distinguishing emancipatory from non-emancipatory claims about capitalism's boundaries. As I've already explained, the first criterion is *nondomination*. Capitalism's institutional separations entrench deep-seated relations of domination, along lines of gender, race/ethnicity, and class. No proposal to revise those institutional boundaries is normatively acceptable if it reinforces or exacerbates such domination. The nondomination principle rules out proposed alternatives that institutionalize the subordination of a designated group or groups of social actors.

The second criterion is *functional sustainability*: any proposal has to be sustainable. It has to be able to become institutionalized in a social order with the capacity to stabilize itself over time. It can't be set up in a way that generates constant turmoil, and it can't be premised on dynamics that lead it to destabilize its own preconditions of existence. We don't require (or want!) perfect, rigid stability, of course. But we do need sustainability.

The third criterion is *democracy*. Any acceptable proposal must be able to be institutionalized in such a way that participants remain able to reflect on it, question it, decide whether it's working for them or not, and change it if necessary.

My view is that the three criteria should be used together, as a toolkit. To be acceptable, a proposed structural transformation must satisfy all three. I suspect that, if we apply them in that way, we'd discover that some projects that today present themselves as emancipatory do not in fact pass muster.

Jaeggi: This is certainly a helpful toolkit, and I do like the mix of deontological, functional, and quasi-ethical requirements. Still, I'm concerned about the somewhat "external" and freestanding character of it. I'm still convinced there might be a more immanent approach that involves looking directly at the very dynamics of these struggles. We might be able then to assess the emancipatory potential of these movements by referring to their regressive or non-regressive dynamics. The framework of a crisis analysis should give us a clue here. Boundary struggles do not spring up out of nowhere; they are motivated by problems and crises such that existing practices and institutions "no longer function," because they erode their own resources for sustaining themselves or they run up against problems or contradictions they cannot resolve. And, as we discussed in chapter 3, we might distinguish adequate and non-adequate ways to address a crisis in terms of learning processes or the absence of learning blockages.

Fraser: Well, I remain eager to see how you develop your intuitions about learning processes and learning blockages. But I don't see anything freestanding or external about my proposal, which *does* derive from the framework of a crisis analysis. The contents of my "toolkit" flow directly from the account I gave of capitalism's crisis tendencies in chapters 1 and 2. What I said there was that boundary struggles respond to crisis tendencies of the Polanyian type that are inherent in capitalist societies. They respond, that is, to the built-in tendency of a capitalist economy to destabilize its own "non-economic" background conditions of possibility: social reproduction, public power, sustainable natures, and a habitable planet. In crisis periods, the established regime of accumulation loses its ability to soften and defuse these contradictions. Processes and relations that seemed unproblematic before now appear dysfunctional, unjust, and/or bad, and become subject to contestation. Drawing on the normative resources available to them, social actors invoke ideals, values, and principles that are entrenched in the institutional order they inhabit: especially, principles of freedom, equal citizenship, and the public good associated with the political; ideals of care, mutual aid, and solidarity associated with social reproduction; values of harmony, sustainability, and stewardship associated with socioecology; and norms of rationality, equal exchange, and choice associated with economy. These normative resources are embedded in the very texture of social life in a capitalist society, which is why they are accessible to its inhabitants. But, in crisis periods, people use them in a different and potentially explosive way – not just to dispute specific actions within a given, "proper" sphere, but to impugn social relations elsewhere, in the "wrong" sphere, or to problematize the divisions between spheres. These claims themselves must be vetted, not simply taken at face value. The criteria I just evoked for that purpose (nondomination, functional sustainability, and democracy) are themselves generalizations of the first-order norms that participants use – which means that they too are accessible to them. Far from being freestanding or external, they stand in a relation of immanence to capitalist society, even as they also have the capacity to point beyond it.

Jaeggi: There's no denying that your criteria are perfect for engaging in a normative heuristic of existing social movements. Since, as you said, the picture is complicated, we could try and spell this out with respect to existing social struggles and movements. Why don't we start with anarchism, which has become quite trendy among young leftists in the Global North?

Anarchism

Fraser: That's a good starting point, with the potential to yield some important insights. The forms of neo-anarchism I encounter these days, including among some of my students, seem to me to fall short on all three criteria. That's clearly the case with the functionality criterion. Just imagine applying that test to the Occupy Wall Street-type of encampment, which is a "constant meeting," where everything is decided by consensus, with no voting, no leaders, and no organizational structure. If this practice is intended to prefigure a new form of societal organization, it is hard to see how it could be sustainable over time, given the burn-out factor. And the practice also falls short on the non-domination criterion, as it privileges those who are in a position to invest lots of time in assemblies – people who don't have day jobs, children, or other demanding commitments – while providing no way to protect the interests of those who do have such commitments and cannot participate continuously. Obviously, this runs afoul of the democratic criterion as well. But perhaps what I'm saying here is not fully fair. Perhaps we should distinguish anarchism as a program for restructuring social organization from anarchism as a transitional organizing modus.

Jaeggi: Yes, we should consider anarchism from both of those angles. And we shouldn't be too hard on the Occupy movement, which had to organize everything necessary to sustain a lengthy stay at Zuccotti Park. Moreover, some of the issues you raised are not specific to anarchism; they are problems for social movements in general. Grassroots movements are complicated to organize, especially in the face of outside pressure. Present-day society is hardly amenable to just setting people free for a while to get organized and mobilized. All types of movements involve people who are under various kinds of constraints. I would say there are a lot of anarchist experiments today that are actively trying to find different solutions to the problem of domination, with efforts to devise ways of avoiding certain kinds of

180

Critique of "coalition"

gender structures and various kinds of hierarchies, as well as efforts to think about alternative forms of representation beyond traditional, "bourgeois" forms. There are also attempts to deal with the problem of involving people who don't have the same amount of free time as students, who are typically the most active in these kinds of projects.

Fraser: You may be right that I underestimate the level of awareness of these problems and the thoughtfulness with which they have sometimes been treated in the anarchist tradition. But I still have criticisms of anarchism both as a form of organizing and as a program. As a form of organizing, the anarchist strategy tends to be more about evading, circumventing, or working around power than about confronting it head-on, and I don't believe there can be any major structural change that doesn't actually confront power. Confronting power requires counter-power, and counter-power requires organization. How are you going to take the fight to the multinational corporations, to the militarist hegemonic powers, or to the WTO if you insist on spontaneity at the cost of organization? It is as if we've gotten this idea that, since we disapprove of the Leninist party model of organization, we should do away with organization altogether. That's a complete *non-sequitur*. I'm not invested in defending a particular organizational solution here. But I do want to insist that there's a huge amount of room between vanguardist organization and no organization. Movements that are serious about social transformation need to explore that in-between territory.

Jaeggi: Again, it's not that this concern is absent from these discussions. There has been a lot of work put into the problem of single issues and how social movements can link up or reconnect to address the broader picture. Some of these discussions even go under the label of "addressing the question of organization anew," inventing new forms of organizing that critically reflect upon the failures of the old, avant-garde types of organization and its authoritarianism, while trying to come up with modes of effectively organizing resistance to power.

Fraser: Fair enough. But let's not exaggerate the fruits of these discussions, which, as far as I know, haven't actually generated viable answers. One symptom is the constant appeal to the term "coalition" in contemporary social movement circles. That term is truly ubiquitous. Truth be told, however, it serves more as a placeholder for an organizational strategy than as an actual strategy. Its use is only very rarely coupled with serious reflection on the programmatic basis of a given coalition or the specific forms of coordination its practice requires. What is the relation between a coalition and a political party or a trade union? Can social movements "in coalition" replace or circumvent the need for unions and parties? There's very little real discussion of these issues.

The constant stress on "movements" as opposed to parties or organizations is itself a clue that something has gone wrong on the organizational front. After all, we live in an era where social movements erupt in spectacular ways, occupy public space, capture public attention, and then suddenly disappear without leaving a trace. *Podemos* in Spain is an exception: they've tried to convert the *Indignados* movement into an actual political party. I'm not idealizing them, but that's a very interesting effort. I say this in the context of another symptom: the widespread "NGO-ization" of politics. In recent decades, the NGO has become a substitute for the party or the organization. This is highly problematic for many reasons that have been widely noted, first and foremost by Sonia Alvarez.[6]

Another idea is a "movement of movements." That was the self-understanding of the World Social Forum, which was an impressive effort to create a public space for communication among a vast array of disparate struggles against neoliberalism across the globe. Impressive as it was (or, possibly, still is), the WSF remained deeply divided over what exactly it meant to be a "movement of movements." Should the WSF be an umbrella? Should anyone be able to speak for it? Should it adopt a programmatic vision of "another world?" Should it develop a strategic view about how its constituent movements might coordinate their struggles? Or should one simply sit back and wait for all of that to emerge spontaneously? These are key organizational questions. And I'm sorry to say that the influence of neo-anarchism (including among many who would themselves disclaim that label) has hampered our efforts to answer them.

Jaeggi: We can give these experiments a lot of credit for trying to resolve these organizational problems – after all, these problems can't be solved from the armchair but only in practice, through trial and error – and yet we can still say that some versions of anarchism fall short as a political and theoretical program. As a project for re-shaping the basic institutions of society, the anarchist program can still be accused of naïveté for failing to take sufficient account of the coordination needs of modern industrialized society. For example, there is a certain kind of small-scale communalism that has become fashionable again. But if we don't want to turn back from the mode of production and level of development we have achieved, then this kind of strategy is simply not an option. Also, the idea of affecting change by localized, "pre-figurative" politics ties in with that old-school Marxist critique that anarchist collectivism ultimately becomes a "petit-bourgeois" form of practice, because, however non-hierarchical its internal organization, each collective will still be an enterprise competing with others on the (free) market. In the end, these collectives just end up replacing individuals and firms as the main actors in what is otherwise the same market system – that is, unless some additional overarching structure can be instituted which regulates the relations between actors.

Fraser: I agree. To me, it is inconceivable that we could have a desirable society, whether capitalist or postcapitalist, that does not give a major role to planning. *Contra* orthodox Communism, planning can and should be democratic. It does not require a *nomenklatura* or rule by a class of technical "experts." But how can we possibly deal with an issue like climate change without some very large-scale planning? A systemic blockage of that scale cannot possibly be left to this little collective or that little collective. *Contra* anarchism, the ecological crisis does not arise from too much organization, but rather from too little. Granted, some issues are best addressed locally, but others require large-scale global planning, and even global governance structures. I don't know whether Marx and Engels were serious about the state "withering away," but I don't see how that's possible if, by "the state," we mean democratically accountable institutions that deploy public power to coordinate social interaction in ways that inhibit perverse, unintended effects.

Moreover, having large-scale forms of governance does not mean we can't also have movements toward more localized forms of production and collective management. I am very strongly in favor of locavorism in terms of food. But I would insist that it's only by having in place the right kind of large-scale global governance and organization that we can create the conditions under which devolution to the local is possible. National social democracy was possible, after all, only thanks to the Bretton Woods international framework. We would need an analogue of that to make locavorism possible in a way that is coherent, sustainable, democratic, and just. Failing that, there's no avoiding domination – as, for example, when people with access to good soil have plenty to eat, while those in the desert go without.

183

De-growth movements

Jaeggi: One thing I took from our previous discussions is the idea that, were we to define the kind of socialism that we would endorse, a very good formula would be: it's democratic control over the social surplus. This posits a deep internal relation between economy and democracy. It doesn't simply mean democratic control of the capitalist tiger, or the democratic taming of the tiger; instead, it's actually "within" the tiger itself. In other words, if we are involved in decisions about what we produce, how we produce, and where we invest the social surplus, then we are no longer just regulating the economy from the outside but transforming the economy from within. This is a radical transformation of what capitalism is, and I'm very happy with this formulation.

I also take it that you would still favor some form of industrial society. The "de-growth" movement has gained quite some momentum, and it could be seen as a model boundary struggle, putting ecological concern, but also personal life, before the imperatives of the market and competition more generally. Not all, but some, of those activists favor some notion of de-industrialization. But you appear to take industrial society as a matter of fact: this is what we have reached, this is what we are confronted with, and there will be no socialism that is not a transformation *within* industrial society. You also mentioned that even local production and distribution can only work if we have some kind of overarching framework. So, I would be interested in what you would grant to at least some kind of de-growth idea, because this is one of the major discussions in the anti-capitalist Left right now.

Fraser: As you know, I spent fall semester of 2016 at the research center on "Post-Growth Societies" in Jena, Germany. As that name suggests, they reject the term "de-growth" in favor of "post-growth." And that distinction really matters. The first thing I learned when I got there is that "post-growth" does not mean that society should not grow, still less that it has to shrink. The idea is rather that society should not be built on a hard-wired growth imperative, which operates as a blind necessity or irresistible "force of nature," pre-empting the possibility for *us* to decide whether or not to grow, how much and how fast to grow – which is, of course, precisely what capitalism does. That's already an interesting subtlety, and I think it makes good sense.

However, we should also consider what exactly is meant by

"growth" in this discourse. What precisely should be growing or not growing? In capitalism, what must necessarily grow is not human wealth or well-being but *capital*. That interpretation of growth (that capital must grow endlessly and without limit) is one that we should forthrightly reject. But it doesn't necessarily follow that we should be producing less, especially in light of the huge levels of deprivation and poverty in the world. The real question is not *how much* is being produced but *what* is being produced, and how and to whose benefit. These so-to-speak qualitative questions are the heart of the matter. We cannot confine ourselves to questions framed in exclusively quantitative terms, such as "growing" versus "not growing."

We also need to unpack what we mean by "industrial society." I'm happy that some things I use are produced industrially; other things, not so much. For example, I'm glad airplanes are industrially produced. I wouldn't want to board one that somebody just built out of their garage; I'm glad there are standards, regulations, controls, and inspections aimed at ensuring their durability and safety. Food, however, is another matter. I'd be glad to see the end of industrial farming of animals and of mass production of genetically engineered crops. Once again, we should focus on the qualitative question: *Which* goods are we talking about? How is their production organized, and by whom? Is someone profiting from it at the expense of others? Is the work safe and rewarding, or is it demeaning and deadening? Is it democratically organized? Is surplus being extracted from it for the benefit of corporate shareholders? Does it rest on a hidden abode of unwaged and expropriated labor? Is its energic basis ecologically sustainable?

What I'm getting at is that the phrase "industrial society" doesn't adequately capture what's important. Nor does the category of "growth." In my view, you can't be "for" or "against" these things. You need to use other terms to get to the real questions.

Postcolonial, decolonial, and indigenous movements

Jaeggi: To continue with social movements and struggles – for quite some time now, there have been profound critiques of Western modernity within the Left. On the level of theory, this has come by way of postcolonialism. But there are also indigenous movements that many on the Left sympathize with, and these may not fit easily into your idea of socialism as democratic control of the social surplus. They might not want the kind of industrialized society and state

185

institutions you support, even if they are qualified by "de-" or "post-growth" ideas. The Left has had to undergo an important learning process as it comes to terms with the notion that it's not as easy as Marx thought, and all these "pre-modern" kinds of upheavals and movements are responding to a certain kind of discontent that might not just wither away once we've defined the problem in socialist terms and forwarded a socialist solution. Granted, we haven't achieved socialism yet, so we don't know how these concerns would be addressed and would be solved in different ways. Yet it could still be the case that our ideas about socialism rest on a sectarian conception of modernity, which is biased against legitimate and desirable views of a good life.

On the other hand, I don't mean to endorse those exaggerated critiques that insist that all received ideas about equality, non-domination, democracy, or freedom are still in the grip of the "imperialist" tendency to homogenize forms of life that are radically different, and these forms of life must be allowed to rely on their own kinds of knowledge, drawn from their own traditions, practices, and cultural forms. I would, of course, grant that we cannot and should not pretend to be "in the same boat" with those whose perspectives and experiences have been neglected through the legacy of colonialism and imperialism. But an adequate solution cannot be one that effectively replaces the asymmetry produced by colonialist ideology with another asymmetry brought on by the restriction of analysis and judgment for the sake of avoiding ethnocentrism. Here I strongly sympathize with Uma Narayan's observation that "refusing to judge" is no solution, as it can all too easily turn into yet another "'Western' gesture that confirms the moral inequality of Third World cultures by shielding them from moral and political evaluations that 'Western' contexts and practices are subject to."[7] If that's right, as I believe it is, then the real task is to foster transcultural critique and dialogue, which doesn't refrain from judging forms of life but is very cautious to do this on an equal footing.

What is your position here? I ask not only because these movements have an important presence worldwide, but also because there is a substantial portion of the contemporary Left that reflects upon and even leans toward this kind of critique.

Fraser: I agree entirely with your view of these matters, including the last point about the need for real debate on an equal footing – although that is easier said than done. But let me make two further points. The first has to do with the relation between capitalism and cultural pluralism; the second, with asymmetrical power. I credit the first point to Hartmut Rosa, who argued in a brilliant early paper that capitalism itself is a major obstacle to cultural pluralism.[8] Despite its self-proclaimed dedication to "choice," capitalism's logic is to flatten differences by "culturalizing" them, treating them as consumer or lifestyle options arrayed before us in a tantalizing way, while concealing the fact that all are sitting on a shared platform built around the imperative of maximal accumulation of capital. And that changes the character of the "choices." The constraints of that system are so strong and pervasive that the chance to pursue qualitatively different forms of life is severely restricted. The conclusion I draw is that, while socialism may not be a sufficient condition for a genuine (and desirable) form of cultural pluralism, it is very definitely a necessary condition.

The second point, about asymmetrical power, follows from the same premise about the power of the capitalist world system. It is very unhelpful, in my view, to presume a sharp dichotomous line between "modern Western" civilization and "pre-modern non-Western" societies, as if "Western civilization" were unitary and had emerged autonomously from the head of Zeus, untouched by interaction with "non-Europeans"; and as if the latter's societies were themselves pristine, not already entangled with global forces, in ways both relatively benign and downright lethal. So, if the issue is where we stand now, we need to situate it in relation to the history of capitalism. Capitalism didn't create transregional interaction, of course, but it certainly accelerated and deepened it, and, even more important, it gave it a distinctive shape – both by creating the geography of core and periphery and by establishing the mutually imbricated dynamics of "development" and "under-development." (I am thinking of Walter Rodney's cogent formulation, *How Europe Underdeveloped Africa*.[9]) Here, too, in other words, the imperialist-capitalist world system forms the inescapable frame of reference because (among other things) it generates both "cross-civilizational" fertilization and stark asymmetries of power, which must be thought together.

I understand that some thinkers and activists reject the perspective I'm sketching as itself imperialist. But I'm convinced that that is mistaken. Far from being an external Western imposition, it has been pioneered by thinkers and activists from the Global South – above all, by those who have engaged deeply with supposedly "Eurocentric" frameworks such as Marxism. From what I can see, many of the most interesting recent efforts along these lines are coming out of Latin America – probably because of the strength and sophistication there of both Marxism and indigenous movements. When democratizing, anti-neoliberal movements are informed simultaneously by both those perspectives, sparks fly. In the Andean countries, for example, those movements united urban European-descended populations with indigenous populations behind the Quechua expression "*sumak kawsay*" (usually translated as "*buen vivir*" in Spanish), which suggests non-exploitative relations with nature and among human beings – hence, a "good life" not structured by capitalism's constitutive divisions. And they used this catchphrase in an interesting way: not to demand preservation of traditional life forms, but rather to transform present-day capitalist society for everyone's benefit. They used it to promote a form of life that is "modern" in the sense of being gender-egalitarian and democratic, but also ecologically sustainable, "plurinational," and freed from the treadmill of "growth." Another example is the transnational uprising of the Sioux, who joined with other First Nations peoples and Euro-American radicals in the US and Canada to oppose the Dakota Access Pipeline and other neoliberal extractive projects. In cases like these, indigenous movements are working closely with "Western" ecologists and segments of the "Euro-American" Left. Developments like these go well beyond old categories of "Western" versus "non-Western."

Jaeggi: I would say some of these movements are much more sophisticated than some of the left-wing theorists who tend to romanticize indigenous knowledge.

Fraser: Yes, that's exactly my point. But we shouldn't forget that there are also very sophisticated left-wing forms of postcolonial theory. The Subaltern Studies School was exemplary, at least in its early days, in its re-appropriation of Gramsci, and its effort to theorize the relation between class and caste. There is, in addition, the impressive body of South African neo-Marxist theory on "racial capitalism." And there are towering works that are harder to classify, such as Dipesh Chakrabarty's *Provincializing Europe* and Paul Gilroy's *Black Atlantic*.[10] All of those thinkers have staged deep encounters between elements of the Western Marxist tradition and contexts where capitalist development was more expropriative than exploitative, premised as much on status oppression as on class domination in the narrow sense. One doesn't need to agree with every word to recognize the profundity and importance of such works. I intend my own expanded account of capitalism, which encompasses expropriation as well as exploitation, as a contribution to this strand of critical theorizing.

188

I'm less enthralled, I must confess, with the current of postcolonial thought that is centered on "*de*-coloniality." At least some proponents of this approach seem to imagine that it is possible (and desirable!) to "purify" indigenous culture, to purge the "Western" influences that have "contaminated" it, and thereby to return to something "pristine." And that seems unhelpful to me.

Jaeggi: But how would you characterize these kinds of movements within the expanded conception of capitalism? One could tell a story of Western modernity, which prioritized colonialism and imperialism, but which saw them much more as enterprises of political expansionism and outright domination than, say, driven by the logic of capital. Where do anti-imperialist and indigenous struggles feature on your map of boundary struggles?

Fraser: Here I would recall our discussion of racial and imperial oppression in chapters 1 and 2. There, I analyzed those phenomena as stemming from the joint, overdetermined logic of "the economic" and "the political." Utilizing that double lens, I interpreted expropriation as simultaneously a mechanism of accumulation and an apparatus of domination, premised on politically enforced hierarchies of status. The thrust was to refute the idea that we must choose between economic and political accounts of capitalist imperialism. It is not an either/or but a both/and. On this point, I'm in agreement with many theorists of imperialism and the capitalist world system, including Arendt, Harvey, Arrighi, and Wallerstein.

But it is not just theorists who appreciate this point. Many anti-imperialist struggles have incorporated a double focus, targeting both the economic and political aspects. And many other movements, whose ostensible focus is elsewhere, have an anti-imperialist dimension that encompasses both of those poles. All these activists know very well that capitalism has never lived from exploitation alone, that the exploitation of workers in industrial production in the countries of the core always rested on massive expropriation of cheap energy (including human muscle power), land, raw materials, and other inputs from the periphery. They appreciate too that this remains the case today. Even though the new geography of financialized capitalism has scrambled these distinctions to a considerable degree, illegitimate transfers of value continue in many forms old and new, imperial and neo-imperial – just recall my discussions of environmental load displacement and care deficit displacement in chapter 2. For me, this context is crucial for understanding the stakes of indigenous and

189

postcolonial struggles and for assessing their emancipatory potential. Whatever solutions they (or we!) propose can only be evaluated with this global history in mind.

The triple movement

Jaeggi: Later, I want to talk about *regressive* responses to capitalism. To prepare the way, let's concentrate first on the conceptual level. You've been drawing heavily on Polanyi's idea of a "double movement" between marketization and social protection, along with his thesis that capitalist society can be characterized as an ongoing conflict between these two poles. But you suggested that we revise his idea and think in terms of a "triple movement," which would add an axis of emancipation to Polanyi's original two. I take it that, in order to avoid regressive answers to the disintegrative effects of marketization, we need to include the emancipation pole. How does this triple movement between marketization, protection, and emancipation figure into the question of social struggles as boundary struggles?

Fraser: I didn't realize this until fairly late, but I now see that my concept of boundary struggle owes a lot to Polanyi. He doesn't use that term, of course, but his "double movement" really fits the bill: it's a struggle over the boundary between "economy" and "society." While some social actors seek to extend market logic deep into society, others aim to hold the line. In effect, the struggle is about where economization should stop: one side thinks there are virtually no limits, while the other wants to wall off communities, relations, and habitats whose integrity is threatened by market incursions. In Polanyi's view, the marketizers were the revolutionaries while the protectionists were the conservatives. And yet his sympathies lay squarely with the latter.

But, as I've said before, Polanyi's model is premised on a simplification of capitalism's institutional structure and of the conflicts that structure generates. He allows only for two possibilities: either one is for economy and marketization, or one is for society and social protection. He narrates a substantial chunk of the history of capitalism, from the early nineteenth to the mid twentieth century, in terms of this one fault line, tracing the conflict between free-marketeers and social protectionists. As he tells it, the whole of this epoch centers on that conflict, which progressively sharpens until everything goes up in flames with the rise of fascism and the outbreak of World War II.

190

This is problematic in several respects. On the social-action level, Polanyi overlooks a number of epochal struggles that raged throughout the nineteenth and twentieth centuries: struggles for the abolition of slavery, the emancipation of women, and the overthrow of colonialism and imperialism. These struggles do not fit either pole of the double movement: they sought neither to defend society nor to extend the market. Most aimed rather to overcome entrenched systems of domination, whose grounds did not lie exclusively in one or the other of Polanyi's two domains but rather in the overall institutional configuration of capitalist society, especially in its constitutive divisions of production from reproduction, economy from polity, exploitation from expropriation, core from periphery, and human society from non-human nature. So I think we should understand them as instantiating a third, analytically distinct pole of social movement, which I have called "emancipation." The upshot is that, where Polanyi saw a double movement, I think the reality was (and still is!) a triple movement, in which movements for social protection collide not only with projects of marketization but also with struggles for emancipation.

Jaeggi: Okay, I see the problem on the social-action level. But I gather you think Polanyi's approach also has weaknesses on the social-structural level.

Fraser: Yes, I do. The problem is that his category "society" is really a catch-all, an ill-defined blanket term for everything other than the market economy. As a result, his picture of capitalism's institutional structure is over-simplified. By positing a stark dualism of economy and society, which implies a single boundary, he misses capitalism's triad of constitutive institutional separations (economy/polity, production/reproduction, and human society / non-human nature) and overlooks the complex of boundaries associated with those separations. Certainly, Polanyi was interested in what we would call ecology, social reproduction, and democratic politics. But his conceptual framework clarifies neither their place in capitalist society nor the crisis tendencies associated with them. So, I suggest we replace his dualistic, economy/society view with the expanded conception of capitalism outlined here. In that case, we'd end up with three analytically distinct loci of boundary struggle, each of which attracts contestation in the form of a triple movement.

Jaeggi: Some might say that, by enriching Polanyi in this way, you also take away some of his radicalism. In a certain way, "emancipation" has a place in his picture, as one of the two world-historical resolutions of the struggle he had in view: he speaks of socialism and contrasts it with fascism. Could you say a bit more about how inserting emancipation as a strand into the movement gives a less Manichean picture with multiple tensions and effects of synergy?

Fraser: It's true that Polanyi was very invested in promoting an emancipatory resolution of the crisis he wrote about. But I don't think that his conceptual framework was up to that task. The whole thrust of his analysis, however unintentional, was to counterpose a warm, integrated "society" to a bad, disintegrative "economy." By contrast, he offered no resources for distinguishing socially integrated forms of life that are premised on domination from those that are not. And that left his evident preference for socialism as just that: an ungrounded subjective preference. So I would dispute the claim that, by explicitly introducing the category of emancipation, I am taking away his radicalism. I would say, rather, that I am strengthening it, by supplying the concepts needed to ground it.

But that is not all. By introducing a third, emancipatory pole of social struggle, I am also clarifying how radicalism might emerge in capitalist society. I've used the triple movement to parse conflict scenarios in terms of "two against one." For example, I take social-democratic state-managed capitalism to have devised a new way of synthesizing the two poles that Polanyi understood as mutually incompatible – namely, marketization and social protection. But, as I explained in chapter 2, this synthesis was based on the sacrifice of emancipation; it was built on women's dependency through the family wage, on racial/ethnic exclusions, and on ongoing imperial expropriation. So, it was an alliance of two against one: marketization and social protection against emancipation. In due course, as we saw, that arrangement broke down, and it was replaced by a different two-against-one scenario, which is distinctive of financialized capitalism: in this new scenario, marketization has teamed up with emancipation at the expense of social protection. That sounds perverse, of course, but it really does capture a situation in which mainstream liberal currents of emancipatory social movements have adopted thin, meritocratic, market-friendly understandings of equality and freedom that dovetail perfectly with the projects and legitimation requirements of leading sectors of "cognitive capitalism." It is the dominance of these sectors, including IT, Hollywood, and Wall Street, that has pulverized industry and metastasized debt, promoted austerity and cannibalized working-class living standards throughout the historic core of the capitalist world system. And all this has proceeded under the cover of progressive tropes: "multicultural diversity," "women's empowerment," LGBTQ rights.

The neoliberal project is faltering today, for reasons both structural and political. Its hegemonic alliance of emancipation and marketization/financialization has lost much of its charismatic luster. This is therefore a very good moment to envision another scenario of two-against-one, the only one that has not yet been tried: social protection and emancipation against runaway marketization and financialization. That is certainly my preferred scenario for the present conjuncture. And it grew out of my critical engagement with Karl Polanyi, as filtered through and leavened by my much longer engagement with "the other Karl."[11]

The rise and fall of progressive neoliberalism

Jaeggi: We already mentioned the possibility that social movements can be driven by the symptoms of deep-seated contradictions and crises of capitalism, but nevertheless address these questions in a way that one might count as non-emancipatory or even regressive. These movements are part of a dynamic of social struggle that calls capitalism into question, yet not only are some of these movements not emancipatory, many are quite radically *anti*-emancipatory, even fascist or fundamentalist. How do we assess this situation? Despite the attention given in 2011 to Occupy Wall Street, one could argue that, on a worldwide scale, the majority of anti-capitalist sentiment and mobilization is not leftist. This confronts us with a serious problem.

We've always had conservative critiques of capitalism; some of these express a certain nostalgia for precapitalist forms of life; others are fine with capitalist economy but object to certain forms of social modernity that accompany it. Conservative newspapers can even be more forceful and radical than some leftists in their attacks – for example, with regard to the neoliberalization of universities, since conservatives often have attachments to certain old humanist values.

Yet there are some strands committed to calling the capitalist status quo into question in a very dangerous way, and we need to ask how seriously we should take them. This is one reason why it's important, from the very beginning, to have analytic as well as normative criteria. We can't just think in terms of a simple binary that sorts the forces of capitalism onto one side and the forces against capitalism onto the other side. That's too simplistic. I know that you aim at avoiding

193

this binary in the way you draw out all the ambivalences of the triple movement, but perhaps the grid of affirmative versus transformative struggles needs to be expanded by taking stock of its sinister flip-side. This might reach from affirmation of exactly the wrong aspects of boundaries to deeply regressive inclinations to abolishing them altogether.

One such type of regressive social movement would be fundamentalism, of which there are many varieties, including different strands of Islamic fundamentalism, Christian fundamentalism, or even aspects of Modi's attempts in India to codify a fundamentalist version of Hinduism, which runs entirely contrary to the received development of that religious tradition. Another would be the forms of right-wing populism that have recently been emerging or gathering strength. We've encountered them in Donald Trump's supporters, in pro-Brexit voters, and there are a variety of other movements we've seen gain momentum across Europe, in France, the Netherlands, Denmark, and elsewhere.

Fraser: These are important and pressing questions. We certainly *do* need to understand the surge in regressive right-wing responses to the present crisis and the relative weakness of left-wing emancipatory alternatives. But let's recall what I said before: my conceptual distinction between affirmative and transformative struggles does not equate to the normative distinction between emancipatory and regressive struggles. We already agreed about that and about the need for (non-freestanding, non-external) normative standards.

If we keep that understanding in mind, we can situate both sorts of responses, the regressive as well as the emancipatory, in relation to the current context. Both oppose the boundary configurations instituted by financialized capitalism. Both reject the neoliberal commonsense that has supported that configuration: the elite consensus in favor of "free trade" (really, the free movement of capital) and corporate globalization. Both have deserted the established political parties, which upheld both neoliberal policy and neoliberal hegemony. Both left- and right-wing radical movements are actively searching for new ideologies, projects, and leadership. The result is a widespread unraveling of neoliberal hegemony.

That unraveling provides the inescapable context for addressing your question about the comparative strength of right-wing responses. The necessary first step, in my view, is temporarily to bracket normative considerations, and try to think together such otherwise heterogeneous developments as the Brexit vote, the election of Trump, the

194

surprising strength of Bernie Sanders's challenge to Hillary Clinton in the US Democratic primary, the rising fortunes of ethnonationalist and economic-nationalist parties throughout Europe, and the broad support for Jeremy Corbyn's course change in the British Labour Party. Obviously, these responses differ importantly from one another, including on the normative level. But all of them are effectively saying that neoliberalism isn't working, that there's something deeply wrong with the present way of organizing life and doing business, and that we need to replace it with something dramatically different. And that's an indication that, contrary to what I wrote a few years ago,[12] a real legitimation crisis may be brewing. The sense is widespread now that the political classes and established parties are bankrupt, that they've been captured by private interests and should be booted out. Granted, there is massive disagreement as to who and what should replace them and as to where the blame ultimately lies: Finance? Immigrants? Muslims? The 1%? But anti-neoliberal forces are everywhere on the march, openly rejecting the neoliberal project and severely weakening, if not utterly shattering, its hegemony. What emerges in situations like this is not always pretty. I am reminded of Gramsci's description of an earlier "crisis of authority": "the old is dying and the new cannot be born; in this interregnum, a great variety of morbid symptoms appear."[13] What we're seeing now are the morbid symptoms.

That's the context, in my view, for addressing your question, which I would reformulate as follows: in the void opened up by the unraveling of neoliberal hegemony, why do transformative movements on the Right appear to fare better than those on the Left?

Jaeggi: I'm a little more skeptical about whether these movements are really all somehow united in the claim that neoliberalism is at its end or should be put to its end. In Germany (as well as elsewhere) we have new ethnonationalistic or "völkisch" radical right-wing populist movements. Practically all of them are racist; practically all of them unite under some kind of anti-political correctness and anti-immigration *ressentiment*, usually accompanied by Islamophobia; some are even openly revanchist with respect to Nazi Germany. But only a minority of them is on the protectionist side of the triple movement and against marketization. On economic grounds, a great number of them are clearly defending neoliberal positions – provided, of course, that "we" get rid of the immigrants and refugees, "reclaim our country," and become "German again" (or, as the case may be, French, Polish, Hungarian, Danish, and so forth). There are a lot of inconsistencies in the various claims and programs, in Europe and worldwide. But I don't see a strict anti-neoliberal tendency at work, neither in programs nor in deeds. The strange, alarming, and disturbing thing – a tendency we still do not understand – is rather the odd alliance between economic and political neoliberalism and protectionist, nationalist, anti-modern elements. How could Trump, with his strong alliances with (not only) Wall Street and his desire to abolish what few welfare state protections there were in the US to start with, represent "the end of neoliberalism?" Isn't he rather its continuation?

Fraser: I still want to address your previous question: Why is the Right faring better than the Left in the current conjuncture? But let me try first to answer your objections to my underlying premise that there is a crisis of neoliberal hegemony. You say, first, that support for right-wing European parties is based more on racism than on opposition to neoliberalism; and, second, that Donald Trump is still governing as a neoliberal. Both points turn in part on interpretations of empirical matters. But both could also invite a conceptual confusion by leading us to conflate some important distinctions: first, the distinction between neoliberal policy and neoliberal commonsense; and, second, the distinction between right-wing populist sentiment and the policies pursued in office by those elected on the basis of such sentiment. Let me explain.

Suppose, for the sake of argument, that you are right about Germany: that the rise of the AfD (Alternative für Deutschland) has nothing to do with economic insecurity, but is strictly a matter of racism pure and simple. I'm not sure if that is really the case; I suspect that that party, like virtually all others, appeals to a heterogeneous population, whose various segments support it for different reasons. But, if you are right, that would make Germany an outlier, an exception in the current conjuncture. Elsewhere in Europe, the collapse or weakening of social-democratic and traditional center-right parties has at least as much to do with their joint promotion of "austerity," precarity, and high unemployment as with principled, hard-core racism. This is clear in France, where both the Socialist and center-right parties have bled support to the Right and the Left after trying for decades to curtail labor protections and social entitlements – a job that will now fall to a banker and political outsider who will govern without a political party. It is true, as well, in the UK, where popular rebellion against the ravages of financialization, promoted by both "New Labour" and the Conservatives, finally found a voice in the Brexit campaign, especially in the deindustrialized North. The proof, in both cases, is the striking volatility of majority-nationality working-class voters. They shifted back and forth between Mélenchon and Le Pen in France and from Brexit to Corbyn in the UK. What this shows is that, far from displaying any principled attachment to racism, the voters in question have acted opportunistically, seeking the most effective vehicle for registering protest in the context at hand.

As far as I can determine, this is the case as well in Italy, Greece, Spain, Sweden, and Denmark, where ethnonationalist movements have thrived in the wake of social insecurity following neoliberalization – forced on them in some cases by Germany, it must be said; and where left-wing vehicles for expressing protest have been weak or compromised. That these movements focus their ire on immigrants does not prove that the overwhelming majority of their supporters are incorrigible racists, although some of them undoubtedly are. Before casting all of them into the same basket of "deplorables," as Hillary Clinton notoriously did, I would want to consider what else they may want to express and what other political vehicles are available to them for expressing it. Could it be that fear of immigrants expresses the not-so-far-fetched anxiety that things are out of control?

It's another matter, in any case, what such right-wing populist movements will do if and when they come to power. If the past is any guide, the politicians they elect will make deals with global finance to continue neoliberal policy in some other guise. But that does not refute the claim that the sentiments fueling their rise are anti-neoliberal. It simply underlines the point that a collapse of neoliberal hegemony does not by itself entail the end of neoliberal policy.

The poster child for this point is the United States, the only country in the Global North outside of east-central Europe where an anti-neoliberal ethnonational movement has come to power – or, rather, seemed to. You are right, of course, that, since assuming the presidency, Donald Trump has failed to pursue the economic populist policies on which he campaigned. Far from it! Having temporized on NAFTA, he has neither lifted a finger to rein in Wall Street nor taken a single serious step to implement large-scale, job-creating public infrastructure projects or otherwise encourage manufacturing. And, far from proposing a tax code reform whose principal beneficiaries would be working-class and middle-class families, he has signed on to the boilerplate Republican version, designed to funnel more wealth to the 1% (including to himself and his family). But none of this refutes the claim that he won the presidency by campaigning as a *reactionary populist*. On the contrary, this is a classic case of bait and

197

switch. Having surreptitiously replaced economic nationalism with neoliberalism upon assuming office, Trump has doubled down on the recognition front, issuing a slew of ever more vicious and exclusionary provocations. The result is that voters who thought they were electing a reactionary populist have in fact gotten something else, namely a *hyper-reactionary neoliberal*.[14] (I could go into more detail about that later, if you wish.)

Here, I want only to insist on a simple point: the fact that workers who vote for right-wing populists get betrayed by those whom they elect does not refute the idea that they are looking for social protection. Of course, many of them misconceive what it is that they need protection from – putting the onus on immigrants instead of on finance; and their understanding of what exactly it will take to protect them is often faulty. But, in voting for Trump, an important segment of working- and middle-class Americans wanted (among other things) the abrogation of "free-trade" agreements, and large-scale public infrastructure projects to create well-paid manufacturing and construction jobs. More than eight million of them, including those who delivered the Electoral College to Trump, had voted for Obama in 2012 (when he campaigned from the Left, borrowing Occupy rhetoric), and many of those had voted for Sanders in the Democratic primaries of 2016. In all three cases, these voters responded consistently to class-based distributive appeals, whereas the recognition dynamics they signed on to along the way varied widely. Thus, they too exhibited a volatility that belies the idea that they are nothing but card-carrying racists.

Jaeggi: I agree with you that these movements are a symptom of a crisis and that the usual liberal response of moral condemnation is wholly inadequate. It is not enough to say that they are morally wrong or outrageous, or that they represent an unexpected and contingent falling back from "progressive" achievements. This much is true. So, whether or not it is rightly viewed as a rejection of neoliberalism, the current wave of right-wing populism might still be understood as a symptom of some underlying crisis, problem, or contradiction within the recent development of neoliberalism, even if these movements are reacting and giving expression to it in a way that is fatally flawed. But then the question is why this reaction took the regressive, reactionary form that it did, as opposed to a more emancipatory one. This can't be explained by an egocentric pursuit of self-interest: just think of the fact that (in your country) those who are most dependent on a functioning system of health insurance and social welfare

choose politicians who are openly trying to destroy it! Some kind of
ideology-theoretical approach seems to be called for here. How does
it come about that the social suffering and indignation brought on
by the present crisis did not generate emancipatory movements but
instead gave rise to reactionary, authoritarian, and even proto-fascist
impulses? What are the mechanisms at work here? We should not
insinuate that those voting for right-wing authoritarian populism do
this without any "reason" (or, let's say, "occasion"), but nor should
we take their motives at face value. This further raises the question of
what a left-wing answer would be, and why the Left has not been able
to address these issues or offer a viable alternative.

Fraser: I agree that the dismissive response is wrong – and, I would
add, *counterproductive.* Right-wing populists *do* have genuine grievances, which deserve to be validated. And reactionary populist movements *are* responding to a real underlying crisis, which also requires
acknowledgment. The problem, as you suggest, lies in the way the
grievances are expressed, the movements' mistaken diagnosis of the
root causes, their resort to scapegoating and pseudo-solutions.

Why, you ask, have such positions become so attractive to so many
in the present context? Well, there is a lot to be said on that subject,
but one key factor is the worldwide decline of the Left in the course
of the last several decades. Newly radicalized and politicized actors
simply do not have much access to secular, left-wing worldviews that
could offer anti-capitalist and anti-imperialist interpretations of the
present crisis. And in the absence of left-wing alternatives, the Right
becomes the go-to option for those who want radical change.

But that is not the whole story. There's also a darker aspect,
which we should have the courage to explore. I mean neoliberalism's
hegemonization – or "recuperation," to use Boltanski and Chiapello's
term – of major currents of what was once the Left.[15] To say this
is to invoke a cousin of what you called an "ideology-theoretical
approach," but it is a version that owes more to Gramsci than to
Althusser or the Frankfurt School and that invites analysis in terms of
the triple movement.

Jaeggi: It's not only about the Left leaving a vacuum open for the
Right by failing to develop a good strategy. In your view, somehow the
Left has become hampered in its ability to address these issues, right?

Fraser: Yes, that's right. It has to do with the "two-against-one"
scenario I sketched before. As I said, social democracy was based

on a two-against-one alliance of marketization and social protection against emancipation, while financialized capitalism has generated an alliance of marketization and emancipation against social protection. And that second alliance has divided the social forces that a serious Left must unite. It has cut the proponents of emancipation off from the manufacturing-sector workers and rural communities who are reeling from financialization and gravitating to right-wing populism. Actually, it's worse than that. More than just cutting them off, the new alliance has set dominant currents of emancipatory movements in direct opposition to people who could (and should!) be among their most important allies in crafting a left-wing response to the current crisis.

Let me explain how this came about. In the decades since the 1970s, two different sets of struggles unfolded at about the same time in many countries of the capitalist core. The first set pitted labor against capital, which sought to break unions, drive down real wages, relocate manufacturing to low-wage regions in the semi-periphery, and precaritize work. This was an old-fashioned class struggle, which has mainly been won by capital, at least for now. But unfolding in parallel to it was a second front, which pitted the forces of emancipation (in the form of "new social movements," such as feminism, multiculturalism, anti-racism, LGBTQ rights, etc.) against defenders of "old-fashioned" family values and lifeworlds, many of whom were also on the losing end of the first struggle and resented the cultural "cosmopolitanism" associated with the new globalizing economy. Caught up in the second struggle, and largely oblivious to the first, hegemonic currents of the progressive movements dropped the ball on political economy, ignoring the structural transformations underway. Worse still, they drifted to meritocratic and individualist ways of framing their agendas – think, for example, of "lean-in" feminisms dedicated to "cracking the glass ceiling" so as to enable "talented" women to climb the higher rungs of the corporate ladder. Such currents abandoned efforts to understand gender domination structurally, as grounded in the capitalist separation of production from reproduction. And they abandoned less privileged women, who lacked the cultural and social capital to benefit from lean-in and who therefore remained stuck in the basement.

What I have called "progressive neoliberalism" emerged from the collision of those two sets of struggles.[16] Surprising as the term may sound, it aptly names the hegemonic bloc that dominated US politics throughout the period from Clinton through Obama. And there are variants elsewhere as well. In each case, hegemonic currents of

emancipatory movements (such as feminism, anti-racism, multiculturalism, and LGBTQ rights) became allied – in some cases consciously and deliberately, in other cases not – with neoliberal forces
aiming to financialize the capitalist economy, especially the most
dynamic, forward-looking, and globalized sectors of capital (such as
Hollywood, IT, and finance). As usual, capital got the better of the
deal. In this case the "cognitive capitalist" sectors used ideals like
diversity and empowerment, which could in principle serve different
ends, to prettify policies that devastated manufacturing and what
were once middle-class lives. In other words, they used the charisma
of their progressive allies to spread a veneer of emancipation over
their own regressive project of massive upward redistribution.

Jaeggi: I was always convinced that you addressed this question of
what Hester Eisenstein called *liaisons dangéreuses* with real insight.[17]
(In fact, you've always been at your best as a critical theorist seeking
to clarify "the struggles and wishes of the age.") Nevertheless, there
were a lot of people who reacted to your accusations – namely,
that parts of the feminist movement have bought into progressive
neoliberalism – by saying you're only giving half the story, that there
have always been strands of feminism that reject this connection.
Queer theory, for instance, cultivates a strong critique of established
power structures and seems very intent on criticizing its own entanglements with hegemonic projects, as in the critique of "pink-washing,"
"homo-nationalism," and so on.

Fraser: Certainly, not all feminists were won over to the neoliberal
cause. But those who were, whether knowingly or otherwise, constituted the largest, most visible segment of the movement, while those
(like me!) who resisted were confined to the margins. Certainly, too,
progressives in the neoliberal bloc were its junior partners, far less
powerful than their allies from Wall Street, Hollywood, and Silicon
Valley. Yet they contributed something essential: charisma, a "new
spirit of capitalism." Exuding an aura of emancipation, this new
"spirit" charged neoliberal economic activity with a frisson of excite-
ment. Now associated with the forward-thinking and the liberatory,
the cosmopolitan and the morally advanced, the dismal suddenly
became thrilling. Thanks in large part to this ethos, policies that
fostered a vast upward redistribution of wealth and income acquired
the patina of legitimacy.

In any case, the reaction of those feminists you describe was
defensive. What they understood as an "accusation" was actually an

attempt to understand the construction of *hegemony* – the process by which the patently regressive class project of neoliberalism gained a measure of "consent" by reinflecting and drawing in important currents of progressive movements. Need I add that it is essential to understand how hegemony works if we want to figure out how to build a counter-hegemony?

Jaeggi: Even if some of these "liaisons" are non-intentional or even at odds with what these movements were aiming for, they remain unintended consequences of social transformations taking place on a deeper level. Putting this in the framework of the triple movement gives it a lot more analytical depth than, say, Nina Power's sardonic remark that "capitalism is a girl's best friend."[18] But don't you agree that, while "Third Way" progressives like Clinton, Blair, and Schröder did their part to solidify the neoliberal project, it was figures like Reagan and Thatcher who set the whole thing in motion?

Fraser: Yes, that's right. Progressive neoliberals did not dream up neoliberal political economy. That honor belongs to the Right: to its intellectual luminaries Friedrich Hayek, Milton Friedman, and James Buchanan; to its visionary politicians, Barry Goldwater and Ronald Reagan; and to their deep-pocketed enablers, Charles and David Koch, among others. But the right-wing "fundamentalist" version of neoliberalism could not become hegemonic in countries whose commonsense was still shaped by social-democratic or New Deal thinking, the "rights revolution," and a slew of social movements descended from the New Left. For the neoliberal project to triumph, it had to be repackaged, given a broader appeal, linked to other, non-economic aspirations for emancipation. Only when decked out as *progressive* could a deeply *regressive* political economy become the dynamic center of a new hegemonic bloc.

I would stress three further points. First, neoliberalism is not just an economic policy; it is also a *political project* that strives to achieve hegemony by assembling a historic bloc. The favored strategy is to link its plutocratic, expropriative politics of distribution to a politics of recognition that can win broad support. Consequently, and this is my second point, neoliberalism is not monolithic; rather, there are progressive and regressive strands of it. The difference turns on recognition. Whereas both variants promote a distributive politics that chiefly benefits the 1%, one of them articulates that program with an apparently inclusive politics of recognition, while the other conjoins it instead to an explicitly exclusionary alternative. Finally,

202

it was especially the *progressive* strand of neoliberalism that succeeded in becoming hegemonic, defeating not only anti-neoliberal forces, but also *reactionary* neoliberal forces. The winning strategy linked a deeply inegalitarian, anti-labor politics of distribution to a modern, "forward-looking," and apparently emancipatory politics of recognition.

That was certainly the case in the United States. There, progressive neoliberalism achieved hegemony in the 1990s, when Bill Clinton assumed the presidency. Parallel formations emerged elsewhere around that time, in Latin America, Europe, and in the UK; the paradigm case was Tony Blair's "New Labour," but there was also Gerhard Schröder in Germany. In the US, the Clintonite wing of the Democratic Party quietly disarticulated the old New Deal coalition that had united organized labor, immigrants, African-Americans, the urban middle classes, and some fractions of big industrial capital for several decades. In its place, they forged a new alliance of entrepreneurs, bankers, suburbanites, "symbolic workers," new social movements, Latinos, and youth, while retaining the support of African-Americans, who felt they had nowhere else to go. Bill Clinton won the presidency by talking the talk of diversity, multiculturalism, and women's rights. Once in office, however, he walked the walk of Goldman Sachs, deregulating the banking system and negotiating the free-trade agreements that accelerated deindustrialization.

The combination of progressive recognition and regressive distribution was sufficiently powerful at least for a while to defeat the Right (the Republicans in the US, the Conservatives in the UK), whose counter-project combined regressive distribution with reactionary (ethnonationalist, anti-immigrant, pro-Christian) recognition. But the progressive neoliberal victory came at a price. What was thrown under the bus were the declining industrial centers, especially the so-called "Rust Belt," once the stronghold of New Deal social democracy, but now the region that delivered the Electoral College to Donald Trump in 2016. That region, along with newer industrial centers in the South, took a major hit as financial deregulation and free-trade policies destroyed manufacturing centers over the last two decades.

Even as those communities were being devastated, the progressive-neoliberal bloc was diffusing a recognition ethos that was superficially egalitarian and emancipatory – centered on ideals of "diversity," women's "empowerment," LGBTQ rights, post-racialism, multiculturalism, and environmentalism. However, those ideals were interpreted in a specific, limited way that was fully compatible with the Goldman Sachsification of the US economy. Protecting the environment meant carbon trading. Promoting home ownership meant subprime loans bundled together and resold as mortgage-backed securities. Equality meant meritocracy. The reduction of equality to meritocracy was especially fateful. The progressive-neoliberal aim was not to abolish social hierarchy but to "diversify" it, "empowering" "talented" women, people of color, and sexual minorities to rise to the top. And that ideal was inherently *class-specific*: geared to ensuring that "deserving" individuals from "underrepresented groups" could attain positions and pay on a par with the straight White men *of their own class*. The feminist variant is telling but not unique. Focused on "leaning in" and "cracking the glass ceiling," its principal beneficiaries could only be those already in possession of the requisite social, cultural, and economic capital.

Progressive neoliberalism was perfectly incarnated by Hillary Clinton in 2016, and it became the principal target of Trump's campaign. The whole election was, in fact, a referendum on progressive neoliberalism. If we want to understand Trump's victory, that of the Brexit campaign, and the strong showing of right-wing populist parties elsewhere we need to understand what those who voted for them were so upset about – what they were determined to put an end to.

Jaeggi: This is indeed a challenging analysis! So, what we are faced with is more than a simple backlash against women's emancipation, anti-racism, LGBTQ rights, and all the other movements. This may help explain why right-authoritarian and right-populist movements spend so much energy on discrediting the left-liberal cultural elite and minority politics. In Germany, for example, we are seeing intense attacks on "genderism" and on "politically correct," queer, multicultural elites, who are cast as rootless cosmopolitans without "Vaterland" (and now even without gender), which evokes strong memories of antisemitic stereotypes.[19] The usual left-wing explanation is that this is just rhetoric aimed at stirring up emotions, when in fact it's really about the economy and protectionist opposition to neoliberalism. But that is much too superficial. I would say your picture goes a bit deeper in that it does not dismiss either side of the phenomenon. If the problem here is not just neoliberalism but *progressive* neoliberalism, then, in an odd way, neopopulist leaders are actually picking up on something when they lash out against multiculturalism and other progressive causes. It's not just pent-up racism and it's not even simply a misplaced reaction to neoliberalism as such; rather, in the picture you're describing, these movements are targeting a real aspect of the situation. As much as we on the Left support the impulses behind these progressive movements, there is nevertheless a link we have to acknowledge between the form they have taken and neoliberalism – a kind of "alliance" – which has contributed to the situation we're now faced with. This is an important point and an interesting analysis. There is a connection to be spelled out that, in your view, brings into focus why "political correctness" might not be as absurd a target for the new Right.

Fraser: You've stated the basic idea with perfect clarity and genuine insight. The recognition side of the story is not mere ideology, but the very real self-assertion of a social stratum, whose ascension is based at once in the shift to postindustrial, cognitive, globalizing capitalism and in its own self-understanding as culturally and morally superior to the parochial working-class communities whom those shifts have left behind. So, yes, it is both recognition and distribution – or, better yet, a specific way in which those two aspects of justice got interlinked in the era of financialized capitalism. Right-wing populist movements are rejecting the whole package. And, in so doing, they are simultaneously targeting two real, consequential components of a single historic bloc whose hegemony diminished their chances – and those of their children – to live good lives.

Jaeggi: This analysis casts an interesting light on a debate that is raging in Europe. Didier Eribon and others have argued that the Left has abandoned the "social question" and should now get back to it.[20] The ensuing discussion should lead to a much-needed process of self-reflection. But I doubt that we could now simply "return" to the social question. That seems to me to underestimate the real scope and character of the crisis. After all, fighting for all-gender bathrooms did not cause the decline of the Rust Belt, nor will the abolition of political correctness solve the problems of the "abandoned poor." Nor will a simple "return to class issues" do the job. We should not become nostalgic for "traditional" working-class politics, but should take our bearing from the New Left moment – the moment when social critique and artistic critique (to use Boltanski and Chiapello's concept) have been united.[21] This is what I would call an "emancipatory" moment and a more solid ground for emancipatory politics.

Fraser: On this point, I mostly agree. Certainly, there's no going back to old-style class politics. That approach always assumed a narrow definition of class and class struggle, as I said at the outset.

205

So, I would focus on broadening what we mean by the "social question" in a way that makes visible our hidden abodes. The crisis of financialized capitalism has as much to do with ecology, democracy, and social reproduction as with the organization of paid labor. Those matters must be at the center of any left-wing politics that hopes to challenge the current regime. I would also focus on broadening what we mean by "the working class." I was very struck by the sharp contrast between the way that category was invoked by Donald Trump, on the one hand, and by Bernie Sanders, on the other. The "working class" Trump conjured was White, straight, male, and Christian, based in mining, drilling, construction, and heavy industry, whereas the "working class" Sanders wooed was broad and expansive, encompassing not only Rust-Belt factory workers, but also domestic, public-sector, and service workers, including women, immigrants, and people of color – not just the exploited, but also the expropriated and the evicted. I don't mean to idealize Sanders, who is in some ways a bit of a throwback. But his expansive view of "the working class" is already well in advance of the sectors of the Left that you just invoked.

Jaeggi: I want to make another remark, in hopes of pushing the analysis a bit further. It relates to the fact (and we agree on this) that we are confronted with, and should focus our analysis on, crisis tendencies. Even if your analysis of the "alliances" leading up to progressive neoliberalism is correct, I would still maintain that a deeper, crisis- or contradiction-oriented analysis should go beyond this level. If our aim is to locate the causes for the transformations in question (let's say, in a materialistic spirit), we shouldn't be looking at these movements and counter-movements alone. We should look also at the emergence of "cognitive capitalism," along with a political and economic dynamic that prevented the emancipatory transformation required to respond adequately to it.

You have actually spelled out the material causes for the so-called "cultural turn" earlier. And I like this approach. I would also say that what we might call "cultural liberalization" with respect to family values, LGBTQ rights, even minority rights, has become possible through deep-seated economic and social transformations. I don't want to argue for some kind of one-dimensional determinism here, since certainly the influences go in both directions. The "creative sector" and its innovative potential draws its vitality from the creative impact of new and liberalized forms of life, and vice versa: the latter, too, are made possible in part through the new social settings that unfold with a new economy, with its focus on communicative skills, cooperation, and other dimensions of neoliberal subjectivation. In other words, progressive neoliberalism is a tendency "in the world," brought about by material conditions, and it would be a mistake to reduce it to a case of misguided political judgments or wrongly chosen alliances.

Yes, social movements do have their role within the transformations in question. But they also require a certain momentum; they rely on "passive elements" (as Marx would say) and ruptures within the institutions and practices of a certain society. If both LGBTQ rights and the decline of the Rust Belt have their roots in the same process of social and economic transformation – that is, if the opening for anti-discrimination rights is the result of a transformation that at the same time leads to a crisis for industrialized regions – this doesn't put them in "direct opposition." Nor is one directly or indirectly responsible for the other. Getting rid of gendered toilets won't bring back a single job in Wisconsin. These two issues – Oliver Nachtwey calls them "horizontal" versus "vertical" equality – are not connected to each other in a direct or causal way.[22] It's only on a symbolic level, on the level of the economy of attention, that they are in competition. This is not an unimportant level, to be sure. But again, paying attention to the underlying transformations, in my view, also means that one shouldn't overestimate the role of the Left here. I would maintain this, even though I do find your analyses always very fruitful and would sign on to a substantial portion of them.

Fraser: I'm unsure whether you meant to suggest that we disagree about the importance of relating political-hegemonic analysis of social struggles to analysis of objective, systemic crisis. My own view, argued repeatedly throughout this book, is that a critical theory of crisis needs both of those levels. So, I don't think we disagree there. But perhaps we conceive the linkages between them differently.

In any case, I'm very struck by what you've just said about the "material basis" of progressivism. I like the idea of a two-way synergy between cultural liberalization and cognitive capitalist innovation. I also appreciate the idea that, while Rust Belt decline and LGBTQ rights are rooted in the same set of macro-transformations, they need not be mutually antithetical. That accords perfectly with my own strong sense that aspirations for emancipation and for social protection, which are currently posed as mutually antithetical, can in fact be rendered compatible and mutually supporting. That's actually one of the most fundamental political aims of my analysis: to disclose the possibility of a counterhegemonic alliance between the social forces that are now arrayed against one another as antagonists. But, as I said, it's only by understanding how that opposition was first constructed that we can glimpse a path by which it could be deconstructed – via a new reconfiguration of the triple movement.

I want to stress one further point about the habitus of the progressive professionals and symbolic workers whom you've just described: their confidence that they represent the advance guard of humanity's progression to moral cosmopolitanism and cognitive enlightenment. This sense of cultural superiority has been central to this stratum's identity and posture. But it also functions as a Bourdieusian strategy of "distinction,"[23] imbuing progressive neoliberalism with a superior "tone," which has devolved all too easily into moralizing, finger-pointing, and talking down to rural and working-class people, with the insinuation that they were culturally backward or stupid. It is not hard to understand why this generated *ressentiment*. The insult of status hierarchy compounded the injury of class domination. Right-wing populists like Trump have exploited that sentiment.

Jaeggi: I think you can find old-fashioned left-wing radicals who share this kind of *ressentiment* as well, I assure you! And I agree completely about the moralism and the finger-pointing. Moralism is always a sign of the weakness of the Left, of its fading out into some kind of humanitarianism.

But I think many of the activists who call out racist or sexist discourse would probably advance a different interpretation of what they are doing. I for my part agree that the gesture is often terribly moralistic. But I think we also agree that the power relations keeping racism, sexism, and homophobia in place are built on a rather intricate web of individually quotidian slurs, jokes, improper advances, and microaggressions. With this in mind, much of what appears to be moral condescension can also be read as a reflection of the kinds of social phenomena that need to be addressed; the aim is to alter power relations, not simply dole out moral blame. I also think the observable moralism is partly created by the absence of a broad movement that embodies a different praxis, and that helps set the stage for an encounter between the masses of "normal" people and some isolated liberal elites chiding them.

Fraser: I'm in agreement with your last point. To call out progressives for their condescension is not at all to imply that racism, sexism, homophobia, Islamophobia, and other forms of discrimination are unreal or unimportant. But it does suggest that much of the current opposition to those injustices assumes a shallow and inadequate view of them – that it grossly exaggerates the extent to which the problems are inside people's heads, while missing the depth of the structural-institutional forces that undergird them. Certainly, this criticism does not apply to the left-wing segments of the opposition, which represent the minority. For the broader progressive mainstream, however, it is all too apt.

Let me explain what I mean by reference to race, which remains a burning political issue in the United States. You might not know it from observing the current obsession with microaggressions, but racial oppression in the US today is not at bottom a matter of demeaning attitudes or bad behavior, although these surely exist. The crux is rather the racially specific impacts of deindustrialization and financialization in the period of progressive-neoliberal hegemony, as refracted through long histories of systemic oppression. In this period, Black and brown Americans, who had long been denied credit, confined to inferior segregated housing, and paid too little to accumulate savings, were systematically targeted by purveyors of subprime loans and consequently experienced the highest rates of home foreclosures in the country. In this period, too, minority towns and neighborhoods that had long been systematically starved of public resources were clobbered by plant closures in declining manufacturing centers; their losses were reckoned not only in jobs but also in tax revenues, which deprived them of funds for schools, hospitals, and basic infrastructure maintenance, leading eventually to debacles like Flint – and, in a different context, to the Lower 9th Ward of New Orleans.[24] Finally, Black men long subject to differential sentencing and harsh imprisonment, coerced labor, and socially tolerated violence, including at the hands of police, were in this period massively conscripted into a "prison-industrial complex," kept full to capacity by a "war on drugs" focused on possession of crack cocaine and by disproportionately high rates of unemployment, all courtesy of bipartisan legislative "achievements," orchestrated largely by Bill Clinton. Need one add that, inspiring though it was, the presence of an African-American in the White House failed to make a dent in these developments?

What I'm trying to get at here is the depth at which racism is anchored in contemporary capitalist society – and the incapacity of progressive-neoliberal moralizing to address it. (This is equally the case for sexism and other axes of domination that are structurally grounded in capitalist society.) As I understand them, the structural bases of racism have as much to do with class and political economy as with status and (mis)recognition. Equally important, the forces that are destroying the life chances of people of color belong to the same dynamic complex as those that are destroying the life chances of Whites – even if some of the specifics differ.

I offer this analysis as a corrective to the shallow moralizing that prevails today in progressive circles. What should distinguish the Left from such postures is a focus on the fundamental structural bases of social oppression. By framing the problem in terms of capitalism, understood as an institutionalized social order, the Left should insist that racism (for example) has structural bases in capitalist society, that it must be fought not only culturally but also institutionally, by transforming the constitutive separations we've discussed throughout this book. That's the alternative to progressive moralism that I support – not dismissing racism and sexism as "superstructural," but insisting that they are structural and deeply imbricated with class (and gender) domination, that they can neither be understood nor overcome in abstraction from the latter. That's an additional advantage of our expanded view of capitalism as an institutionalized social order. It shows that we don't actually need to pit class domination and status hierarchy against one another. Both are part and parcel of capitalist society, co-products of its structural divisions. Both can and must be opposed together.

Jaeggi: Maybe we can dig a bit deeper into the conditions for the weakness of the Left. For sure, it is not just bad judgment regarding whom to team up with. This unfortunate alliance between neoliberalism and emancipation – can it still be framed in terms of recognition and redistribution? Isn't it the case that the struggle for cultural hegemony is part of the *liaisons dangéreuses* and also part of the anger and *ressentiment* you are referring to? Isn't the neglect of the working class also a neglect in the "cultural" dimension, a misrecognition in terms of their lifestyle, form of life, and – if you will – "culture?" The working class, the abandoned poor, and the "non-bohemian" segments of the precariat are not only economically deprived; they are also culturally deprived.

It's not simply that the established voices have dropped the class issue. They've also been actively promoting, and even in some ways sensationalizing, cultural issues in media and television, particularly with regard to issues of sexuality and non-heteronormative or non-cis gender identities. If we're talking about cultural hegemony, these are the kinds of issues that "sell": they're interesting enough, they're sexy enough, and they're "bohemian" enough to attract public attention, whereas the "totally boring" struggles of the working class can't get attention unless they're portrayed as meth dealers or in some other sensational way. In Germany in the 1970s, there was a famous left-wing book by Erika Runge based on interviews with working-class women.[25] It was a huge bestseller then, but you couldn't imagine someone doing this now – being that interested in the fate and everyday struggles of working-class women. (Arlie Hochschild is an exception, but, in fact, the attention that her recent book, *Strangers in Their Own Land*, received had a lot to do with the aftermath of the US election.[26])

But then, getting back to the question of redistribution and rec-ognition: Isn't the neglect of class struggle also a neglect in terms of recognition? I doubt that these two issues – the redistribution issue and the recognition issue – can be separated. The anger you referred to is not simply an anger caused by economic deprivation. After all, Trump is certainly not a member of the "working class" when it comes to income, wealth, resources, and opportunities, but he speaks to them with respect to certain elements of habitus and lifestyle. So, his appeal has to do not only with the way he speaks to economic grievances (which he is not going to address anyway – quite the oppo-site) but with a certain charisma at the cultural level. He's sort of an "underclass billionaire" – he has the language, he has the attitude, he has the *ressentiment* – and so there's something about it that doesn't seem to be fake.

Fraser: Actually, there's a huge revival of interest now in "the working class," its culture, politics and self-understanding. Unfortunately, however, the term is still usually defined in the narrow, old-fashioned way, which has the effect of suggesting that the problems of that class are something different from and in competition with the problems of women, immigrants, and people of color!

I gather that's also the notion that you have in mind when you speak about the non-recognition of working-class culture – and of the deep appeal of Donald Trump to those who imagine that they see under-appreciated facets of themselves writ large in him. That's a fascinating idea and well worth exploring. But let me suggest another hypothesis, which points in a different direction, by aiming to explain why Trump appealed to those who might *not* think he resembles them. I'm thinking especially of White women. I assume you know that a majority of them voted for him, about 52 percent in fact, notwithstanding the Access Hollywood tapes, in which he boasted of

being able to "grab [women] by the pussy" with impunity. It's doubt-
ful that women's votes for Trump were based on identification. His
appeal might lie instead in his pugnaciousness, his readiness to fight at
the drop of a hat. That's the point at which the image of the predator
morphs into that of the protector, someone who's in your corner
and has your back. For people who are being expropriated and who
feel not just neglected or unrecognized but *exposed* and *unprotected*,
that's pretty powerful stuff. And it sits right on the intersection of
distribution and recognition, implicating them both.

Since you asked about those categories, I want to say a bit more
about how I am using them here, in conjunction with some Gramscian
concepts, to analyze our current hegemonic crisis. My strategy is not
to separate distribution and recognition, but rather to parse the construction and deconstruction of a hegemonic commonsense, and with
it the rise and fall of an associated historical bloc – all with a view to
assessing the prospects for an emancipatory social transformation.
Recognition and distribution are central to this analysis for historical
reasons. Since at least the mid twentieth century in the United States
and Europe, capitalist hegemonies have been forged by combining
views about those two different aspects of justice. What made Trump
and Trumpism possible was the discrediting of progressive neoliberalism's distinctive normative nexus of distribution and recognition.
By parsing the construction and break-up of that nexus, we can
clarify not only Trumpism, but also the prospects, post-Trump, for a
counterhegemonic bloc that could resolve the crisis. Let me illustrate
the point by returning once more to the United States.

Prior to Trump's rise to power, US political commonsense was
highly restricted – built, as I said before, around the opposition
between two variants of neoliberalism: one progressive, the other
regressive. What was offered, in other words, was a clear choice
between two different politics of recognition, but only one (neoliberal)
politics of distribution: you could choose between multiculturalism
and ethnonationalism, but you were stuck, either way, with financialization and deindustrialization. This left a *gap* in the hegemonic
organization of political life: an empty, unoccupied zone, where an
egalitarian, pro-labor, anti-neoliberal distributive politics might have
taken root. And that left a sizable segment of Americans, victims of
financialization and globalization, without a political voice. Given
the social processes that were all the while grinding away at their
life conditions, it was only a matter of time before someone would
proceed to occupy that empty space and fill the gap.

There were some rumblings in this direction in 2007/8 (with the financial crisis and Obama's election) and again in 2011 (with the eruption of Occupy Wall Street). But the hegemonic order remained largely intact, at least on the surface. Then, in 2015/16, the earthquake finally struck. The usual scripts were up-ended by a pair of outsiders, causing both major political establishments to appear to collapse. Challenging their respective party apparatchiks (bosses, pundits, *éminences grises*, and big donors), both Trump and Sanders excoriated neoliberalism's "rigged economy," but espoused two sharply divergent views of recognition. The immediate result was to put two new political options on the table: *reactionary populism* and *progressive populism*. But neither of those options actually materialized. Sanders's loss to Hillary Clinton removed the progressive-populist option from the ballot. And once in power, as I already said, Trump dropped his economic populism, while doubling down on his reactionary politics of recognition, which became hugely intensified and ever more vicious. What we have gotten, as I said before, is a *hyper-reactionary neoliberalism.*

However, hyper-reactionary neoliberalism is not a new hegemonic bloc. It is rather an unstable, chaotic amalgam. That's due partly to Trump's psychology and partly to his dysfunctional co-dependency with the Republican Party establishment. But there is also a deeper problem. By shutting down the economic-populist face of his campaign, Trump is effectively trying to reinstate the very hegemonic gap he helped to explode in 2016. Ironically, he is being joined in that endeavor by the Clintonite wing of "the resistance," which hopes to revive progressive neoliberalism in some new guise, and thereby to return the public sphere to its previous state as a populism-free zone. However, neither the Clintonites nor Trump himself can suture the hegemonic gap, in my opinion. The populist cat is out of the bag and is not about to slink quietly away. The result is an unstable interregnum, with no secure hegemony.

That's the situation confronting the Left today. I want to consider whether it offers an opening for the construction of a counterhegemonic bloc. If so, the likeliest candidate seems to me to be some new variant of *progressive populism* – one that combines an egalitarian, pro-working-class distributive program with an inclusive, nonhierarchical vision of a just recognition order – or, as I said before, emancipation plus social protection.

Jaeggi: I do have one additional question. If we want to talk about the triple movement and a new alliance between emancipation and social protection, we need a left-wing response to the question about what social protection in a globalized world should look like – who should be protected or who belongs in the "circle" of people who are counted under social protection. People like Trump, Le Pen, or Nigel Farage answer quite simply that we need to go back to the nation-state and that national borders should provide the means for defining those who should be socially protected, and clearly part of the appeal of these movements has to do with the idea of protecting the economy within national borders. This idea of returning to national protection also carries some appeal among certain left-wing voices, and so the motivation behind it is something that the Left will have to address.

Fraser: This is a pressing and difficult question. I'm convinced, for starters, that the genie of globalization is too far out of the bottle to be put back in. That's one reason why Brexit and Trump (among others) cannot deliver on their promises to working-class voters. In the UK, the short- and medium-term consequences of Brexit will not be social protection at all but increased exposure to globalization, because, absent its EU agreements, the Brits (or what's left of them, given Scottish and Northern Irish unhappiness) will be hanging out there on their own. The same is true for the US: the moment Trump scrapped the Trans-Pacific Partnership, China announced that it would pursue its own regional trade deal with the Asian countries. So, it's not as if you can actually protect yourself simply by tearing up these agreements, even though – it is true – they are stacked in favor of capital and against workers. In the absence of transnational or global coordination, what you get is rival national or regional protectionisms. And this is dangerous. Just think of the late 1920s and 1930s, when escalating competition among national protectionisms led directly to world war.

In sum, social protection cannot be envisioned today in a national frame. As I noted earlier, even state-managed capitalism – which synthesized marketization with social protection – required Bretton Woods and other forms of international coordination. And, of course, that approach did nothing to counteract the vast discrepancies in state capacity to deliver social protection, which are the enduring legacy of colonialism. Quite the contrary! The state-managed model worked by siphoning value from periphery to core; in effect, it made metropolitan protection dependent on (post-)colonial exposure to predation. So, it cannot be a model for us. Moreover, we face some pressing issues, such as climate change and financial regulation, which simply cannot be handled at the national level. These issues really do demand some form of global governance. Lastly, as we discussed in chapters 1 and 2, capitalism is and always has been a global dynamic. Whatever solutions we might develop – even ones designed to promote certain kinds of autonomy at the national or local level – these have to be developed with this global dynamic in mind.

Going forward

Jaeggi: I want to press you one last time on the assumptions behind your diagnosis. Your claim is that it is this progressive-neoliberal alliance that has created this backlash of reactionary protectionism, but there is also a possible explanation that it has merely opened a floodgate of much more substantial regressive tendencies that were already present and latent. We might also give a thought to the possibility that racism has a dynamics and a power of its own. When Horkheimer and Adorno were faced with National Socialism, they concluded that there are dramatically regressive potentials *built into* the very process of civilization and enlightenment. They came to situate the fundamental problem on a level running deeper than capitalism itself. But, even if we grant that these tendencies are bound up with dynamics particular to capitalism, from the point of view of ideology critique, one could still say that something like sexism was not only functionally necessary to justify women's indispensable contribution of unpaid reproductive labor. Sexism, like racism, has long served as a means to compensate (White) male workers in an extra-economic sphere for the material exploitation they suffered. So, the current pain might not come from seeing progressivism team up with the neoliberal enemy of one's class, but from progressivism taking away the "consolation prize" of male privilege or White supremacy.[27] Maybe to some this "consolation prize" has become the most real thing, a source of warped recognition and perceived stability. So, increasing inequality and precarity might be bearable, but only so long as that symbolic hierarchy which posits White males on top remains in place. Now that a partially successful emancipation movement is appearing to erode this, we witness a defensive reaction by those desperate to keep in place an outlived ideological structure.

Fraser: I appreciate the depth of the question you raise and the thoughtfulness with which you address it. I can see some truth in the view you attribute to Horkheimer and Adorno, but with one major qualification: I'd locate the source of the deep regressive tendencies in capitalism, not in civilization or enlightenment. I can also see some *"h as to offer = a counter-good*

truth in the "consolation prize" hypothesis. But what follows from that politically? I'd say that a viable left-wing response (whether progressive populist or democratic socialist(has to offer a counter-good] to those whose consolation is presently threatened; and that this has to be something more existentially substantial and psychically compelling than "male privilege" or "White-skin privilege." A posture that is exclusively defensive is not the answer. It takes away existing "consolation" while offering nothing in return. To paraphrase Marx: the goal is not to "pluck . . . the imaginary flowers on the chain . . . in order that man shall continue to bear that chain without fantasy or consolation, but so that he shall throw off the chain and pluck the living flower."[28]

Jaeggi: Let's say we accept your diagnosis – that we're faced with a reactionary social protectionism against a collapsing progressive neoliberalism. What do we do now? We don't want to be complacent, and we don't want to take the kind of moralizing stance that will only create an even greater backlash from the Right. At the same time, it's also clear that most of the Left finds itself in a defensive position. As problematic as progressive neoliberalism has been, isn't there a certain priority, given the current situation, to defending the progress that has been made, however imperfect? One can fault these movements for not being forward-looking enough or not offering a valid alternative, but it's also clear we now have to protect the most vulnerable, those who might become targets of these right-wing populist movements. There seems to be some urgency in fending off the racism, xenophobia, and misogyny that are resurgent now. So how do we meet this immediate need to defend existing progress without losing sight of the deeper-lying problems of progressive politics?

Fraser: My instinct is to seize the moment and go on the offensive. I already suggested that neither hyper-reactionary neoliberalism nor progressive neoliberalism will be able to (re)establish a secure hegemony in the coming period and that we face a chaotic, unstable interregnum, which, as you say, is fraught with danger. Nevertheless, there could be an opening now for the construction of a counterhegemonic bloc around the project of *progressive populism*. By combining in a single project an egalitarian, pro-working-class economic orientation with an inclusive nonhierarchical recognition orientation, this formation would have at least a fighting chance of uniting the *whole* working class: not just the fractions historically associated with manufacturing and construction, whom reactionary populists and traditionalist leftists have mainly addressed, but also those portions of the broader working class who perform domestic, agricultural, and service labor – paid and unpaid, in private firms and private homes, in the public sector and civil society – activities in which women, immigrants, and people of color are heavily represented. By wooing both segments, the expropriated as well as the exploited, a progressive populist project could position the working class, understood expansively, as the leading force in an alliance that also includes substantial segments of youth, the middle class, and the professional–managerial stratum.

For that to happen, working-class supporters of Trump and of Sanders would have to come to understand themselves as allies – differently situated victims of a single "rigged economy," which they could jointly seek to transform. What speaks in favor of this possibility, in the US at least, is the fact that, between the supporters of Sanders and those of Trump, something approaching a critical mass of American voters rejected the neoliberal politics of distribution in 2015/16. What speaks against it are the deepening divisions, even hatreds, long simmering but recently raised to a fever pitch by Trump, which appear to validate the view, held by some progressives, that all Trump voters are "deplorables" – irredeemable racists, misogynists, and homophobes. Also reinforced is the converse view, held by many reactionary populists, that all progressives are incorrigible moralizers and smug elitists who look down on them while sipping lattes and raking in the bucks. The prospects for progressive populism depend on successfully combating both of those views. That's where I propose to focus – as I've actually already been doing throughout this chapter.

Jaeggi: I wonder whether it might not help to revisit a concept that you have used and that has been around for a while with respect to the diagnosis of our time: the concept of *ressentiment*. It seems as though it's more than a *façon de parler*; it's another tool for understanding the inner structure of those dynamics that misdirect social suffering and indignation toward reactionary, authoritarian, and proto-fascist impulses instead of emancipatory movements. I think that this cannot be explained by the ruthless pursuit of self-interest alone, notwithstanding the exclusionary nationalistic tendencies, since people have chosen a politics that openly betrays their interests (Trump, after all, made no secret of his plans to eliminate Obamacare). Even to the extent that you have convincingly sketched out reasons for the hatred of the so-called left-liberal cultural elite, this still doesn't turn it into a rational decision. And you didn't mean to suggest that these

217

political affects were legitimate (after all, to understand doesn't mean to excuse). So, I would say that, even though their real interests are not satisfied, their *ressentiment* is.

This is what makes the concept interesting for an analysis of our situation. Provided that we conceive it not merely as a sociopsychological concept, but as a form of "affect" that is genuinely social, we can examine the deeper structural causes for *ressentiment* as part of a more comprehensive analysis of crisis and regression. *Ressentiment* is what I would call a second-order affect: the starting material of *ressentiment* is not a certain social situation per se, the absence of certain desired social gratifications or goods, but rather a situation normatively judged as bad, undeserved, and unjustified – a situation of indignation and outrage. But there is another element that Max Scheler has pointed to in his brilliant analysis: *ressentiment* always occurs in combination with a feeling of impotence, the feeling of powerlessness.[29] And, again, this powerlessness is not merely the impotence against a first-order problem – for example, that I cannot change being unemployed or that I have no health insurance. Rather, the powerlessness which triggers *ressentiment* is the impotence or inability even to express one's feeling of indignation or outrage. Within a neoliberal culture of "taking responsibility," one can easily see how people see themselves in a situation in which even their indignation is banned. But this powerlessness is also ascribed to and projected onto the "left-elite." The supposed "thought ban" – the fact that political correctness prevents them from expressing their vindictive and envious feelings toward those whom they believe "don't deserve" their respective resources, attention, and public recognition – then becomes (as it must) one of the main fronts. This is why we might expect *ressentiment* to be felt even by those who are neither objectively deprived nor objectively powerless, and why it can be directed against those who, objectively speaking, do not have much power at all. Incidentally, at least one study shows that Trump's primary supporters score high with respect to "authoritarianism" across diverse social and economic statuses.[30]

But it is also clear that *ressentiment* is a defense mechanism. When the limits of order begin to break down (e.g., the dissolution of gender identities or national borders), the precarious work and life situation, as well as the more generalized experience of impotence and precarious social orientation, brings forth the need to be "master in one's own house" ("Build the wall!"). This can only be satisfied in the imagination. Authoritarian *ressentiment* is urgently directed against those who are blamed for having violated and dissolved "the sanctity

218

of the home" and turned "our homeland" into a strange place. But then, to feel "alienated" by this kind of "Heimatverlust" ("loss of home") is itself an instance of an ideological blockage of reality and a denial of the real causes of being alienated. This is what makes it into a moment of regression. Talking about *ressentiment* as a mode of regression here seems to be helpful in order to understand how these emotions are "real" but still illusory.

So, while you oppose closing ranks with progressive neoliberalism and its tendency to frame things in moralizing "us" versus "them" terms, we should still ask whether these reactionary impulses stem from a *ressentiment* against progressive-neoliberal moralizing that in itself is a regressive answer to the conceived crisis. *Not* closing ranks with progressive neoliberals to defend what emancipatory achievements have been made then might present its own dangers.

Fraser: What you say about regression is very interesting and worth developing. But I disagree with the political conclusion you draw from it, which is a variant of the old idea of "lesser evil-ism." This is the Left's habitual posture, dusted off every few years, of ventriloquizing liberal objectives and squelching its own, out of fear of a Trump or an AfD. Although aimed at saving us from "the worst," that strategy actually fertilizes the soil that germinates new and ever more dangerous bogeymen, which in turn justify further deferments – and on and on, in a vicious circle. When it wins, its policies serve not to diminish but rather to stoke populist rage. You yourself have said that the *ressentiment* felt by many right-wing populist supporters is a response to real grievances, even if much of it is currently misdirected toward immigrants and other scapegoats. The proper response from *us* is not moral condemnation but political validation, while redirecting the rage to the systemic predations of finance capital.

That response also serves to answer the suggestion that we should now close ranks with the neoliberals to ward off fascism. The problem is not only that reactionary populism is not (yet) fascism. It is also that, seen analytically, liberalism and fascism are not really two separate things, one of which is good and the other bad, but two deeply interconnected faces of the capitalist world system. Although they are by no means normatively equivalent, both are products of unrestrained capitalism, which everywhere destabilizes lifeworlds and habitats, bringing in its wake both individual liberation and untold suffering. Liberalism expresses the first, liberatory side of this process, while glossing over the rage and pain associated with the second. Left to fester in the absence of an alternative, those sentiments fuel authoritarianisms of every sort, including those that really deserve the name "fascism" and those that emphatically do not. Without a Left, in other words, the maelstrom of capitalist "development" can only generate liberal forces and authoritarian counterforces, bound together in a perverse symbiosis. Thus, far from being the antidote to fascism, (neo)liberalism is its partner in crime. The real charm against fascism (whether proto- or quasi- or real) is a left-wing project that redirects the rage and the pain of the dispossessed toward a deep societal restructuring and a democratic political "revolution." Until very recently, such a project could not even be glimpsed, so suffocatingly hegemonic was neoliberal commonsense. But, thanks to Sanders, Corbyn, Mélenchon, Podemos, the early SYRIZA – imperfect as all of them are – we can again envision an expanded set of possibilities.

In general, then, I'm opposed to closing ranks. In fact, my preferred scenario is just the opposite: namely, separation in the service of realignment. Where you seek unity with the liberals, I would like to see the Left seek to precipitate two major shifts. First, the mass of less privileged women, immigrants, and people of color have to be wooed away from the lean-in feminists, the meritocratic anti-racists and anti-homophobes, and the corporate diversity and green-capitalism shills who hijacked their concerns, inflecting them in terms consistent with neoliberalism. This is the aim of a recent feminist initiative, which seeks to replace "lean-in" with a "feminism for the 99 percent."[31] Other emancipatory movements should copy that strategy.

Second, declining working-class communities have to be persuaded to desert their current crypto-neoliberal allies. The trick is to convince them that the forces promoting militarism, xenophobia, and ethnonationalism cannot and will not provide them with the essential material prerequisites for good lives, whereas a progressive-populist bloc just might. In that way, one might separate those right-wing populist voters who could and should be responsive to such an appeal from the card-carrying racists and alt-right ethno-nationalists, who are not. I am certain that the former outnumber the latter by a wide margin. I don't deny, of course, that reactionary populist movements draw heavily on loaded rhetoric and have emboldened formerly fringe groups of real White supremacists. But I reject the far too hasty conclusion that the overwhelming majority of reactionary-populist voters are forever closed to appeals on behalf of an expanded working class of the sort evoked by Bernie Sanders and theorized here. That view is not only empirically wrong but counterproductive, likely to be self-fulfilling.

220

Jaeggi: I appreciate your attempts to differentiate. And yes, of course, if we don't want to give up, we need to watch out for possible re-alignments. It's true, too, that left-wing politics has to be offensive, demanding more to make even the tiniest increments of progress.) At the same time, going on the offensive cannot mean just deepening the confrontation on the same terms as before. Nor can it mean following the same strategy of "closing ranks" against regressive movements in a more forceful or radical way. It is necessary, rather, to develop an alternative project and an emancipatory social movement that can attract those who are not hardcore fascists and that speaks to their real grievances. On these points, we agree.

But let me ask a provocative question. It almost sounds like there is some way in which you think that our current situation opens up more prospects for the Left than there were before.) Maybe "optimism" is too strong a word, but to the extent that these events have disturbed the security of neoliberal hegemony, perhaps you see an opening for the Left to break away from the kind of politics that have led to this situation. For my part, I still find the massive shift toward radical right-wing, nationalistic, racist, and sexist politics too disturbing to maintain much optimism; and, as I already said, it is still unclear to me whether we really are "breaking away from neoliberalism."

Fraser: Well, I've already said that neoliberalism persists as policy, including under Trump. What has crumbled is progressive-neoliberal *hegemony*. It's precisely that combination that defines the present conjuncture: on the one hand, an ongoing, decades-long assault on living standards in the broadest sense, which transcends "the economic"; on the other hand, the delegitimation of the regime and the parties that have perpetrated or supported that assault. That's the background against which I interpret your question. Does this conjuncture contain new opportunities for the Left, opportunities that were not available before the unraveling of progressive-neoliberal hegemony?

I want to say three things in response to that question. The first is that, for the overwhelming majority of people, any gains delivered by progressive neoliberalism have been very small. This is not only true for those who have defected to right-wing populism. It holds as well for those who have stuck with the progressive or center-left parties – parties that hijacked their claims while advancing neoliberalization. I mean the mass of women, immigrants, people of color, and non-cis and non-hetero people. Granted, these groups won some significant rights on paper. But those rights were won just as neoliberalization was

221

eroding the necessary material conditions for their exercise. The vast majority did not fully share in the benefits, which went overwhelmingly to the professional–managerial stratum and the 1%. Members of these groups have a lot to gain from a Left, which is why so many of them have been attracted to Sanders, Mélenchon, Podemos, and Jeremy Corbyn. It's a mistake to think defensively, about what they now have to lose. They can and should be wooed by the Left, as should the winnable working-class fractions of reactionary populism. One should adopt this sort of "optimism," if that's what it is, less as an empirical prediction than as a pragmatic presupposition of our action. To assume the alternative, "pessimistic" stance is to foreclose possibilities and ensure defeat.

That was point one, and here is point two: We've talked previously about the objective side of crisis. We talked about the near-implosion of the global financial order in 2007/8; we've talked about climate change; we've talked about the crisis of social reproduction, about the terrible deterioration of living conditions and lifeworlds and people's capacity to care for their families under this neoliberal assault. That's the objective crisis. What we now have is the crisis at the level of hegemony – the social action or participant side of crisis. For a long time, this side of crisis did not appear, and I for one wondered when it would appear. Now it has appeared.

Jaeggi: But on the wrong terms! And with possibly dangerous outcomes.

Fraser: Well, history doesn't always unfold the way we want it to! Nevertheless, we now have not only an objective system crisis but also a hegemonic political crisis. I repeat: as a *hegemonic* project, neoliberalism is finished; it may retain its capacity to dominate, but it has lost its ability to persuade. And I can't pretend to be unhappy about that. But that doesn't mean that I am in a position to make any predictions about what will happen next. What are the chances that the progressive-populist protection-plus-emancipation scenario I've been proposing will actually come to pass? What are the chances that the current crisis will galvanize struggles of sufficient breadth and vision to transform the present regime in an emancipatory direction? I have no way of knowing. And it's much too soon to hazard a guess. But I will say this: I didn't see many openings for the emergence of a new Left before, and I do see some now.

And here, finally, is point three: the roots of all of these crisis phenomena, the social as well as the structural, lie in the multiple, deep-seated contradictions of capitalism that our expanded conception has brought to light. The crisis phenomena we've been discussing represent the acute form those contradictions assume today, in financialized capitalism. If that is right, then this crisis will not be resolved by tinkering with this or that policy. The path to its resolution can only go through the deep structural transformation of this social order. What is required, above all, is to overcome financialized capitalism's rapacious subjugation of polity to economy, reproduction to production, non-human nature to "human society" – but this time without sacrificing either emancipation or social protection. This in turn requires reinventing the institutional separations that constitute capitalist society. Whether the result will be compatible with capitalism at all remains to be seen.

Jaeggi: I certainly admire your vigor. But this sounds a bit like the old left-wing strategy that hopes for a "sharpening of the contradictions." This strategy didn't always work out. Rosa Luxemburg's alternative between "socialism or barbarism" might not exhaust the realm of options. What we agree about, nevertheless, is that we live in an open situation. And without an emancipatory project that goes beyond the alternatives people seem to be stuck with today, things might get ugly.

Fraser: The contradictions are sharpening whether we want them to or not, that old anti-Left canard notwithstanding. The real issue is how we respond to the sharpening – and to the ugly stuff that comes in its wake. On that, I believe we agree. If we fail to pursue a transformative politics now, we will prolong the present interregnum. And that means condemning working people of every gender, persuasion, and color to mounting stress and declining health, to ballooning debt and overwork, to class apartheid and social insecurity. It means immersing them, too, in an ever-vaster expanse of morbid symptoms – in hatreds born of resentment and expressed in scapegoating, in outbreaks of violence followed by bouts of repression, in a vicious dog-eat-dog world where solidarities contract to the vanishing point. To avoid that fate, we must break definitively both with neoliberal economics and with the various politics of recognition that have lately supported it – casting off not just exclusionary ethnonationalism but also liberal-meritocratic individualism. Only by joining a robustly egalitarian politics of distribution to a substantively inclusive, class-sensitive politics of recognition can we build a counterhegemonic bloc that could lead us beyond the current crisis to a better world.

223

Notes

(handwritten: "Neo-Polanyian conception of capitalist crisis")

Introduction ✓

1 Rahel Jaeggi, *Alienation*, ed. Frederick Neuhouser and trans. Frederick Neuhouser and Alan E. Smith (New York: Columbia University Press, 2014). Nancy Fraser, "Marketization, Social Protection, Emancipation: Toward a Neo-Polanyian Conception of Capitalist Crisis," in *Business as Usual: The Roots of the Global Financial Meltdown*, ed. Craig Calhoun and Georgi Derlugian (New York University Press, 2011), pp. 137–58; "Can Society Be Commodities All the Way Down? Post-Polanyian Reflections on Capitalist Crisis," *Economy and Society* 43, no. 4 (2014): 541–58; and *Fortunes of Feminism: From State-Managed Capitalism to Neoliberal Crisis* (London: Verso, 2013).

2 Rahel Jaeggi, *Critique of Forms of Life*, trans. Ciaran Cronin (Cambridge, MA: Harvard University Press, forthcoming), and "What (If Anything) Is Wrong with Capitalism? Dysfunctionality, Exploitation, and Alienation: Three Approaches to the Critique of Capitalism," *Southern Journal of Philosophy* 54, Spindel Supplement (2016): 44–65. Nancy Fraser, "Behind Marx's Hidden Abode: For an Expanded Conception of Capitalism," *New Left Review* 86 (2014): 55–72.

3 G. A. Cohen, *Why Not Socialism?* (Princeton University Press, 2009).

4 Jürgen Habermas, *The Theory of Communicative Action*, 2 vols., trans. Thomas McCarthy (Boston: Beacon Press, 1984–7 [1981]).

5 For a thoughtful discussion on this, see Timo Jütten, "Habermas and Markets," *Constellations* 20, no. 4 (2013): 587–603.

6 Jürgen Habermas, *The Lure of Technocracy*, trans. Ciaran Cronin (Cambridge: Polity, 2015), p. 88.

7 Axel Honneth, *Freedom's Right: The Social Foundations of Democratic Life*, trans. Joseph Ganahl (Cambridge: Polity, 2014).

8 Fredric Jameson, *Postmodernism, or, The Cultural Logic of Late Capitalism* (Durham: Duke University Press, 1991); Carlo Vercellone, "From Formal Subsumption to General Intellect: Elements for a Marxist Reading of the Thesis of Cognitive Capitalism," *Historical Materialism* 15, no. 1 (2007): 13–36.

(handwritten: Carlo Vercellone) 224

9 Max Horkheimer, "Postscript" [to "Traditional and Critical Theory"], in *Critical Theory: Selected Essays*, trans. Matthew J. O'Connell (New York: Continuum, 1999), p. 249.

10 Rahel Jaeggi, "A Wide Concept of Economy: Economy as a Social Practice and the Critique of Capitalism," in *Critical Theory in Critical Times: Transforming the Political and Economic Order*, ed. Penelope Deutscher and Cristina Lafont (New York: Columbia University Press, 2017).

11 Nancy Fraser, "Struggle over Needs: Outline of a Socialist-Feminist Critical Theory of Late-Capitalist Political Culture"; Nancy Fraser and Linda Gordon, "A Genealogy of 'Dependency': Tracing a Keyword of the US Welfare State"; and "After the Family Wage: Gender Equity and the Welfare State" – all (reprinted) in Fraser, *Fortunes of Feminism* (London: Verso, 2013).

12 Nancy Fraser, "From Redistribution to Recognition? Dilemmas of Justice in a 'Postsocialist' Age," *New Left Review* 212 (1995): 68–93; and Nancy Fraser and Axel Honneth, *Redistribution or Recognition? A Political-Philosophical Exchange*, trans. Joel Golb, James Ingram, and Christiane Wilke (London: Verso, 2003).

13 Jaeggi, *Critique of Forms of Life*.

14 Karl Marx, "Letter to A. Ruge," September 1843, in *Karl Marx: Early Writings*, trans. Rodney Livingstone and Gregor Benton (New York: Vintage Books, 1975), p. 209.

1 Conceptualizing Capitalism

1 Peter A. Hall and David Soskice (eds.), *Varieties of Capitalism: The Institutional Foundations of Comparative Advantage* (Oxford University Press, 2001).

2 Karl Marx, *Capital*, vol. I [1867], trans. Samuel Moore and Edward Aveling, in *Karl Marx and Frederick Engels: Collected Works*, vol. XXXV (London: Lawrence & Wishart, 2010), p. 179.

3 Theodor Adorno, "Beitrag zur Ideologienlehre" [1954], in *Soziologische Schriften I, Gesammelte Schriften*, vol. VIII (Frankfurt am Main: Suhrkamp, 1997), p. 465.

4 Max Weber, *The Protestant Ethic and the Spirit of Capitalism*, trans. Talcott Parsons (New York: Routledge, 2005 [1930]), e.g., p. 124.

5 Werner Sombart, *Der modern Kapitalismus. Historich-systematische Darstellung des gesamteuropäischen Wirtschaftslebens von seinen Anfängen bis zur Gegenwart*, 3 vols. (Munich: Duncker & Humblot, 1902–28).

6 Elizabeth Gaskell, *North and South* (Ware: Wordsworth Editions, 1994 [1855]).

7 Nancy Fraser, "What's Critical About Critical Theory? The Case of Habermas and Gender," *New German Critique* 35 (Spring/Summer 1985): 97–131. Reprinted in Fraser, *Fortunes of Feminism* (London: Verso, 2013).

8 Karl Polanyi, *The Great Transformation: The Political and Economic Origins of Our Time* (Boston: Beacon Press, 2001 [1944]), pp. 45–70.

9 See, e.g., James C. McKinley, Jr., "Conservatives on Texas Panel Carry the Day on Curriculum Change," *New York Times*, March 13, 2010, A10.

10 See, e.g., Valerie Vande Panne, "Life without Money in Detroit's Survival Economy," *Bloomberg*, January 12, 2017, at https://www.bloomberg.com/

news/features/2017–01–12/life-without-money-in-detroit-s-survival-econo my; Liz Alderman, "Paying in Olive Oil," *New York Times*, September 24, 2015, B1.

11 See, e.g., Immanuel Wallerstein, *Historical Capitalism, with Capitalist Civilization* (London: Verso, 1996), esp. pp. 26–43.

12 Polanyi, *The Great Transformation*, esp. pp. 71–80, 136–40, 201–6; Nancy Fraser, "Can Society Be Commodities All the Way Down? Post-Polanyian Reflections on Capitalist Crisis," *Economy and Society* 43, no. 4 (2014): 541–58.

13 See Rahel Jaeggi, *Critique of Forms of Life*, trans. Ciaran Cronin (Cambridge, MA: Harvard University Press, forthcoming); Jaeggi, "What (If Anything) Is Wrong with Capitalism? Dysfunctionality, Exploitation, and Alienation: Three Approaches to the Critique of Capitalism," *Southern Journal of Philosophy* 54, Spindel Supplement (2016): 44–65.

14 Polanyi, *The Great Transformation*, esp. pp. 71–80. For this reading of Polanyi, see Fraser, "Can Society Be Commodities All the Way Down?"

15 G. W. F. Hegel, *Elements of the Philosophy of Right*, trans. H. B. Nisbet and ed. Allen W. Wood (Cambridge University Press, 1991 [1821]). I [Fraser] read this work as arguing, *contra* social contract theory, that society cannot be contract all the way down, and as invoking that argument to establish the necessity of embedding "Abstract Right" within the broader context of "Ethical Life." For a detailed interpretation along these lines, see Michel Rosenfeld, "Hegel and the Dialectics of Contract," *Cardozo Law Review* 10 (1989): 1199–1269.

16 Piero Saffra, *The Production of Commodities by Means of Commodities: Prelude to a Critique of Economic Theory* (London: Cambridge University Press, 1975).

17 Karl Marx, *Capital*, vol. II [1893], ed. Frederick Engels, in *Karl Marx and Frederick Engels: Collected Works*, vol. XXXVI (London: Lawrence & Wishart, 2010), p. 394.

18 Polanyi, *The Great Transformation*, pp. 71–80.

19 See, e.g., Karl Marx, *Capital*, vol. I [1867], trans. Samuel Moore and Edward Aveling, in *Karl Marx and Frederick Engels: Collected Works*, vol. XXXV (London: Lawrence & Wishart, 2010), pp. 510–12; Marx, "Chapter Six. Results of the Direct Production Process" [c.1864], in *Karl Marx and Frederick Engels: Collected Works*, vol. XXXIV (London: Lawrence & Wishart, 2010), pp. 339–471, esp. pp. 424–42.

20 Polanyi, *The Great Transformation*, pp. 59–80.

21 See Marx, *Capital*, vol. I, pp. 270–307.

22 Rahel Jaeggi, "A Wide Concept of Economy: Economy as a Social Practice and the Critique of Capitalism," in *Critical Theory in Critical Times*, ed. Penelope Deutscher and Cristina Lafont (New York: Columbia University Press, 2017), pp. 160–79, 173–5.

23 Marx, *Capital*, vol. I, pp. 704–61.

24 Marx, *Capital*, vol. I, pp. 185–6.

25 Marx, *Capital*, vol. I, pp. 704–7.

26 David Harvey, "The 'New' Imperialism: Accumulation by Dispossession," *Socialist Register* 40 (2004): 63–87.

27 Friedrich Engels, *Origins of the Family, Private Property and the State*, selections in *The Marx–Engels Reader*, ed. Robert C. Tucker (New York: W. W. Norton, 1978).

28 Alexandra Kollontai, *Selected Writings* (New York: W. W. Norton, 1977); Sylvia Pankhurst, "A Constitution for British Soviets: Points for a Communist Programme," *Workers' Dreadnought* (June 19, 1920), at http://libcom. org/library/constitution-british-soviets-points-communist-programme-syl via-pankhurst; and Pankhurst, "Cooperative Housekeeping," *Workers' Dreadnought* (August 28, 1920), at http://libcom.org/library/co-operative- housekeeping-sylvia-pankhurst; Mariarosa Dalla Costa and Selma James, "Women and the Subversion of Community," in *Materialist Feminism: A Reader in Class, Difference, and Women's Lives*, ed. Rosemary Hennessey and Chris Ingraham (New York: Routledge, 1997), pp. 33–40; Juliet Mitchell, "Women: The Longest Revolution," *New Left Review* 40 (December 1966): 11–37; and Angela Y. Davis, "The Approaching Obsolescence of Housework: A Working-Class Perspective," in Davis, *Women, Race and Class* (New York: Random House, 1981), and "Reflections on the Black Woman's Role in the Community of Slaves," *The Massachusetts Review* 13, no. 2 (1972): 81–100. Other major figures of the "second wave" include Silvia Federici, *Revolution at Point Zero: Housework, Reproduction, and Feminist Struggle* (Oakland: PM Press, 2012); Christine Delphy, *Close to Home: A Materialist Analysis of Women's Oppression* (London: Verso, 2016); Eli Zaretsky, *Capitalism, the Family and Personal Life* (New York: Harper & Row, 1976); Maxine Molyneux, "Beyond the Domestic Labor Debate," *New Left Review* 116 (1979): 3–27; Heidi Hartmann, "The Unhappy Marriage of Patriarchy and Capitalism: Toward a More Progressive Union," *Capital & Class* 3, no. 2 (1979): 1–33; Bonnie Fox (ed.), *Hidden in the Household: Women's Domestic Labor under Capitalism* (New York: Women's Press, 1980); Linda Nicholson, *Gender and History* (New York: Columbia University Press, 1986). Many key texts, including classic essays by Margaret Benston, Gloria Joseph, and Iris Marion Young, are collected in *Materialist Feminism*, ed. Hennessey and Ingraham. See also Nancy Holmstrom, ed., *The Socialist Feminist Project: A Contemporary Reader in Theory and Politics* (New York: Monthly Review Press, 2002); and Shahrzad Mojab, ed., *Marxism and Feminism* (London: Zed Books, 2015).

29 Lise Vogel, *Marxism and the Oppression of Women: Toward a Unitary Theory* (Chicago: Haymarket, 2014 [1983]). For "social reproduction feminism," see Barbara Laslett and Johanna Brenner, "Gender and Social Reproduction: Historical Perspectives," *Annual Review of Sociology* 15 (1989): 381–404; Kate Bezanson and Meg Luxton (eds.), *Social Reproduction: Feminist Political Economy Challenges Neoliberalism* (Montreal: McGill-Queen's University Press, 2006); Isabella Bakker, "Social Reproduction and the Constitution of a Gendered Political Economy," *New Political Economy* 12, no. 4 (2007): 541–56; Cinzia Arruzza, "Functionalist, Determinist, Reductionist: Social Reproduction Feminism and its Critics," *Science & Society* 80, no. 1 (2016): 9–30; Susan Ferguson, Genevieve LeBaron, Angela Dimitrakaki, and Sara R. Farris, eds., "Symposium on Social Reproduction," *Historical Materialism* 24, no. 2 (2016): 25–163; and Tithi Bhattacharya (ed.), *Social Reproduction Theory: Remapping Class, Recentering Oppression* (London: Pluto, 2017).

30 Maria Mies, *Patriarchy and Accumulation on a World Scale: Women in the International Division of Labour* (London: Zed Books, 1986).

31 Maria Mies and Veronika Bennholdt-Thomsen, *The Subsistence Perspective: Beyond the Globalised Economy* (London: Zed Books, 2000); Maria

Mies and Vandana Shiva, *Ecofeminism*, 2nd edition (London: Zed Books, 2014).

32 Nancy Fraser, "Marketization, Social Protection, Emancipation: Toward a Neo-Polanyian Conception of Capitalist Crisis," in *Business as Usual: The Roots of the Global Financial Meltdown*, ed. Craig Calhoun and Georgi Derlugian (New York University Press, 2011), pp. 137–58; Fraser, "Can Society Be Commodities All the Way Down?"

33 James O'Connor, "The Second Contradiction of Capitalism, with an Addendum on the Two Contradictions of Capitalism," in O'Connor, *Natural Causes: Essays in Ecological Marxism* (New York: Guilford Press, 1998), pp. 158–77; John Bellamy Foster, "Marx's Theory of Metabolic Rift: Classical Foundations for Environmental Sociology," *American Journal of Sociology* 105, no. 2 (1999): 366–405; Jason W. Moore, *Capitalism in the Web of Life: Ecology and the Accumulation of Capital* (London: Verso, 2015); and Joan Martinez-Alier, *The Environmentalism of the Poor: A Study of Ecological Conflicts and Valuation* (Cheltenham: Edward Elgar, 2003). Other major works in this tradition include Andre Gorz, *Ecology as Politics* (New York: South End Press, 1980); Ariel Salleh, "Nature, Woman, Labor, Capital," *Capitalism, Nature, Socialism* 6, no. 1 (1995): 21–39; Alan Dordoy and Mary Mellor, "Eco-socialism and Feminism: Deep Materialism or the Contradictions of Capitalism," *Capitalism, Nature, Socialism* 11, no. 3 (2000): 41–61; Neil Smith, "Nature as Accumulation Strategy," *Socialist Register* 43 (2007): 16–36; and Andreas Malm, *Fossil Capital: The Rise of Steam Power and the Roots of Global Warming* (London: Verso, 2016).

34 See Foster, "Marx's Theory of Metabolic Rift."

35 Andreas Malm, "Who Lit This Fire? Approaching the History of the Fossil Economy," *Critical Historical Studies* (2016): 216–48, and the essays in *Anthropocene or Capitalocene? Nature, History, and the Crisis of Capitalism*, ed. Jason W. Moore (Oakland: PM Press, 2016).

36 Donna J. Haraway, "A Cyborg Manifesto: Science, Technology, and Socialist-Feminism in the Late Twentieth Century," in *Simians, Cyborgs, and Women: The Reinvention of Nature* (New York: Routledge, 1991 [1985]), pp. 149–81.

37 Ellen Meiksins Wood, "The Separation of the Economic and the Political in Capitalism," *New Left Review* 1, no. 127 (1981): 66–95.

38 Giovanni Arrighi, *The Long Twentieth Century: Money, Power and the Origins of our Times* (London: Verso, 1994).

39 I [Fraser] read Polanyi and Arendt as having analyzed the political contradictions of liberal capitalism. Whereas the former analyzed the intractable political conflicts that wracked European societies struggling to protect themselves from the ravages of the "self-regulating market," the latter dissected the political deformations visited on European states as the expansive, trans-territorial logic of their economically driven colonial projects ran up against the territorial logic of political rule. Habermas did something analogous for state-managed capitalism, diagnosing its tendency to produce "legitimation crises": Polanyi, *The Great Transformation*; Hannah Arendt, *The Origins of Totalitarianism* (New York: Harcourt, Brace, Jovanovich, 1973), especially the under-appreciated middle section on imperialism; and Jürgen Habermas, *Legitimation Crisis*, trans. Thomas McCarthy (Boston: Beacon Press, 1975). For the political contradictions of financialized capi-

talism, see Wendy Brown, *Undoing the Demos: Neoliberalism's Stealth Revolution* (Brooklyn: Zone Books, 2015); Colin Crouch, *The Strange Non-Death of Neoliberalism* (Cambridge: Polity, 2011); Stephen Gill, "New Constitutionalism, Democratisation and Global Political Economy," *Pacifica Review* 10, no. 1 (1998): 23–38; Wolfgang Streeck, *Buying Time: The Delayed Crisis of Democratic Capitalism* (London and Brooklyn: Verso, 2014); Streeck, "The Crises of Democratic Capitalism," *New Left Review* 71 (2011): 5–29; Streeck, "Citizens as Customers: Considerations on the New Politics of Consumption," *New Left Review* 76 (2012): 27–47; and Nancy MacLean, *Democracy in Chains: The Deep History of the Radical Right's Stealth Plan for America* (New York: Viking, 2017). Also Nancy Fraser, "Legitimation Crisis? On the Political Contradictions of Financialized Capitalism," *Critical Historical Studies* 2, no. 2 (2015): 1–33.

40 Marx, *Capital*, vol. 1, pp. 704–7.

41 David Harvey, *The New Imperialism* (Oxford University Press, 2003); Harvey, "The 'New' Imperialism"; Rosa Luxemburg, *The Accumulation of Capital* (New York: Routledge, 2003 [1913]); see also Klaus Dörre, "Social Classes in the Process of Capitalist *Landnahme*: On the Relevance of Secondary Exploitation," *Socialist Studies* 6, no. 2 (2010): 43–74.

42 For an account that extends the concept of primitive accumulation beyond initial stockpiling, see the chapter on "Extended Primitive Accumulation," in Robin Blackburn, *The Making of New World Slavery: From the Baroque to the Modern, 1492–1800* (London: Verso, 2010).

43 C. L. R. James, *The Black Jacobins* (London: Penguin Books, 1938); W. E. B. Du Bois, *Black Reconstruction in America, 1860–1880* (New York: Harcourt, Brace, 1935); Eric Williams, *Capitalism and Slavery* (Chapel Hill: University of North Carolina Press, 1944); Oliver Cromwell Cox, *Caste, Class and Race: A Study of Social Dynamics* (New York: Monthly Review Press, 1948); Stuart Hall, "Race, Articulation and Societies Structured in Dominance," in UNESCO, *Sociological Theories: Race and Colonialism* (Paris: UNESCO, 1980), pp. 305–45; Walter Rodney, *How Europe Underdeveloped Africa* (Washington, DC: Howard University Press, 1981); Angela Y. Davis, *Women, Race, and Class* (London: The Women's Press, 1982); Cedric Robinson, *Black Marxism* (Chapel Hill: University of North Carolina Press, 1999). Other major contributions to the Black-Marxist tradition include Manning Marable, *How Capitalism Underdeveloped Black America* (Brooklyn: South End Press, 1983); Barbara Fields, "Slavery, Race and Ideology in the United States of America," *New Left Review* 1, no. 181 (May–June 1990): 95–118; Robin D. G. Kelley, *Hammer and Hoe: Alabama Communists during the Great Depression* (Chapel Hill: University of North Carolina Press, 1990), and *Race Rebels: Culture, Politics, and the Black Working Class* (New York: Free Press, 1996); David Roediger, *The Wages of Whiteness* (Brooklyn: Verso, 1999); Cornel West, "The Indispensability Yet Insufficiency of Marxist Theory" and "Race and Social Theory," both in *The Cornel West Reader* (New York: Basic Civitas Books, 1999), pp. 213–30 and 251–67, respectively; Adolph Reed, Jr., "Unraveling the Relation of Race and Class in American Politics," *Political Power and Social Theory* 15 (2002): 265–74; and Keeanga-Yamahtta Taylor, *From #Black Lives Matter to Black Liberation* (Chicago: Haymarket, 2016).

44 Moore, *Capitalism in the Web of Life*.

45 Polanyi, *The Great Transformation*, pp. 144–5.
46 Georg Lukács, "Reification and the Consciousness of the Proletariat," in *History and Class Consciousness: Studies in Marxist Dialectics*, trans. Rodney Livingstone (Cambridge, MA: MIT Press, 1971), pp. 83–222.
47 See, e.g., Jaeggi, "A Wide Concept of Economy." For the practice account of forms of life, see Jaeggi, *Critique of Forms of Life*.
48 Fraser, "What's Critical About Critical Theory?"
49 Jürgen Habermas, *Between Facts and Norms: Contributions to a Discourse Theory of Law and Democracy*, trans. William Rehg (Cambridge, MA: MIT Press, 1996), pp. 39–40.
50 See Jens Beckert, "Die sittliche Einbettung der Wirtschaft. Von der Effizienz und Differenzierungstheorie zu einer Theorie wirtschaftlicher Felder," *Berliner Journal für Soziologie* 22, no. 2 (2012): 247–66.
51 Nancy Fraser, "Distorted Beyond All Recognition: A Rejoinder to Axel Honneth," in Nancy Fraser and Axel Honneth, *Redistribution or Recognition? A Political-Philosophical Exchange*, trans. Joel Golb, James Ingram, and Christiane Wilke (London: Verso, 2003), pp. 216–18.

2 Historicizing Capitalism ✓

1 Thomas Kuhn, *Structure of Scientific Revolutions*, 2nd edition (University of Chicago Press, 1962); Richard Rorty, *Philosophy and the Mirror of Nature* (Princeton University Press, 1979), pp. 320–32.
2 Karl Marx and Frederick Engels, *The German Ideology* [1845–6], in *Karl Marx and Frederick Engels: Collected Works*, vol. V (London: Lawrence & Wishart, 2010), pp. 36–7. See also Louis Althusser, *Ideology and Ideological State Apparatuses* in *Lenin and Philosophy and Other Essays* (New York: Monthly Review Press, 1971).
3 Göran Therborn, *Between Sex and Power: Family in the World, 1900–2000* (New York: Routledge, 2004).
4 Max Weber, "Religious Rejections of the World and Their Directions," in *From Max Weber: Essays in Sociology*, ed. H. H. Gerth and C. Wright Mills (New York: Oxford University Press, 1946), pp. 323–59; Jürgen Habermas, *The Theory of Communicative Action*, vol. I, trans. Thomas McCarthy (Boston: Beacon Press, 1984 [1981]), pp. 243–71.
5 Brian Milstein, "Thinking Politically about Crisis: A Pragmatist Perspective," *European Journal of Political Theory* 14, no. 2 (2015): 141–60.
6 For an extensive discussion of these dynamics of problem-solving, see Rahel Jaeggi, *Critique of Forms of Life*, trans. Ciaran Cronin (Cambridge, MA: Harvard University Press, forthcoming), esp. part two, ch. 4, and part four.
7 Alain Lipietz, "Behind the Crisis: The Exhaustion of a Regime of Accumulation," *Review of Radical Political Economics* 18, nos. 1–2 (1986): 13–32; Robert Boyer, *La Théorie de la Régulation: une analyse critique* (Paris: La Découverte, 1986); Robert Boyer and Yves Saillard (eds.), *Régulation Theory: The State of the Art* (New York: Routledge, 2002); Michel, Aglietta, *A Theory of Capitalist Regulation: The US Experience*, trans. David Fernbach (London: Verso, 2015 [1976]).
8 Stephen Gill, "New Constitutionalism, Democratisation and Global Political Economy," *Pacifica Review* 10, no. 1 (1998): 23–38.

9 Immanuel Wallerstein, *The Modern World-Systems Analysis* (Durham: Duke University Press, 2004).

10 David Harvey, "The 'New' Imperialism: Accumulation by Dispossession," *Socialist Register* 40 (2014): 63–87.

11 Nancy MacLean, *Democracy in Chains: The Deep History of the Radical Right's Stealth Plan for America* (New York: Viking, 2017).

12 Colin Crouch, *Post-Democracy* (Cambridge: Polity, 2004).

13 Wolfgang Streeck, *Buying Time: The Delayed Crisis of Democratic Capitalism*, trans. Patrick Camiller (London: Verso, 2014).

14 Jürgen Habermas, *The Theory of Communicative Action*, vol. II, trans. Thomas McCarthy (Boston: Beacon Press, 1987 [1981]), pp. 356–73.

15 Ava Baron, "Protective Labor Legislation and the Cult of Domesticity," *Journal of Family Issues* 2, no. 1 (1981): 25–38; Nancy Woloch, *A Class by Herself: Protective Laws for Women Workers, 1890s-1990s* (Princeton University Press, 2015).

16 Paul Ginsborg, *Family Politics: Domestic Life, Devastation and Survival, 1900–1950* (New Haven: Yale University Press, 2014).

17 Wolfgang Streeck, "Citizens as Customers," *New Left Review* 76 (2012): 27–47.

18 Luc Boltanski and Ève Chiapello, *The New Spirit of Capitalism*, trans. Gregory Elliott (London: Verso, 2013).

19 Nancy Fraser, "The End of Progressive Neoliberalism," *Dissent*, January 2, 2017 (https://www.dissentmagazine.org/online_articles/progressive-neoliberalism-reactionary-populism-nancy-fraser).

20 Arlie Russell Hochschild, "Love and Gold," in *Global Woman: Nannies, Maids, and Sex Workers in the New Economy*, ed. Arlie Russell Hochschild and Barbara Ehrenreich (New York: Henry Holt and Co., 2003), pp. 15–30.

21 Nancy Fraser, "Contradictions of Capital and Care," *New Left Review* 100 (2016): 99–117; Courtney Jung, *Lactivism: How Feminists and Fundamentalists, Hippies and Yuppies, and Physicians and Politicians Made Breastfeeding Big Business and Bad Policy* (New York: Basic Books, 2015), esp. pp. 130–1; Sarah Kliff, "The Breast Pump Industry Is Booming, Thanks to Obamacare," *Washington Post*, January 4, 2013 (https://www.washingtonpost.com/news/wonk/wp/2013/01/04/the-breast-pump-industry-is-booming-thanks-to-obamacare/); Mark Tran, "Apple and Facebook Offer to Freeze Eggs for Female Employees," *The Guardian*, October 15, 2014 (https://www.theguardian.com/technology/2014/oct/15/apple-facebook-offer-freeze-eggs-female-employees); Anna North, "Is Egg Freezing Really a Benefit?" *New York Times*, October 15, 2014 (https://op-talk.blogs.nytimes.com/2014/10/15/is-egg-freezing-really-a-benefit); Michael S. Schmidt, "Pentagon to Offer Plan to Store Eggs and Sperm to Retain Young Troops," *New York Times*, February 4, 2016 (https://www.nytimes.com/2016/02/04/us/politics/pentagon-to-offer-plan-to-store-eggs-and-sperm-to-retain-young-troops.html); Rebecca Mead, "Cold Comfort: Tech Jobs and Egg Freezing," *New Yorker*, October 17, 2014 (https://www.newyorker.com/news/daily-comment/facebook-apple-egg-freezing-benefits); Natalie Lampert, "New Fertility Options for Female Soldiers," *The Atlantic*, February 29, 2016 (https://www.theatlantic.com/health/archive/2016/02/fertility-women-soldiers/471537).

22 Maria Mies, *Patriarchy and Accumulation on a World Scale: Women in the International Division of Labor* (London: Zed Books, 1998).

23 Marx and Engels, *The German Ideology*, p. 31.

24 Walter Benjamin, "Theses on the Philosophy of History," in *Illuminations: Essays and Reflections*, ed. Hannah Arendt and trans. Harry Zohn (New York: Schocken Books, 2007 [1950]), pp. 253–64, 259.

25 John Bellamy Foster, "Marx's Theory of Metabolic Rift: Classical Foundations for Environmental Sociology," *American Journal of Sociology* 105, no. 2 (1999): 366–405.

26 Philippe Descola gives a brilliant account of this, as does Carolyn Merchant in her classic book, which also discloses the gender subtext of these developments. See Philippe Descola, *Beyond Nature and Culture*, trans. Janet Lloyd (University of Chicago Press, 2014), and Carolyn Merchant, *The Death of Nature: Women, Ecology, and the Scientific Revolution* (San Francisco: HarperOne, 1990 [1980]).

27 William Cronon, *Nature's Metropolis: Chicago and the Great West* (New York: W. W. Norton & Co., 1992).

28 James O'Connor, "Capitalism, Nature, Socialism: A Theoretical Introduction," *Capital, Nature, Socialism* 1, no. 1 (1998): 11–38.

29 Jason W. Moore, *Capitalism in the Web of Life: Ecology and the Accumulation of Capital* (London: Verso, 2015).

30 Moore, *Capitalism in the Web of Life*.

31 For the distinction between "somatic" and "exosomatic" energy regimes, see J. R. McNeill, *Something New Under the Sun: An Environmental History of the 20th Century* (New York: W. W. Norton, 2000), pp. 10–16.

32 Jason W. Moore, "Potosí and the Political Ecology of Underdevelopment, 1545–1800," *Journal of Philosophical Economics* 4, no. 1 (2010): 58–103.

33 Andreas Malm, "The Origins of Fossil Capital: From Water to Steam in the British Cotton Industry," *Historical Materialism* 21 (2013): 15–68.

34 Alf Hornborg, "Footprints in the Cotton Fields: The Industrial Revolution as Time–Space Appropriation and Environmental Load Displacement," *Ecological Economics* 59, no. 1 (2006): 74–81.

35 See, e.g., Mike Davis, "The Origins of the Third World," *Antipode* 32, no. 1 (2000): 48–89; Alf Hornborg, "The Thermodynamics of Imperialism: Toward an Ecological Theory of Unequal Exchange," in Hornborg, *The Power of the Machine: Global Inequalities of Economy, Technology, and Environment* (Lanham, MD: AltaMira, 2001), pp. 35–48; Joan Martinez-Alier, "The Ecological Debt," *Kurswechsel* 4 (2002): 5–16; John Bellamy Foster, Brett Clark, and Richard York, "Imperialism and Ecological Metabolism," in Foster et al., *The Ecological Rift: Capitalism's War on the Earth* (New York: Monthly Review Press, 2011), pp. 345–74.

36 Joan Martinez-Alier, *The Environmentalism of the Poor: A Study of Ecological Conflicts and Valuation* (Cheltenham: Edward Elgar, 2003).

37 Timothy Mitchell, "Carbon Democracy," *Economy and Society* 38, no. 3 (2009): 399–432.

38 Mitchell, "Carbon Democracy."

39 Larry Lohmann, "Financialization, Commodification and Carbon: The Contradictions of Neoliberal Climate Policy," *Socialist Register* 48 (2012): 85–107.

40 Lohmann, "Financialization, Commodification and Carbon."

41 Martin O'Connor, "On the Misadventures of Capitalist Nature," in *Is Capitalism Sustainable? Political Economy and the Politics of Ecology*, ed. Martin O'Connor (New York: Guilford Press, 1994), pp. 125–51; Martinez-Alier, *The Environmentalism of the Poor*.

42 Karl Marx, *Capital*, vol. I [1867], trans. Samuel Moore and Edward Aveling, in *Karl Marx and Frederick Engels: Collected Works*, vol. XXXV (London: Lawrence & Wishart, 2010), p. 739.

43 Judith Shklar, *American Citizenship: The Quest for Inclusion* (Cambridge, MA: Harvard University Press, 1991).

44 See, e.g., Ruy Mauro Marini, *Dialéctica de la dependencia* (Mexico City: Ediciones Era, 1973).

3 Criticizing Capitalism

1 Philippe Van Parijs, "What (if Anything) Is Intrinsically Wrong with Capitalism?" *Philosophica* 34 (1984): 85–102.

2 Karl Marx, *Capital*, vol. III [1894], in *Karl Marx and Frederick Engels: Collected Works*, vol. XXXV (London: Lawrence & Wishart, 2010), pp. 209–30.

3 Daniel Bell, *The Cultural Contradictions of Capitalism* (New York: Basic Books, 1996 [1976]).

4 Joseph A. Schumpeter, *Capitalism, Socialism, and Democracy* (New York: Routledge, 2003 [1943]), pp. 121–63.

5 Rahel Jaeggi, "What (if Anything) Is Wrong with Capitalism? Dysfunctionality, Exploitation, and Alienation: Three Approaches to the Critique of Capitalism," *Southern Journal of Philosophy* 54, Spindel Supplement (2016): 44–65.

6 G. W. F. Hegel, *Elements of the Philosophy of Right*, ed. Allen W. Wood and trans. H. B. Nisbet (Cambridge University Press, 1991 [1821]), pp. 264–7 (§§240–4).

7 Thomas McCarthy, "The Critique of Impure Reason: Foucault and the Frankfurt School," in *Critique and Power: Recasting the Foucault/Habermas Debate*, ed. Michael Kelly (Cambridge, MA: MIT Press, 1994), p. 248.

8 Max Horkheimer, "Traditional and Critical Theory," in *Critical Theory: Selected Essays*, trans. Matthew J. O'Connell (New York: Continuum, 1999 [1937]), pp. 188–243.

9 Karl Marx, *Capital*, vol. I [1867], trans. Samuel Moore and Edward Aveling, in *Karl Marx and Frederick Engels: Collected Works*, vol. XXXV, p. 204.

10 Karl Marx, *Critique of the Gotha Program* [1875], trans. David Forgacs, Rodney Livingstone, Krystyna Livingstone, et al., in *Karl Marx and Frederick Engels: Collected Works*, vol. XXIV (London: Lawrence & Wishart, 2010), pp. 83–8.

11 Georg Lohmann, "Zwei Konzeptionen von Gerechtigkeit in Marx' Kapitalismuskritik," in *Ethik und Marx: Moralkritik und normative Grundlagen der Marxschen Theorie*, ed. Emil Angehrn and Georg Lohmann (Königstein im Taunus: Athenaeum Verlag, 1986), pp. 174–94.

12 See Rahel Jaeggi, *Alienation*, trans. Frederick Neuhouser and Alan E. Smith (New York: Columbia University Press, 2014), pp. 22–5, 36–7.

13 Georg Simmel, *The Philosophy of Money*, trans. Tom Bottomore, David

Frisby, and Kaethe Mengelberg (New York: Routledge, 2011 [1900]); Werner Sombart, *Der modern Kapitalismus. Historich-systematische Darstellung des gesamteuropäischen Wirtschaftslebens von seinen Anfängen bis zur Gegenwart*, 3 vols. (Munich: Duncker & Humblot, 1902–28).

14 Max Weber, *Economy and Society*, 2 vols., ed. Guenther Roth and Claus Wittich (Berkeley: University of California Press, 1978 [1922]).

15 Hartmut Rosa, *Social Acceleration: A New Critical Theory of Modernity*, trans. Jonathan Trejo-Mathys (New York: Columbia University Press, 2013).

16 See Jaeggi, *Alienation*, pp. 11–16.

17 Karl Marx, "Estranged Labor," *Economic and Philosophic Manuscripts of 1844*, trans. Martin Milligan and Barbara Ruhemann, in *Karl Marx and Frederick Engels: Collected Works*, vol. III, trans. Jack Cohen, Clemens Dutt, Martin Milligan, Barbara Ruhemann, Dirk J. Struik, and Christopher Upward (London: Lawrence & Wishart, 2010), pp. 270–82.

18 Jürgen Habermas, *Between Facts and Norms: Contributions to a Discourse Theory of Law and Democracy*, trans. William Rehg (Cambridge, MA: MIT Press, 1996), pp. 99–104, 118–31.

19 See Rahel Jaeggi, *Critique of Forms of Life*, trans. Ciaran Cronin (Cambridge, MA: Harvard University Press, forthcoming). For a fuller account of Jaeggi's theory of "appropriation" as a necessary corollary to human freedom, and how alienation can become an impediment to it, see Jaeggi, *Alienation*, esp. pp. 35–40.

20 Karl Marx, *Outlines of the Critique of Political Economy (Grundrisse)* [1857–8], trans. Ernst Wangermann, in *Karl Marx and Frederick Engels: Collected Works*, vol. XXVIII (London: Lawrence & Wishart, 2010), pp. 384–93.

21 Marx, *Outlines of the Critique of Political Economy (Grundrisse)*; Marx, *Capital*, vol. I, pp. 241, 638–40.

22 Jaeggi, *Alienation*.

23 For an account of social freedom as we find it in Hegel, see Frederick Neuhouser, *Foundations of Hegel's Social Theory: Actualizing Freedom* (Cambridge, MA: Harvard University Press, 2003); for an approach that spells out the institutional spheres of social freedom, see Axel Honneth, *Freedom's Right: The Social Foundations of Democratic Life*, trans. Joseph Ganahl (Cambridge: Polity).

24 Max Horkheimer and Theodor W. Adorno, *Dialectic of Enlightenment*, trans. John Cumming (New York: Continuum, 1999 [1944]).

25 Horkheimer and Adorno, *Dialectic of Enlightenment*.

26 Herbert Marcuse, *Eros and Civilization: A Philosophical Inquiry into Freud* (Boston, MA: Beacon Press, 1966).

27 Hannah Arendt, *The Human Condition*, 2nd edition (University of Chicago Press, 1998 [1958]), pp. 191–4, 230–47.

28 See Jaeggi, *Critique of Forms of Life*, chs. 5 and 6.

29 Hegel, *Elements of the Philosophy of Right*, pp. 264–7 (§§240–4).

30 Editor's note: The "Speenhamland system" was a 1795 reform to the Elizabethan Poor Law that aimed to subsidize the wages of the rural poor should they fall below subsistence levels; it would be repealed in 1834. Leaving laborers with little incentive to work and employers with little incentive to offer a living wage, the Speenhamland system created a dynamic of pauperization and demoralization that would serve as a pretext for the

subsequent establshment of a free labor market system. See Karl Polanyi, *The Great Transformation: The Political and Economic Origins of Our Time* (Boston: Beacon Press, 2001 [1944]), pp. 81–107.

31 Bell, *The Cultural Contradictions of Capitalism*.

32 Jürgen Habermas, *Legitimation Crisis*, trans. Thomas McCarthy (Boston: Beacon Press, 1975); *The Theory of Communicative Action*, 2 vols., trans. Thomas McCarthy (Boston: Beacon Press, 1984–7 [1981]).

33 James O'Connor, "The Second Contradiction of Capitalism, with an Addendum on the Two Contradictions of Capitalism," in O'Connor, *Natural Causes: Essays in Ecological Marxism* (New York: Guilford Press, 1998), pp. 158–77; "Capitalism, Nature, Socialism: A Theoretical Introduction," *Capital, Nature, Socialism* 1, no. 1 (1998): 11–38; Lise Vogel, *Marxism and the Oppression of Women: Toward a Unitary Theory* (Chicago: Haymarket, 2014 [1983]).

34 Nancy Fraser, "Marketization, Social Protection, Emancipation: Toward a Neo-Polanyian Conception of Capitalist Crisis," in *Business as Usual: The Roots of the Global Financial Meltdown*, Possible Futures 1, ed. Craig Calhoun and Georgi Derlugian (New York University Press, 2011), pp. 137–58.

35 Nancy Fraser, "Can Society Be Commodities All the Way Down?" *Economy and Society* 43, no. 4 (2014): 541–58.

36 Nancy Fraser, "A Triple Movement? Parsing the Politics of Crisis after Polanyi," *New Left Review* 81 (May–June 2013): 119–32.

37 Rahel Jaeggi, "'Resistance to the Perpetual Danger of Relapse': Moral Progress and Social Change," in *From Alienation to Forms of Life: The Critical Theory of Rahel Jaeggi*, ed. Amy Allen and Eduardo Mendieta (University Park: Penn State University Press, forthcoming).

38 For a complete account of the social dynamics of learning processes, see Jaeggi, *Critique of Forms of Life*.

39 Alastair MacIntyre, "Epistemological Crises, Dramatic Narrative, and the Philosophy of Science," *The Monist* 60, no. 4 (1977): 453–72.

40 Anthony Giddens, *Central Problems in Social Theory: Action, Structure, and Contradiction in Social Analysis* (London: Macmillan Education, 1979), pp. 131–64.

41 Brian Milstein, "Thinking Politically about Crisis: A Pragmatist Perspective," *European Journal of Political Theory* 14, no. 2 (2015): 141–60.

42 Nancy Fraser, "Abnormal Justice," *Critical Inquiry* 34, no. 3 (2008): 393–422.

4 Contesting Capitalism ✓

1 Herbert Marcuse, *An Essay on Liberation* (Boston: Beacon Press, 2000 [1969]).

2 Karl Marx, "On the Jewish Question" [1843], in *Karl Marx and Frederick Engels: Collected Works*, vol. III (London: Lawrence & Wishart, 2010), pp. 146–74.

3 Diane Elson, "Market Socialism or Socialization of the Market?" *New Left Review* 172 (1988): 3–44.

4 Nancy Fraser, "From Redistribution to Recognition? Dilemmas of Justice in

a 'Postsocialist' Age," *New Left Review* 212 (July/August 1995): 68–93; and *Scales of Justice: Reimagining Political Space in a Globalizing World* (New York: Columbia University Press, 2009), pp. 22–3.

5 André Gorz, *Strategy for Labor: A Radical Proposal*, trans. Martin A. Nicolaus and Victoria Ortiz (Boston: Beacon Press, 1967). See also Fraser's adaptation of Gorz's idea in Nancy Fraser, "Social Justice in the Age of Identity Politics: Redistribution, Recognition, and Participation," ch. 1 of Fraser and Axel Honneth, *Redistribution or Recognition? A Political-Philosophical Exchange*, trans. Joel Golb, James Ingram, and Christiane Wilke (London: Verso, 2003).

6 Sonia E. Alvarez, "Advocating Feminism: The Latin American Feminist NGO 'Boom,'" *International Feminist Journal of Politics* 1, no. 2 (1999): 181–95.

7 Uma Narayan, *Dislocating Cultures: Identities, Traditions, and Third World Feminism* (New York: Routledge, 2013), p. 150.

8 Hartmut Rosa, "Cultural Relativism and Social Criticism from a Taylorian Perspective," *Constellations* 3, no. 1 (1996): 39–60.

9 Walter Rodney, *How Europe Underdeveloped Africa* (London: Bogle-L'Ouverture Publications, 1973). See also Manning Marable's equally cogent reformulation, *How Capitalism Underdeveloped Black America* (Cambridge, MA: South End Press, 1983).

10 Dipesh Chakrabarty, *Provincializing Europe: Postcolonial Thought and Historical Difference* (Princeton University Press, 2000); Paul Gilroy, *The Black Atlantic: Modernity and Double Consciousness* (Cambridge, MA: Harvard University Press, 1993).

11 Nancy Fraser, "Why Two Karls Are Better than One: Integrating Polanyi and Marx in a Critical Theory of the Current Crisis," working paper for the DGF-Kollegforscher-innengruppe Postwachstumsgesellschaften, no. 1/2017, Jena (2017).

12 Nancy Fraser, "Legitimation Crisis? On the Political Contradictions of Financialized Capitalism," *Critical Historical Studies* 2, no. 2 (2015): 157–89.

13 Antonio Gramsci, *Selections from the Prison Notebooks*, ed. and trans. Quintin Hoare and Geoffrey Nowell Smith (New York: International Publishers, 1971), p. 276.

14 Nancy Fraser, "From Progressive Neoliberalism to Trump – and Beyond," *American Affairs* 1, no. 4 (2017): 46–64.

15 Luc Boltanski and Ève Chiapello, *The New Spirit of Capitalism*, trans. Gregory Elliott (London: Verso, 2013), pp. 446–7.

16 Nancy Fraser, "Progressive Neoliberalism versus Reactionary Populism: A Hobson's Choice," in *The Great Regression*, ed. Heinrich Geiselberger (Cambridge: Polity, 2017). A shorter version appeared as "The End of Progressive Neoliberalism," *Dissent* (2017).

17 See Hester Eisenstein, "A Dangerous Liaison? Feminism and Corporate Globalization," *Science & Society* 69, no. 3 (2005): 487–518; Nancy Fraser, "Feminism, Capitalism, and the Cunning of History," *New Left Review* 56 (2009): 97–117.

18 Nina Power, *One-Dimensional Woman* (Winchester: Zero Books, 2009), p. 21.

19 For analyses of anti-genderism and its relation to the recent wave of right-

wing populism and authoritarianism, see Sabine Hark and Paula Irene Villa (eds.), *Anti-Genderismus* (Bielefeld: transcript Verlag, 2015). For an illuminating analysis, see Eva von Redecker, "'*Anti-Genderismus*' and Right-Wing Hegemony," *Radical Philosophy* 198 (July/August, 2016): 2–7.

20 Didier Eribon, *Returning to Reims*, trans. Michael Lucey (Los Angeles: Semiotext(e), 2013).

21 Boltanski and Chiapello, *The New Spirit of Capitalism*, pp. 38–40.

22 Oliver Nachtwey, *Die Abstiegsgesellschaft: Über das Aufbegehren in der regressiven Moderne* (Berlin: Suhrkamp, 2016).

23 Pierre Bourdieu, *Distinction: Social Critique of the Judgment of Taste*, trans. Richard Nice (New York: Routledge, 1986).

24 Editor's note: Fraser is referring here to two famous cases in which majority-Black communities in the US suffered grave harms due to the systematic failure of federal, state, and local governments to invest in the maintenance and repair of crumbling infrastructure. In 2014, the 100,000 residents of Flint, Michigan – once a proud center of automobile manufacturing, but now an icon of deindustrialization and urban decay – were exposed to high levels of lead contamination in the water supply, as a result of such deprivation. The Lower 9th Ward is the largely Black neighborhood in New Orleans that suffered the most extensive damage when Hurricane Katrina struck the US in August 2005. The handling of Hurricane Katrina was notorious not only for the massive lack of preparedness, poor coordination, and slow and inadequate response, but also for the long-term failure of the government to build and maintain the levees needed to protect the neighborhood from storm surges.

25 Erika Runge, *Frauen* (Frankfurt am Main: Suhrkamp, 1969).

26 Arlie Russell Hochschild, *Strangers in Their Own Land: Anger and Mourning on the American Right* (New York: The New Press, 2016).

27 See von Redecker, "'*Anti-Genderismus*' and Right-Wing Hegemony."

28 Karl Marx, *Contribution to the Critique of Hegel's Philosophy of Law*, trans. Jack Cohen, Clemens Dutt, Martin Milligan, Barbara Ruhemann, Dirk J. Struik, and Christopher Upward, in *Karl Marx and Frederick Engels: Collected Works*, vol. III, p. 178.

29 Max Scheler, *Ressentiment*, trans. Louis Coser (Milwaukee: Marquette University Press, 1994 [1915]).

30 Matthew C. MacWilliams, *The Rise of Trump: America's Authoritarian Spring* (Amherst: The Amherst College Press, 2016); see also Peter E. Gordon, "The Authoritarian Personality Revisited: Reading Adorno in the Age of Trump," *boundary 2* 44, no. 2 (2017): 31–56.

31 Linda Martin Alcoff, Cinzia Arruzza, Tithi Bhattacharya, et al., "Women of America: We're Going on Strike. Join Us SoTrump Will See Our Power," *The Guardian*, February 6, 2017, at https://www.theguardian.com/commentisfree/2017/feb/06/women-strike-trump-resistance-power; Linda Martin Alcoff, Cinzia Arruzza, Tithi Bhattacharya, et al., "We Need a Feminism for the 99%: That's Why Women Will Strike This Year," *The Guardian*, January 27, 2018, at https://www.theguardian.com/commentisfree/2018/jan/27/we-need-a-feminism-for-the-99-thats-why-women-will-strike-this-year.

Index